THE Lee Bros.
CHARLESTON
KITCHEN

ALSO BY MATT LEE AND TED LEE

The Lee Bros. Southern Cookbook

The Lee Bros. Simple Fresh Southern

THE Lee Bros. CHARLESTON KITCHEN

MATT LEE & TED LEE

CLARKSON POTTER/PUBLISHERS

NEW YORK

All rights reserved.
Published in the United States by
Clarkson Potter/Publishers,
an imprint of the Crown Publishing
Group, a division of
Random House, Inc., New York.
www.crownpublishing.com
www.clarksonpotter.com

CLARKSON POTTER is a trademark
and POTTER with colophon is a
registered trademark of Random
House, Inc.

Library of Congress Cataloging-in-
Publication Data
Lee, Matt.
The Lee Bros. Charleston kitchen /
Matt Lee and Ted Lee. — 1st ed.
p.   cm.
Includes index.
1. Cooking, American—Southern
style.   2. Cooking—South
Carolina—Charleston.   I. Lee,
Ted.   II. Title.
III. Title: Lee Brothers Charleston
kitchen.
TX715.2.S68L4448   2012
641.5975—
dc23   2012013331

ISBN 978-0-307-88973-7
eISBN 978-0-7704-3395-6

Printed in China

Photographs on pages 10, 12, 15,
32, 64, 66, 94, 95, 96, 100, 102,
103, 121, 171, and 173 copyright
© 2013 Matt Lee and Ted Lee.
Photographs on pages 53, 84, 133,
151, 168 reprinted with permission
Map illustrations copyright © 2013
by David Cain
Design by Stephanie Huntwork
Jacket design by Stephanie Huntwork
Jacket photography by Squire Fox

10 9 8 7 6 5 4 3 2 1

First Edition

THIS BOOK IS DEDICATED
TO OUR FAMILIES

CONTENTS

WELCOME!

WE ARE WALKING THROUGH NEAT ROWS OF COLLARD GREENS AT
Joseph Fields Farm on Johns Island, thirteen miles south of downtown Charleston. It's just after 8:00 A.M. on an early March morning and the sun struggles against a low fog. Carrying wooden produce crates, we step across furrows of sandy dirt, leaving deep footprints as we follow behind farmer Joseph Fields and a farm manager. They cut whole heads of collards at the stalk with pocket knives and toss heavy bunches of greens into our crates.

We're hosting an oyster roast tonight, an impromptu gathering at our test kitchen on Wentworth Street, to welcome a former roommate who popped into town on business. We called some people yesterday, and they called some more, and there's got to be nearly forty of us now. (By party time we may be fifty.) No problem: oysters for that many is easy in Charleston. Our beloved *Crassostrea virginica,* earthy and generously salty, grow one upon another in clustered, torch-shaped forms in intertidal marshes of the coastal plain. A single cluster may have four or eight or more bantam-sized oysters clinging to it. These aren't white-tablecloth "singles," but they are the correct, perfect oyster for the outdoor roast, where guests crowd a plywood table as shovelfuls come off the fire, and then set about the task of breaking the clusters apart, shucking around to find all the treasure within. Seafood markets in the area sell these oysters in white woven bushel bags—a single bushel might hold three hundred oysters but cost less than thirty dollars.

By far the larger challenge for this many people is the collards. You've got to offer some sustenance other than bivalves and beer at an oyster roast—something you learn from growing up here (and also that a good-sized bunch of collards might only feed two people, two and a half if you're lucky). Hence the journey to the farm: we need collards, lots of them. And while we might be able to buy twenty-five heads of New Jersey, California, or North Carolina–grown collards from a supermarket downtown, driving twenty-six miles round-trip for local collards . . . well, that's just what Charlestonians do, honoring special occasions with the best, freshest ingredients we can find. Joseph Fields' organic collards, just-picked, are our insider tip.

As we follow Mr. Fields down the row, we watch as he pinches off the top of the plant—a bright-green, bud-like form sprouting immature yellow flowers—and pops it in his mouth. "Collard tops—tastiest part of the plant," he says, and offers the next ones to us. And he's right: these shoots are tender like pea greens, but with an astonishing pepperiness—like horseradish and chiles in the same bite. In all our years growing up here, and cooking, eating, and writing here as adults, we've never encountered—or considered—collard tops.

By the time our crates are full, the fog has lifted and chickens are scrabbling the ground near where we've parked our car. We pay Mr. Fields and say our goodbyes. In the car, we can't shake those collard tops—something virtually absent from the marketplace, but so plentiful if you know where to look. We get to thinking how we might focus that peppery flavor of the tops in a pot of greens, by backing off on the bacon and amping up the peppers. That'll be the day's experiment—and the greens we serve at the oyster roast.

CHARLESTON HAS ALWAYS BEEN FOR US A PLACE OF DISCOVERIES, firsts, and small miracles in the realm of food. For kids born here, food is like language, a body of knowledge absorbed almost unconsciously; you taste your first oyster before you're two years old, and by the time you're five it's just what you eat. But we were born in New York, and we moved to Charleston with our parents and our sister when we were eight and ten. We had so much catching up to do.

Our family landed in a 1784 townhouse on Rainbow Row, a stretch of East Bay Street where almost every house is attached, and each stucco façade is painted a different pastel hue (ours was warbler-yellow). The upper floors had an expansive view of Charleston Harbor that stretched past the boatyard of the Carolina Yacht Club to Fort Sumter in the distance, and we could take in the seagulls, the dolphins, the container ships cruising the middle distance. In the immediate foreground was—still is—the baseball diamond at the Hazel V. Parker Playground, a park where we joined

the phalanxes of kids riding around on BMX bikes and skateboards. It was here, climbing a tree that grew on the fence line between the playground and the yacht club, that we tasted mulberries for the first time. Our new friends showed us to look for the ripest, purple-black ones and we experienced their strangely mellow-sweet berry flavor. We ate until our teeth turned blue and our shirts were stained. There was also new vocabulary to learn: *benne,* for the sesame found in salty-sweet, molar-sticking candy and in tiny little crisp cookies; *scuppernongs,* grapes as syrupy-sweet as the word was funny to say, with a range of flavors depending on their ripeness. In time, we could tell just by feeling them which ones we would like best. We learned that peanuts could be eaten wet, boiled to a bean-like consistency, and in short order we discovered loquats, too—fuzzy yellow-skinned fruits you could peel, eating the small amount of sweet-tart flesh that clung to the seeds. Or you could pop the whole thing in your mouth, munch on it, and then spit out the skin and the seeds.

We weren't aware as children that these discoveries would add up to any understanding of Lowcountry food and traditions, and even the skills we learned in Charleston that would've been unthinkable in our New York lives—fashioning a drop-line from string and chicken necks to lure blue crabs, or throwing a cast-net to catch shrimp—we certainly didn't perceive in the context of the kitchen. We can't remember who cooked or ate what we caught. It was just fun, outdoor sport. But in hindsight, we can't help thinking that our acclimation to Charleston had a profound effect on the sense of wonder we bring to our kitchen today, to the feeling that—whether we're at the stove, out on the water, chatting with a historian, or dining in a newly opened restaurant—we're constantly learning, or seeing something from the past in a new light.

In this book we hope to show you not only what it's like to grow up here and learn to cook here, but also how we are continually inspired by this place. You'll see that our encounter with Mr. Fields that morning in March yielded Matt's Four-Pepper Collards (page 100), a new standard in our kitchen. A day out on the Stono River with a crabber friend, Fred Dockery, spurred us to tackle conch (crabber's bycatch, for which there's a minor market in the area) in the kitchen for the first time; but it was the wisdom of another fisherman, Thomas Backman, that made our Conch Fritters (page 150) delicious.

You'll note that many ideas in this book emerge from time we've spent with farmers and fishermen, but we also pay respect here to Charleston institutions past and present. We'd never have the gumption to ask Martha Lou Gadsden, the chef and owner of Martha Lou's Kitchen, if we could publish her recipe for Long-Cooked Green Beans (page 106). But you can bet that our own recipe is our attempt

to emulate the satisfying beans she makes. Our tributes to bygone restaurants may be even more interpretive, more speculative. Our Deviled Crabs are a mash-up of techniques gleaned from two sources: one was a former cook at Henry's, the much-beloved seafood restaurant that was Charleston's Galatoire's from the fifties until the eighties; the other, a recipe credited in a rare community cookbook to the Edisto Motel, a destination restaurant about an hour south of town as mythic in the minds of Charlestonians of a certain age as the defunct nightclub King Street Garden & Gun Club, or the specialty-foods emporium Harold's Cabin (our city's Zabar's), which lasted from the 1950s to the 1980s.

You'll find a revivalist streak in our book, because we repeatedly come across recipes in old cookbooks (or simple mentions of dishes in Charleston memoirs) that we've literally never seen in any dining room or on any restaurant table in town. So we'll get curious about it, and head into the test-kitchen. Often we're astonished that these delicious ideas and methods fell out of fashion. We hope our Salsify "Oysters" (page 97)—perfect lightly fried veggie puffs that, true enough, look exactly like fried oysters—and Syllabub with Rosemary-Glazed Figs (page 206) will bring back these wonderful food ideas to dinner tables. During our own lifetimes, we witnessed Peach Leather (page 210) fall off the radar. Why? It's such a triumph—a candy made from fresh peaches that kids and adults both love, and that's super-easy to make!

Other recipes in this book are simple meditations on a Charleston season—compositions of ingredients that come together at the same time, and practically beg you to put them together on the plate. Skillet Asparagus with Grapefruit (page 93) channels the overlap in earliest spring of backyard grapefruit season with the first tender asparagus (the area of Mt. Pleasant was once known in markets all along the East Coast for producing among the tastiest and earliest crop). Similarly, Butterbeans with Butter, Mint, and Lime (page 110) are simply the flavors of a Southern summer, thrown together, to flatter one another. Sometimes recipes are just fortuitous; during mulberry season, a friend gave us the most tender, precious cut of venison from his game freezer, which became Mulberry-Glazed Venison Loin (page 189). Thirty years later that mulberry tree, the one from the playground, is still there!

TODAY, PEOPLE ALL OVER THE WORLD see Charleston as a great food town, and it's consistently cited by national magazines and television shows as a top dining destination in the United States. For the most part, the coverage refers to the restaurants, and by that barometer it is truly remarkable how, in just the last decade, the sheer variety of different experiences to be had in the Holy City have multiplied.

It's never been a more exciting town to dine out in. We have food trucks. Real pho. Mixologists.

But if you're talking about home cooking, Charleston has *always* been known as a world-class destination for food. The national success and relevance of early cookbooks of this region, like Sarah Rutledge's 1847 *The Carolina Housewife,* and *Two Hundred Years of Charleston Cooking* (Charlestonian Blanche Rhett's 1931 gathering of prominent families' recipes, tested by New York editor Lettie Gay) was notable. A close read of both those cookbooks reveals a vigor and inventiveness from kitchen to kitchen, applied to the region's raw materials and traditions. The diverse viewpoints captured in those early recipes belie attempts to enshrine Charleston recipes as museum pieces.

Twentieth-century tributes to the city's food culture have been plentiful, and sometimes hilarious. We're guessing it was Rhett's book that inspired the B. Altman department store in 1939 to open "Charleston Gardens," a restaurant in their Fifth Avenue flagship, and later in branch locations in Short Hills, NJ, St. Davids, PA, and White Plains, NY (some locations lasted into the late 1980s). In 1951, upon the publication of the next definitive Charleston cookbook, *Charleston Receipts* (which set off its own brushfire of worldwide acclaim, with huge feature stories in the *New York Herald Tribune, National Geographic,* and *Harper's Bazaar*), B. Altman devoted an enormous expanse of windows on Fifth Avenue to a thoroughly stylized Charleston installation, with Spanish moss–strewn wrought-iron gates, sweetgrass baskets, jars of pickles, and many, many copies of the book.

What seems exceptional in light of all the attention is that Charlestonians don't perceive the culinary education we get from living here to be out of the ordinary, even as so many customs quietly endure today: the parish hall tea rooms open their doors every spring, rice is preeminent, jars of loquat liqueur cure in homes downtown. True, we might have bought soup bunches from a street vendor decades ago, but we can still find them at the Piggly Wiggly. We still purchase our fish directly from the fisherman, who guts the sheepshead and triggerfish on the same dock where his boat is tied up, while a crew of attentive brown pelicans (endangered species when we were growing up; they are now flourishing) in the water below feed on the spoils. And our orientation toward food isn't a trend we're trying on this season, it's just life here.

We're not a "foodie" town; we're a food town, pure and simple. And this is despite the fact that until relatively recently, Charleston kitchens were highly imperfect places—quite miserable, actually. Forget the romanticized B. Altman window display, or the kitchens you might have seen in shelter magazines from the post–Hurricane Hugo era, with their commercial-style ranges, two dishwashers, and half-acre of granite countertop. As Frances Hamby, Charleston's preeminent society caterer (who's seen the inside of nearly every kitchen south of Broad in the sixty years she's been in business), explained to us, the classic Charleston kitchen until recently had very little counter and cupboard space, a rickety old staircase to a basement, a minuscule gas stove (largely ignored in favor of the toaster oven), and a refrigerator "from the Dark Ages." And that was just the twentieth century; in the period immediately following the Civil War, the Charleston kitchen was often haunted by the pall of menial labor and privation, with hair-curling heat and humidity the only constant. And before the Civil War? The Charleston kitchen was typically where enslaved people toiled, and was considered such a fire hazard that the "kitchen house" was almost always built separate from the main house.

That karmic distance between kitchen and dining room can be felt today; the reason so many Charleston kitchens in the historic district have a shoehorned feel is that the original separate brick kitchen houses were eventually rented out for needed income, while the gap (called the "hyphen") between the main house and the kitchen house was framed out—often in slapdash fashion—to become the new kitchen.

We mention this because it's important to recognize that Charleston's food culture has flourished over the last couple centuries despite many grave limitations— and may in fact be conditioned by them, to positive effect. Charlestonians tend to see culinary pursuits as part of a broader landscape, rarely confined to the kitchen and dining room; it is impossible to capture the culinary spirit of the Lowcountry without including the gardening, hunting and fishing, the outdoor oyster roasts, crab cracks, funerals, wedding parties, and lowcountry boils that are the defining features of life here. The vibrant food culture seems to transcend equipment, comfort, and space deficiencies.

Learning about this town is a great, lifelong pleasure. From our forays into the little-known corners of Charleston's food history—from the deep past on through to the present—we've unearthed many of the personalities and recipes that show Charleston's food reality to be even more extraordinary and more diverse than the city gets credit for. We've reexamined the conventional wisdom about Charleston's hallowed culinary monuments and uncovered some flavors, stories, and concepts that haven't been aired recently, including some twists and turns in the narrative that might change the way our fellow Charlestonians view their own history. We intend this book to evoke Charleston as it is today and as it may have been, while remaining fresh and relevant to people who love to cook, wherever they happen to be.

So if you're new to Charleston, please know that it's never too late to start loving it. The perfect place to begin would be an oyster roast, because more than a feast, it's a ritual stretching back through most every wave of newcomers, to the native Americans. When you eat oysters from these waters over live fire, you're connecting with people who've lived here for hundreds of years. And while the first impression of our town (the clippety-clop horse-carriages, the wrought-iron gates, the righteousness of the architecture) might lead you to believe that Charleston entertaining is all about engraved save-the-dates and mother's silver on the sideboard, just ask anyone who lives here: the outdoor, rustic-as-heck, shuck-your-own roast is the *thing*, and it says a lot about Charleston's paradoxes and contrasts that the same ease and grace will be brought to an oyster roast as to high holidays with family.

A roast typically happens in the country, on a creekside where there's a bonfire raging, four cinderblocks at the corners of the fire roughly describing a "pit," and a sheet of metal balanced over the top to use as a cooking surface. Shovel the oysters onto the hot metal, cover them with wet burlap to steam in their shells, and transfer them to the shucking table as soon as you see the first shells' hinges peek open.

But at our roast for fifty, we're in a narrow downtown backyard, using a standard kettle grill, which is an imperfect, but workable, substitute for a pit. And we've already learned some new things this afternoon, namely that the bright-blue City of Charleston recycling bins are excellent for icing down two cornelius kegs from the Charleston Beer Exchange.

Got your beer? Good. Here's an oyster knife and an old garden glove. Don't know how to shuck? Just watch your neighbor when the next shovelful comes off the fire. Pick up a steaming craggy cluster, shuck your way around it with the knife. Taste these warm, briny little morsels. This is the flavor of the Lowcountry, and you've arrived in its capital, Charleston. Welcome!

DRINKS

THE LEADING EDGE OF HOSPITALITY IS THE DRINK OFFERED TO A guest upon walking in the door, and so our cookbook begins with recipes for beverages of all sorts.

In a place as warm and steamy as Charleston, the drinks—whether a tall glass of iced tea or a walloping cocktail—are refreshment, medicine, and muse. Charlestonians tend to move deliberately and rapidly to the bar upon joining a party, and they know well how to navigate through a crowded room to return for the refill.

The city has a long and vibrant beverage history, and in particular a strong connection to the Portuguese island of Madeira, whose fortified wines were among the only wines of European origin that traveled well across the Atlantic in the era of the sailing ships. Clubs formed around the connoisseurship of Madeira, and clubs with various other purposes (music, the arts, fraternity, ethnic affiliation) often rallied around a single punch recipe that served as the mascot beverage of the organization. Tea has been grown in the Charleston area almost continuously since the eighteenth century and appears often as a punch ingredient.

What one drinks is a defining flourish of character in Charleston. And people here stick to their tipples—so much so that the professional bartenders hired to serve at functions around town often know exactly what that particular Mrs. Ravenel (there are more than a few in town) will have as soon as she crosses the threshold.

James Bondian consistency, though, is far from the Lee Bros. style; our personal preference with drinks is—as it is with our foods—to match the flavor to the mood and the moment, taking into account the prevailing conditions of temperature, company, scenery, and agenda. We're as hungry for great beverage ideas as we are for the drinks themselves.

This chapter is appropriately kaleidoscopic, as we serve up an overview of appetizing libations, some classic Charleston and others totally new: we reverse-engineer an orange liqueur that was the preferred beverage of a hardy subculture of outdoorsmen, give our own twist to a classic Dark and Stormy (page 23), deliver a ruthlessly elegant Gin and Tonic (page 24), and employ backyard grapefruit and kumquat, fresh from the tree, to bring life and color to clear liquors, leading to all manner of refreshing sparklers and coolers.

Charlestonians' tastes do change, but at a slower pace. Punches, which enjoyed over a century of favor, are on the outs, and fortified wines like Madeira are rare, though a glass of sherry might still be had at the few remaining ladies' teas, put on by grandmothers to celebrate the engagement of a granddaughter. South Carolina finally in 2005 abandoned its mini-bottle mandate (which required all liquor to be dispensed in 1.7-ounce mini-bottles, one per drink, which made mixed cocktails next to impossible), and so in the last couple of years a wave of exuberant cocktail revivalism has swept through Charleston's aspirational bars and restaurants, adding a level of intrigue and some fantastic new ingredients to the bartender's palette.

Every drink has a story—some more than others—but for us, well-balanced flavor is paramount. We aim to balance acidity, sweetness, bitterness, and salt. Yes, a pinch of salt is often all it takes to transform a sweet-leaning beverage into something approaching art.

MUSCADINE SANGRIA

SERVES: 6   TIME: 10 MINUTES PREPARATION, 20 MINUTES CHILLING

Muscadines are the thick-skinned grapes, native to the southern United States, that grow particularly well in the Lowcountry. You find numerous varieties in markets in Charleston—some purple and small as marbles, some bronze-colored and large as Gobstoppers, and others bright green. Whatever the size or color, all have a fun, slightly tropical flavor that puts the bland Thompson Seedless to shame. Every kid here has a memory of eating too many muscadines.

And they're more than just a fresh alternative to seedless table grapes: a pail of muscadines is a taste education in sour-sweet-fruity. Firm, less ripe grapes are sourly sweet, like passionfruit or a Granny Smith apple, while softer ones have a more vanilla-cola taste. The very softest grapes taste almost like coconut cream and raisins if you close your eyes, and there are thousands of gradations of flavor, acidity, sweetness, and oxidation in between. After your first few good muscadine seasons, you learn exactly what degree of muscadine ripeness you prefer; you pick out all those first and then leave the rest of the bucket for your brother or sister.

In this Sangria recipe, we take just the right amount of fresh muscadine juice and blend it with dry, fruity white wine to create an off-dry, delicious punch. Lime slices draw out the citrusy tartness in the grape juice. You'll note we extract the juice from green or bronze-colored grapes, and garnish with purple grapes—a strictly aesthetic choice. If you ain't fussy like that, or if only one variety is available, feel free to use only that one variety.

1 quart (1¼ pounds) ripe green or bronze muscadine grapes

½ cup purple muscadine grapes

2 pinches of kosher salt

1 lime, sliced into thin disks

1 quart ice cubes, plus more for serving

1 (750-ml) bottle dry, fruity white wine, such as pinot grigio or sauvignon blanc

1 cup seltzer

1 Dump 3 cups of the green or bronze muscadines into a food processor, and process them just to a slurry, four to five 3-second pulses. Strain the grapes through a fine-mesh strainer, pressing the pulp to extract the juice; discard the solids. Strain the juice again through a length of cheesecloth doubled over twice. You should have ½ cup muscadine juice.

2 Slice the remaining green or bronze grapes and the purple grapes in half with a sharp knife. Don't worry about the seeds.

3 Sprinkle the salt into the bottom of a pitcher. Scatter about one-third of the halved grapes and the lime slices on top of the salt, then add one-third of the ice on top. Continue to fill the pitcher, alternating layers of fruit and ice, until all the fruit and ice is in the pitcher. Pour the reserved juice, white wine, and seltzer into the pitcher and stir. Transfer to the refrigerator and chill for 20 minutes or until the Sangria is very cold.

4 Pour into glasses over ice, garnishing with halved grapes and lime slices from the pitcher.

THE HUGO   FOR: EACH COCKTAIL   TIME: 3 MINUTES

We named this mixed drink "The Hugo"—our own take on that British colonial classic cocktail the Dark and Stormy—for the category five hurricane that strafed the Caribbean and made landfall on Sullivan's Island, a small beach community just north of Charleston Harbor, at midnight on September 22, 1989. When the storm hit, we were away at college (Ted just three weeks into his freshman year). Our grandmother and her cohorts packed up a friend's big old Mercedes with thermoses of rum and buckets of ice, and headed inland to Macon, Georgia. By the time the storm hit, they were three sheets to the wind.

On televisions in the common rooms of our dorms, we saw the aftermath: the Ben Sawyer Bridge, the small swing-span connecting Sullivan's Island to the mainland, had torqued on its axis and tipped over into the Intracoastal Waterway. A big sloop lay on its side on Lockwood Boulevard. Houses in Summerville and Georgetown were flattened. By comparison, our family fared pretty well—the copper roof of 83 East Bay got peeled back like a sardine can, but it wasn't anything insurance dollars couldn't repair.

Our riff on the Dark and Stormy—as you might imagine, Hugo considering—transforms the soft, tip-'em-back high-ball into a stronger, stiffer affair. We've substituted the ginger beer with peppery-fresh ginger juice. So go easy on these . . . unless of course it's hurricane season, in which case you probably need a few in reserve.

2 ounces (¼ cup) dark rum, such as Mount Gay or Myers's

2 teaspoons fresh ginger juice (from 1½ tablespoons grated fresh ginger pressed through a paper towel)

2 lime wedges

2 teaspoons sugar

Dash of aromatic cocktail bitters, such as Angostura

Splash of seltzer

A rod of peeled fresh ginger (optional)

1 Fill a cocktail shaker with ice cubes. Add the rum, ginger juice, 1 of the lime wedges, the sugar, and bitters, if using. Shake vigorously.

2 Fill a rocks glass with ice cubes. Pour the cocktail over the ice, top off with seltzer, and garnish with the remaining lime wedge and a rod of ginger, if using.

GIN AND TONIC   FOR: EACH COCKTAIL   TIME: 2 MINUTES

n the 1950s, Frances Hamby's life changed when the caterer for a colleague's 400-guest wedding backed out of the job at the last minute. Hamby talked the bride-to-be into letting her cater the event, and when it went off without a hitch, Mrs. Hamby had a new career. Since then, she's been cooking for Charleston graduations, weddings, and funerals, and she has closely studied this city's cocktail-party traditions. Her chicken salad and shrimp salad sandwiches (on Piggly Wiggly "King White" bread, crusts cut off, with Hellmann's mayo) have defined the twilight fare of downtown for the last thirty years, and may in fact be the primary source of nutrition for the city's hardest-working party hounds.

Besides having inspected virtually every kitchen in town, Mrs. Hamby has also taken note of Charlestonians' evolving drinking habits. "People don't want Champagne punch anymore, or coffee punch," she laments, referring to beverages popular in the first part of the twentieth century. "What's popular is gin and tonics and vodka tonics."

Gin and tonics have a particular resonance in a town where the busy wedding season requires everyone to suit up in a malarial, boutonniere-wilting haze. The crystal-clear G&T, which visually registers as an ice cocktail, impresses on first sip, its appetizingly bitter edge riding atop that sweetly herbal gin. It's the perfect refresher for an adult palate.

Nowadays, the restaurants and bars in Charleston are experimenting with a new wave of artisanal gins and tonics, whose exotic flavors are designed more for contemplation than for confidence building. But the key to a great gin and tonic at home is simply to use tonic from small, glass 10-ounce bottles, which deliver a fresher, more sparkly tonic than what is poured from a liter (or, god forbid, 3-liter) plastic bottle. True, the little glass tonics are more difficult to find, and so Schweppes must be commended for continuing to offer them. (Those concerned about wasteful packaging should note that the liter bottle is truly a waste, as the fizz quickly departs; the individual portions conserve usable tonic for far longer.)

The dash of bitters in our version is a grace note you'll almost never find at a Charleston event, but anyone who mixes drinks at home, and owns a bottle of bitters, will recognize that it does no harm; it lends an extra drop of complexity and distinction.

Dash of aromatic cocktail bitters, such as Angostura (optional)

2 ounces (¼ cup) gin

4 ounces (½ cup) tonic water

1 to 2 lime wedges

Fill an 8-ounce glass three-fourths full to the rim with crushed ice. Shake in a dash of bitters, if desired. Pour the gin into the glass. Add the tonic and a squeeze of the lime, and if the drink is for you or close family, smear the lime around the rim of the glass before poking it into the ice with your index finger; if serving company, discard the lime wedge and hang a second wedge on the rim of the glass as a garnish.

MOONSHINE MARTINI   FOR: EACH COCKTAIL   TIME: 2 MINUTES

One of the most exciting beverage developments in the last ten years is the resurgence of craft distilling on the eastern seaboard. After two centuries of decline, entrepreneurs have been inspired to set up distilleries, from the Hudson Valley to the coast of Delaware, to the sea islands of South Carolina, in order to transform sweet, fermentable produce—apples and grapes, corn and rye—into appetizing (and legal!) liquors.

Corn, reputed to be the central ingredient in bootleg booze of the nineteenth and early twentieth centuries, was actually abandoned long ago in favor of cheap sugar. The backyard moonshines we encounter in Charleston freezers are almost certainly made from grocery-store granulated, and at best have a grappa-like headiness to them; at their worst, they may contain other, more dangerous alcohols.

Besides being more costly than sugar, distilling with pure corn takes considerable time and requires more effort, so these days corn whiskey is a de facto hallmark of a quality producer. Taste your first 100 percent corn whiskey and you'll find it easy to stay on the right side of the law. This white lightning tastes richer, smoother, and altogether more delicious than "real" moonshine. Your neighborhood "red dot"—all South Carolina liquor stores must display a big red circle outside the establishment—likely stocks one or two. We prefer the clear corn whiskey to the amber ones aged in oak barrels, as the vanilla-esque flavors of the oak get in the way of the corny sensations.

To celebrate the good stuff, we created this martini, which we season with just a teaspoon of fortified wine, a spicy oxidation note that dries out the inherent sweetness of the corn whiskey. A salty pickled garnish, though optional, will push the savory suggestion into traditional martini territory.

2 ounces (¼ cup) clear corn whiskey

1 teaspoon dry Madeira, dry sherry, or dry vermouth

1 pinch of kosher salt

3 Boiled Peanuts (page 44) or 1 pickled onion, for garnish (optional)

Combine the whiskey, Madeira, and salt in a cocktail shaker filled with ice cubes, and shake vigorously for 10 seconds. Strain the cocktail into a chilled martini glass and garnish with the peanuts, if using.

ROCK AND RYE

TIME: 45 MINUTES

Many Charlestonians have developed an affinity for the syrupy, soul-warming texture of a liqueur, especially in the chill of winter, out on the hunt or working on the water. Former game warden Benjamin Moise recounted for us a distinctive New Year's tradition he kept back in the 1970s and '80s with a commercial rye-based liqueur seasoned with orange, called Mr. Boston Rock & Rye, made in the Roxbury neighborhood of Boston until 1986 (the brand and the beverage continues, now owned by Sazerac Company and produced in Owensboro, Kentucky).

Moise and the Magwood family owned adjacent hummock islands—sandy mid-marsh sites for fishing shacks, with a palmetto tree, maybe a stunted cedar or live oak, and not much more—behind an oceanfront barrier island north of Charleston. And as Moise tells it, in early January, the Magwoods, famous locally as commercial oystermen and shrimpers (see page 138), put on a "Mullet Hunt and Rock & Rye Festival," a gathering of about fifteen hardy friends and their motorboats on the Magwoods' Little Bull Island.

"The Magwood house was built of scrap timber salvaged from shipwrecks, and I remember they had an eight-foot, black-iron wood stove that made the most delicious heat in that low-ceiling thing in winter," said Moise. "Guys would tie up at the back dock, and Andrew Magwood would put on an oyster roast for us. Then he'd go out to the water with a cast net and come back with a bunch of mullet. He'd scale them, roll them in cornmeal, and put 'em in a pan on the stove. A pot of grits had been bubbling all night long, and we'd eat fried fresh mullet, grits, and eggs—it was the best breakfast ever. Then we'd repair to the small boats and hit the beach, bringing Old Mr. Boston Rock & Rye to use as antifreeze."

The tradition ended in 1989, when Hurricane Hugo swept a twenty-foot-high wall of water through the islands, clearing them of everything except a few cedar pilings. Even the heavy iron stove disappeared.

Part of the mystique of commercial Rock & Rye, to this day, is the slice of crystallized orange in the bottom of the bottle. We resolved to bring back the tradition, since the idea of pairing orange with spicy rye whiskey in a winter warmer seems festive and logical. In developing our version, we dialed back the sweetness slightly and boosted the savory rye flavor. Our Rock and Rye is a nice sip on ice, year-round, and a terrific drizzle on vanilla ice cream. But without a doubt, it reaches its highest calling when consumed as a chaser on a cold day, following smoked, pickled, or fried fish.

1 cup sugar

2 pinches of kosher salt

1 navel orange

1 liter American rye whiskey, such as Jim Beam or Old Overholt

1 Stir the sugar and salt with 1 cup of water in a small saucepan and simmer over medium-high heat until the sugar dissolves and becomes syrupy, about 10 minutes.

2 Meanwhile, slice off and reserve the top and bottom of the orange. Cut the orange into ½-inch-thick slices and then cut into half-moons.

3 Reduce the heat under the pan to medium and add the orange half-moons along with the top and bottom slices (the syrup should just barely bubble around the slices at first). Simmer, flipping the slices once or twice as the froth builds, until a nice roasted-orange aroma develops and the flesh has a withered look, about 25 minutes. Allow to cool for a few minutes; then, holding back the candied orange with a wooden spoon,

(recipe continues)

pour the syrup into a large heatproof pitcher. You should have approximately ½ cup orange syrup. Let the candied orange cool in the pan.

4 Pour ½ cup rye from the bottle and reserve for another use; then decant the remainder of the rye into the pitcher with the orange syrup, stirring to dissolve the syrup in the liquor. When the candied orange is cool enough to touch, feed 2 or 3 slices—reserve the remainder for another use, such as garnishing a ½-cup goblet of rye on the rocks—through the neck of the rye bottle (they'll be nice and pliable, and will squeeze through with a firm poke). Pour the flavored rye back into the bottle using a funnel. The liqueur will keep for months at room temperature.

LOWCOUNTRY LIMONCELLO

MAKES: 1 (750-ML) BOTTLE   TIME: 30 MINUTES PREPARATION, 2 DAYS STEEPING

The backyard grapefruit trees that contribute tropical relief to a Charleston winter have an aromatic secret: their glossy green leaves are exquisitely floral in flavor and aroma, and can be used like lime leaves to season curries, marinades, and liquor—to great effect. We make a simple but sophisticated limoncello by steeping the perfumy peels and leaves of backyard grapefruit and orange in clear grape brandy in Mason jars (we get our brandy nearby, from a friend with a muscadine vineyard). Vodka may be used in this recipe, but grape brandy gives the impression of some residual sweetness and binds the flavors seamlessly. When it's obtained locally, it also allows us to make our limoncello from 100 percent Charleston County ingredients.

We sip small amounts of this limoncello cold, as a digestivo after dinner (this idea rose to prominence on the island of Capri, near Naples), but it works very nicely as well in any cocktail that calls for orange-flavored vodka.

1 grapefruit, with 6 to 8 leaves attached to the stem	1 (750-ml) bottle clear grape brandy, like Ciroc "vodka"
1 navel orange	Simple syrup (optional; recipe follows)

1   Using a vegetable peeler, scrape thick curls of zest from the grapefruit, digging deep enough to produce a continuous curl but shallow enough to avoid cutting into the white pith. As long as there is more zest than pith, you're doing great. Remove as many curls of peel as possible and reserve the fruit itself for another use, such as Skillet Asparagus with Grapefruit (page 93). Repeat with the orange.

2   Put the leaves and zest strips in a quart-size Mason jar, pour the brandy into the jar, and seal. Steep at room temperature for 2 days.

3   Season to taste with simple syrup. Leaves and zest may remain in the brandy for several weeks, intensifying the flavor. Strain and discard both once the leaves have lost most of their color. Store in the freezer and serve over ice in small glasses.

SIMPLE SYRUP
MAKES: 1 CUP   TIME: 4 MINUTES

1 cup sugar	½ cup water

In a small saucepan, combine the sugar and water and cook over low heat, stirring with a wooden spoon, until the sugar is completely dissolved, about 2 minutes. Pour into a glass jar or a vessel with a tight-fitting lid, cool to room temperature, and store in the refrigerator. (The syrup keeps for 1 month.)

SUMMER PEACH COOLER   SERVES: 6   TIME: 8 MINUTES

All hail Kim Severson, Atlanta Bureau Chief of the *New York Times,* whose article about peaches in that paper in the summer of 2011 brought to national prominence a phenomenon we'd known anecdotally: that residents of "The Peach State," aka Georgia, cross the border into South Carolina to buy peaches because the fruit that grows in our home state is sweeter.

Yes, folks, there's a peach rivalry between the states! We can't vouch for the Georgia ones, but we know a good peach—syrupy juice and jasmine-like aroma—and the ones grown in upstate South Carolina are so delicious, we'll gladly drive the 3½ hours from our office on Broad Street up to York County. Sanders Peach Stand is to our minds the finest place in the world to buy them, with personalized service and a bonus: in addition to filling your car with peaches for preserving and freezing through the winter months, you can buy signed copies of the terrific novel *Clover,* written by Dori Sanders, who owns the farm with her brothers and sisters.

Our peach cocktails couldn't be simpler. This cooler is a nonalcoholic blend of seltzer and peach purée; the sparkler that follows pairs the sunny flavor of peach with the effervescence of sparkling white wine.

1 pound ripe peaches, peeled and pitted, plus fresh peach slices for garnish

¼ cup lime juice (from about 3 limes)

1 teaspoon sugar, plus more to taste

¾ teaspoon kosher salt

About 1¼ quarts seltzer water

1 Put the peaches in a food processor or blender with the lime juice, sugar, and salt, and process to a very smooth purée.

2 For each drink, pour 6 ounces (¾ cup) seltzer water over ice into a highball glass. With a bar spoon, stir in 3 tablespoons of the peach purée. Garnish with a peach slice.

SUMMER PEACH SPARKLER   SERVES: 4   TIME: 5 MINUTES

This simple Southern spin on the bellini, a classic Italian apéritif, makes an outstanding summer cocktail with just two ingredients—peaches and sparkling white wine. As with the Kumquat Sparkler (page 34), this recipe calls for doctoring the wine with peach purée, so don't splurge on Champagne; just find an inexpensive, dry sparkling wine such as Italian prosecco or Spanish cava.

3 large, ripe peaches, peeled, pitted, and cut into wedges

1 (750-ml) bottle dry sparkling white wine, chilled

1 Put the peaches in a food processor or blender, reserving 4 of the wedges for garnishing the glasses. Process the peaches for about 90 seconds, or until they become a very smooth purée.

2 For each cocktail, pour 1 to 2 tablespoons of the purée into a Champagne flute or wine glass, then fill the glass one-third of the way to the rim with sparkling wine. Stir with a bar spoon to settle the foaming of the wine. Pour in a little more wine, stir again, and finally top off the glass with the sparkling wine. Garnish each with a wedge of peach.

A LEGARE STREET GATE

LOQUAT MANHATTAN

FOR: EACH COCKTAIL   TIME: 3 MINUTES

The loquat trees that drop their small yellow fruits all over downtown Charleston in March and April are perceived to be a nuisance by some people. But many locals (see Holy City Foraging, page 102) know that a simple infusion of whole loquats in a neutral spirit like vodka makes a beautiful aperitif, or a nightcap poured over an ice cube.

Loquat-derived tipples are not unique to the Low-country: Italians make loquat-seed liqueur, which calls for stripping the fruit from the seeds and discarding it, curing the seeds in the sun for weeks, and then steeping them in alcohol; Japanese *biwashu*—more akin to Lowcountry-style methods—preserves the fruit whole, but adds rock sugar to the mix along with clear spirits. The common method in our town is remarkable for its minimalist route to great flavor: We put washed fruit in a clean quart jar, top up with vodka, and let stand. After about three weeks the loquats will have begun to flavor the vodka—a bright, unmistakably cherry-like taste. As the yellow skins of the fruit oxidize, browning in color (which is normal), the liquid also takes on an almond flavor and hue, the flavor becoming more intense the longer you keep it. You may top up the level of the jar with more vodka, but expect the resulting liqueur to have stronger amaretto notes than cherry ones, and then for the flavor to diminish over time.

The cherry-almond character of this elixir inspired us to substitute it for the vermouth in a Manhattan, that classic cocktail of rye whiskey, sweet vermouth, and bitters, with a maraschino cherry and/or orange peel for garnish. Since the cherry taste in the liqueur is pronounced, we skip the maraschino and opt for a solo orange peel.

2 ounces (¼ cup) rye whiskey or bourbon	2 dashes Angostura bitters
1 ounce (2 tablespoons) Loquat Liqueur (recipe follows)	Ice cubes
	1- to 2-inch strip of orange peel (for garnish)

Pour the rye and the loquat liqueur into a bar mixing glass or pint glass, and shake the bitters on top. Fill the glass with ice. With a bar spoon, stir the cocktail for 15 to 20 seconds using a swift circular motion to avoid introducing bubbles into the liquid. Strain the cocktail into a champagne coupe. (If you prefer to serve it over ice, put 1 large or 2 small ice cubes in a rocks glass and pour the cocktail into the glass.) Pinch the orange peel over the cocktail to release its oils onto the surface, brush the rim of the glass with the peel, and drop it in.

LOQUAT LIQUEUR
MAKES: ABOUT 3 CUPS LIQUEUR
TIME: 3 MINUTES PREPARATION,
2 WEEKS STEEPING

4 cups loquats, washed (about 1¼ pounds)	2 to 3 cups vodka, preferably Ciroc

Put the loquats in a quart-size Mason jar. Top up the jar with the vodka and let stand for at least 2 weeks before using (many Charlestonians prefer to wait 1 year). The vodka will keep for a few years at room temperature.

KUMQUAT GIN AND COCKTAILS

Now that Charleston has more than a dozen restaurants with "cocktail programs," as well as a handful of stand-alone bars with bow-tied, suspender-wearing mixologists, our drinking lives in the Holy City have become more interesting than ever. But honestly, translating the craft of these establishments to the home has its challenges: what if you don't have an afternoon to boil beets down to molasses? Where can you find hyssop or sorrel? Or what if you don't have the patience to mail-order in four types of bitters from a dude in Germany?

There are, however, a few easy things you can do to step up your home cocktail game, and making this Kumquat Gin is one of them. It's a simple infusion of a citrus that grows like crazy in downtown Charleston, yet is almost entirely ignored. The kumquat has an otherworldly citrus quality—its flavor is a lot like a mix of orange and grapefruit and lemon, and its peel is the most tasty, sweet, and tender part of the fruit. Like the peach brandy with which Charlestonians of yore used to flavor their punches, Kumquat Gin is something to keep on the bar, in a quart-size Mason jar, for spiking all manner of cocktails.

Here's the recipe for the infused gin, and three cocktail recipes that employ it. The high season for kumquats is winter, and if you don't have some growing in the neighborhood, look for them in markets from January 'til May.

KUMQUAT GIN
MAKES: ABOUT 3 CUPS   TIME: 5 MINUTES PREPARATION, 24 HOURS STEEPING

8 ounces kumquats (about 2 cups), sliced crosswise into ¼-inch-thick coins

2 pinches of kosher salt

1 (750-ml) bottle London dry gin, such as Brokers or Tanqueray

Put the kumquats in a quart-size canning jar and add the salt. Pour the gin into the jar. (You will have about ½ cup leftover gin; reserve and add to the jar as the kumquat gin gets depleted.) Screw the top onto the jar and let steep for 24 hours at room temperature before using. (The gin will keep for up to 6 months at room temperature. Use the sliced kumquats to garnish drinks.)

KUMQUAT SPARKLER
FOR: EACH COCKTAIL   TIME: 2 MINUTES

For festive late winter and early spring celebrations. Don't bother breaking the bank with a costly Champagne; any sparkling white labeled brut (dry)—including French *crémants* de Loire, Spanish cavas, and Italian proseccos—will make a superb substitute.

¾ ounce (1½ tablespoons) Kumquat Gin (recipe above)

1 slice gin-steeped kumquat

5 ounces (generous ½ cup) sparkling white wine, chilled

Pour the gin into a Champagne flute or coupe glass, and add the kumquat slice. Top up the glass with the sparkling white wine and serve.

(recipe continues)

KUMQUATINI

FOR: EACH COCKTAIL   TIME: 3 MINUTES

Alas, we prefer gin martinis—not vodka ones—but we do like ours shaken, not stirred. A subtle orange inflection does a martini good.

½ ounce (1 tablespoon) high-quality dry vermouth, such as Dolin blanc

1 slice gin-steeped kumquat

2 ounces (¼ cup) Kumquat Gin (page 34)

1   Pour the vermouth into a martini glass or Champagne coupe. Swirl it around to coat the inside of the glass entirely and pour out the excess. Add the slice of kumquat to the glass.

2   Fill a cocktail shaker with ice and pour the gin into it. Shake vigorously, then strain the gin into the glass, and serve.

KUMQUAT MARGARITA

FOR: EACH COCKTAIL   TIME: 4 MINUTES

Kumquat Gin is the perfect substitute for the citrusy-sweet Triple Sec in a classic margarita.

1 tablespoon kosher salt (optional)

2 slices gin-steeped kumquat

2 ounces (¼ cup) tequila blanco

1 ounce (2 tablespoons) Kumquat Gin (page 34)

¾ ounce (1½ tablespoons) fresh lime juice

1 teaspoon superfine sugar

1   Scatter salt, if using, on a saucer or plate. Moisten the rim of a rocks glass with one of the kumquat slices, and discard. Dip the moistened rim of the glass into the salt. Fill the glass with ice.

2   Fill a cocktail shaker with ice and add the tequila, gin, lime juice, and sugar, and shake vigorously.

3   Strain the cocktail into the glass. Garnish with the remaining kumquat slice.

KUMQUAT-CHILE BLOODY MARY

SERVES: 2   TIME: 5 MINUTES

One night in our Wentworth Street test kitchen, we got an urge to buzz up local kumquats with some fresh chiles to make a hot sauce. And then it hit: what we were doing was re-creating *yuzu kosho*, the hot and salty chile paste made from chiles and the rind of the Japanese citrus fruit yuzu.

We had traveled to Japan a few years previously to search for the grave of our mother's grandfather, a silk trader who died in 1923, in the Great Kanto earthquake. While there, we discovered the beguiling *yuzu kosho*—a couple dots on a hearty soup, served with an oily fish like hibachi-grilled mackerel, or in a ceramic pot on a table in a pork-only restaurant (they have those in Japan). In Charleston, we use our "kumquat kosho"—*kosho* means "pepper"—as we would hot sauce, dabbed on chilled shrimp or sunny-side-up eggs, and in this fiery, delicious brunch cocktail.

Kumquat Chile Paste is a natural ingredient for adorning a Bloody Mary: its peppery heat hits the high notes with the horseradish, the saltiness suits the savory personality of the beverage, and the zesty citrus works beautifully to round off the edges in the tomato base.

2 cups tomato juice

4 teaspoons Kumquat Chile Paste (recipe follows) or *yuzu kosho*

4 teaspoons fresh lemon juice

1 teaspoon prepared horseradish

⅛ teaspoon freshly ground black pepper

1 rib of celery, cut into a few sticks

1 Fill a cocktail shaker with ice cubes. Combine the tomato juice, chile paste, lemon juice, horseradish, and pepper in a pint glass. Pour the mixture into the shaker and then back and forth a couple times to mix and chill the drink.

2 Fill 2 large tumblers with ice and strain the mixture into the glasses. Garnish with 2 or 3 celery sticks.

KUMQUAT CHILE PASTE

MAKES: ½ CUP   TIME: 25 MINUTES

For our blend of "kumquat kosho" we use jalapeño peppers because we adore their flavor and ubiquity (and mild heat, at least in the grocery-store varieties). Red jalapeños make the prettiest paste if you can obtain them, but the standard green looks great, too. Throw in a habañero for good measure if you want to push the heat quotient to the limit.

4 ounces kumquats, halved lengthwise

6 red or green jalapeño peppers, stemmed and seeded

1½ teaspoons kosher salt or medium-coarse sea salt

1 Set a rack in the middle of the oven and preheat the oven to 300°F.

2 Remove the pithy flesh from each kumquat half with a pinch and a pull, and discard. Lay the kumquat hulls and the pepper pieces on a baking sheet lined with foil. Turn off the oven, put the tray on the middle rack, and close the oven door. Let sit for 10 minutes to partially dehydrate the peppers and kumquats.

3 Remove the sheet from the oven. Chop the peppers and kumquats coarsely, then add both to the bowl of a food processor and process, scraping the sides with a spatula if necessary, until the kumquat is mostly purée and the pepper is reduced to flakes, most of which are smaller than a grain of rice.

4 Transfer the mixture to a small glass jar such as a spice jar, add the salt, and blend with a small spoon. Cover and store in the refrigerator overnight for the flavors to meld. Use judiciously as you would a flavored salt. (The paste will keep in the refrigerator for up to a month.)

SNACKS, HORS D'OEUVRES, and SALADS

IN THIS CHAPTER, WE BEGIN WITH BOILED PEANUTS, THE QUIRKY Southern snack that led us into the food business in the first place. Somehow the smaller finger foods are the enticements we can least resist, for their concentrated goodness (and often their aggressive salt content), but perhaps also because we typically approach them with an empty stomach. In Charleston, an array of savory baked nibbles like Pecan Cheese Wafers (page 55), spiced pecans, mini biscuits, and piped cheese straws or puffs is typically offered to guests along with the cocktails.

Whether homemade or store-bought, hors d'oeuvres and snacks can become the hallmarks of your entertaining style. The Savory Benne Wafers (page 49), tiny addictive sesame bites, are quickly becoming that for us, the way Pepperidge Farm pretzel fish were for our grandmother—always there, in an Imari tureen on her coffee table.

Odds are, however, that it's the more luscious dips and spreads that will work their way into heaviest rotation—a spicy, dippable cheese blend (Henry's Cheese Spread, page 47), a smoky, tangy eggplant dip (page 61), and an herby, spreadable shad roe (page 67) that makes this seasonal indulgence approachable and shareable with a crowd. Like many of these dips and spreads, our Crab Salad (page 58), a year-round treat, can be served with baked crackers, or with endive, celery, and romaine hearts as delivery scoops.

Charleston meals and events are rarely without shrimp, and a batch of Pickled Shrimp with Fennel (page 50), besides making a terrific house present, particularly around the holidays, is a great way to introduce those shellfish to a menu that would otherwise have nothing but meat and vegetables. And our Rice and Ham Croquettes (page 63) are so delicious—crisp on the outside, tender within—that they could pass for a main course if paired with the right vegetable side dish.

BOILED PEANUTS MAKES: 4 POUNDS, ENOUGH FOR 8 FOR SNACKING

TIME: 8 HOURS SOAKING, 8 HOURS BOILING, 2 HOURS COOLING

Boiled peanuts, perhaps more than any other Southern snack, inspire a kind of intense cultural loyalty, one that crosses all lines of class and race. That may be why we missed them so when we moved away from Charleston to colleges in Massachusetts, and it's why, when we began to sell Southern foods by mail order after college (our liberal arts degrees be damned), we used the boiled peanut as the keystone in our little mail-order foods catalogue, which we named "The Lee Bros. Boiled Peanuts Catalogue" (boiledpeanuts.com). Boiled peanuts are associated with the outdoors, and can be purchased in the Charleston area by the side of the road from vendors set up in vacant lots and sandy strips on the way to the beach, adjacent to the ballpark, or at fairgrounds. They are prepared in homes as well, but rarely seen in a restaurant setting (with a few exceptions these days: Hubee-D's, Hominy Grill, The Bar at Husk, and The Wreck).

Like the ungainly name, the damp boiled peanut itself presents a few obstacles to universal enjoyment. Not everyone likes their distinctive grassy flavor or the clammy wetness on the fingers as one picks them apart—and they achieve some exclusivity by being challenging in that respect. Judged on flavor alone, with an open mind, they are divine.

And the smell of peanuts boiling is, to us, part of the pleasure of the process. Our grandmother's landlady, the late Elizabeth Jenkins Young, once remarked to us (in her sonorous variant of the Charleston accent, with a sea island cadence from an upbringing on Edisto Island) that the smell of our peanuts boiling on Gran's stove reminded her of a "sweet potato gone sour." Not that she didn't like them; she proudly displayed her I BRAKE FOR BOILED PEANUTS bumper sticker in the back window of the blue VW Rabbit she won at the 1983 Spoleto Festival auction. But the earthy quality of the peanut, which grows underground and is full of minerals, and the sweetness of it, does in fact suggest the basic character of a sweet potato.

When peanuts are freshly dug, and refrigerated like a fresh vegetable rather than dried, they are called "green" peanuts; and these, when available (usually in the summer months and into the fall), are worth seeking out for their extra tenderness—cut about 4 hours off the boiling time below—and subtlety of flavor. Some green peanuts will be slightly immature, and like a soft-shell crab, may be eaten whole, shell and all.

1½ cups salt, plus more to taste	2 pounds raw peanuts in the shell, or 3 pounds green peanuts

1 In a 10- to 12-quart stockpot, stir ½ cup salt into 2 gallons of water until the salt dissolves, and add the raw peanuts. Use a large dinner plate or two to help submerge the floating peanuts. Allow to soak for 8 hours or overnight. (This step saves a little time boiling, and thus fuel, but if you don't have the luxury of time, skip this step. Skip it also if you're using green peanuts.)

2 Drain the soaking water and fill the pot of peanuts with 2 gallons of fresh water and the remaining cup of salt. Note the level of the water on the side of the pot. Bring to a boil, reduce the heat to low, and simmer, covered, for 6 to 8 hours (or 2 to 3 hours for green peanuts), keeping the water in the pot within an inch or so of its original level with regular additions of water, until the peanuts are soft as a roasted chestnut or softer.

3 When the peanuts have boiled for 3 hours (or 1 hour for green peanuts), sample them to check their texture and salinity. Remove a peanut, and when it is cool enough to handle, crack open the shell and give the kernel a chew, slurping some brine with it. If the

peanut crunches, it should be cooked further. If the brine lacks enough salt, add by ¼-cup amounts; if it is too salty, remove a portion of the water and replace with the same volume of fresh water. Allow an hour for the salinity to equalize before testing again. Sample every hour until the peanuts are pleasantly yielding and as salty and appetizing as a good pickle.

4 When the peanuts are cooked to your satisfaction, turn off the heat and allow them to cool in the pot for an hour (or 30 minutes for green peanuts). When cool enough to handle, drain and eat immediately or store in the shell, in a sealed container, in the refrigerator or freezer. (Boiled peanuts will keep for 7 to 10 days in the refrigerator and for several months in the freezer.)

HENRY'S CHEESE SPREAD

MAKES: 1½ CUPS, ENOUGH FOR 6 TO 8 PEOPLE FOR SNACKING   TIME: 10 MINUTES

When Henry Hasselmeyer and his son-in-law, Walter Shaffer (pronounced SHAFF-er), opened Henry's, a beer parlor at 54 North Market Street, in 1932, they served only beer and deviled crabs (see page 153), baked up by Hasselmeyer's wife in their home on Ashley Avenue and delivered to the establishment on cookie sheets in a long black Packard. By the 1940s, Henry's had evolved into Charleston's most ambitious restaurant, with waiters in white jackets, steaks trucked in from the Kansas City butcher Pfaelzer Brothers, and the house's own fanciful turns on local fish and shellfish: seafood à la Wando (named for a river north of Charleston), flounder à la Gherardi (named, it is variously said, for a rear admiral of the U.S. Navy who served in the Civil War, or for his son, a prominent engineer, who might have been a patron).

Of all the elegant touches at Henry's, which survived until 1985, when the family sold it, our favorite was the iced crudité dish set down on every table at the start of the meal. The plate, a simple steel oval, cradled celery, radishes, green cocktail olives, and an astonishingly good cheese spread. Some have likened this dip to pimento cheese, but it may have been more awesome, with the creamy-fiery thing of p.c., but torqued up by horseradish to a picklish, sinus-clearing intensity. It arrived on the table with little fanfare—it appeared nowhere on the menu (see Henry's Menu, page 123)—but left a deep impression on people who loved Henry's. This latter category included Albert Goldman, the late Elvis biographer, rock-and-roll critic, and frequent contributor to *High Times*—"the voice of the marijuana community"—who praised the cheese spread in his hilariously florid story about Charleston in a 1973 issue of *Travel & Leisure*.

Walter Shaffer's son, Henry, who graduated from the Citadel in 1950 and supervised the kitchen at Henry's for several years in the fifties, loaned us the restaurant's original recipe, typed on an old typewriter, calibrated for a commercial quantity. We've adapted it here for household use, although once you taste it, you may think we're high for ratcheting down the quantity. It's a fabulous spread for asparagus spears, radishes, carrot sticks, and crackers, to name a few. Or stir it into grits or fold it into an omelet!

10 ounces sharp Cheddar cheese, grated (3 cups)	**1 tablespoon prepared horseradish, drained**
2 ounces (¼ cup) lager or ale	**2 teaspoons hot sauce, such as Tabasco or Crystal**
Juice of 1 lemon (3 tablespoons)	**1½ teaspoons dry mustard**
2 tablespoons ketchup	**1 garlic clove, minced**
2 tablespoons Worcestershire sauce	

Combine all the ingredients in the bowl of a food processor and pulse until the mixture is smooth and spreadable. Transfer to a small bowl to serve.

SAVORY BENNE WAFERS

MAKES: ABOUT 150 QUARTER-SIZE WAFERS   TIME: 45 MINUTES, INCLUDING BAKING TIME

Benne is the term for "sesame" in the Bantu dialects of western Africa, and although sesame seeds came to the Lowcountry during the slave trade nearly three centuries ago, the word is still commonly used among Charlestonians, both in home kitchens and on restaurant menus. The crisp Sweet Benne Wafers (page 221) are served with afternoon tea or after-dinner drinks, and sold in tins in grocery stores and gift shops. Homemade Savory Benne Wafers are far rarer, but they're outstanding—an addictive savory cookie for popping by the dozens during the cocktail hour.

We've made these wafers special by pulsing a quantity of toasted sesame seeds with the flour so there's that intense smoky-toasty flavor baked into the cookie. We believe that the thinner we roll the dough, the more delicious they become. Our friend Steven Satterfield, the Savannah-born chef of the restaurant Miller Union, in Atlanta, even advised using a pasta machine to make these, which produces excellent results (make sure you have a liberal amount of flour on hand, as the dough will need to be well dusted before it goes through the rollers). Whether hand-rolled or machine-rolled, these nutty bites are not to be missed.

2 cups all-purpose flour, plus more for dusting

1½ teaspoons kosher salt

¼ teaspoon cayenne

2 tablespoons toasted sesame seeds

¾ cup (1½ sticks) unsalted butter, cut into small pieces, cold

¼ cup ice water

2 teaspoons untoasted sesame seeds

1   Preheat the oven to 325°F.

2   In a food processor, pulse the flour with the salt, cayenne, and 1 tablespoon of the toasted sesame seeds several times until the seeds are pulverized as fine as the flour. Add the cold butter, and continue to pulse until the mixture resembles coarse crumbs with pea-size pieces throughout. Add half of the ice water and pulse a couple times. Add the remaining 1 tablespoon toasted sesame seeds and the remaining ice water, and continue processing in pulses of about 3 seconds duration, just until the mixture comes together in a ball.

3   Dust a cutting board with flour and set the ball of dough on it. Using your hands, flatten the dough and shape it into a patty about 1½ inches thick. Dust the top of the dough with flour, then cut the patty into four small wedges. With a rolling pin, roll each wedge to a uniform ¹⁄₁₆ inch thick (if rolling the dough this thinly and evenly presents a challenge, try rolling each wedge to ¼ or ⅛ inch, and then pass through a hand-crank pasta machine set on the thickest setting). With a quarter-size cookie cutter or a shot glass turned upside down, cut the dough into wafers and transfer to baking sheets lined with parchment paper (you'll need two sheets). Repeat with the remaining dough and any leftovers, and when all the wafers are on the sheets, sprinkle the wafers with the untoasted sesame seeds.

4   Bake until gently browned, 12 to 15 minutes. Remove and let cool completely (although you may want to sneak a few warm ones!). Transfer the wafers to a container with a tight-fitting lid and store at room temperature. (They'll keep for several days.)

PICKLED SHRIMP WITH FENNEL

SERVES: 8   TIME: 30 MINUTES, PLUS 1 HOUR COOLING

We can hear it now: *What? Fennel?* Fennel's not Southern!

One of the more thrilling aspects of delving into the history of agriculture in South Carolina is that you discover vegetables you've never heard of—anybody up for roasted tanya?—and you learn about a few others you might not have perceived to be "Southern." Eggplant, salsify, and yes, fennel, to name a few, have in fact been grown in the Charleston area since the eighteenth century.

We owe much of our understanding of Charleston's veggie past to David Shields, a bow-tied American Studies professor at the University of South Carolina, and a Renaissance man of the highest order (he happens to be an expert on early Russian piano music and still photography from the silent film era). As we eagerly await publication of Shields's magnum opus on vegetables and grains of the South, *The Taste Shall Rise Again,* he has shared with us more than a dozen draft passages, in which we've learned all kinds of cool stuff, such as that in the early 1700s, farmers south of Charleston attempted large-scale commercial olive-oil production. And that when that experiment failed, sesame oil became the salad dressing oil of choice in Charleston in the 1730s. The trade in the oil was so brisk that an export market for it developed, and a commercial sesame oil press was built in Charleston.

History aside, pickled shrimp and fennel are perfectly complementary. After all, we often encounter fennel's close cousins, dill (or dill seed) and celery (or celery seeds), in many preparations of this classic hors d'oeuvre. Served in a bowl for self-service with toothpicks, pickled shrimp may also be a passed hors d'oeuvre on a plate if you use the sturdy bamboo picks found in many party stores these days. One of the advantages of this recipe is that the marinated fennel pushes the pickled shrimp into the cold-salad realm: it's easy enough to strew several of the shrimp and strips or rings of the fennel over butter lettuce to create a pretty appetizer salad.

1 tablespoon plus 1½ teaspoons kosher salt

2 pounds large (21 to 25 count) shrimp, peeled and deveined

½ cup white wine vinegar

1 cup fresh lemon juice (from about 7 lemons)

1 small fresh bird or serrano chile (green or red), sliced very thinly on the bias

1 teaspoon sugar

1 small white onion, thinly sliced

1 small fennel bulb, thinly sliced

1 tablespoon chopped fennel fronds

1 Fill a medium stockpot with 2 quarts of water, add 1 tablespoon of the salt, and bring to a boil over high heat. Prepare an ice bath in a large bowl. When the salted water boils, turn off the heat, add the shrimp, stirring them once or twice to distribute them, and cook until uniformly pink-opaque and just done, about 1 minute. With a slotted spoon, transfer the shrimp to the ice bath. Reserve 2 cups of the shrimp-cooking liquid in a medium bowl.

2 With the slotted spoon, transfer the shrimp to a plate lined with a double thickness of paper towels. (Don't dump the ice bath yet!) Add the vinegar, lemon juice, and chile to the bowl with the shrimp-cooking liquid and whisk in the remaining 1½ teaspoons salt and the sugar until dissolved. Set this bowl of brine in the ice bath (add more ice to the bath if needed), and whisk until the liquid cools to room temperature.

3 Dump the ice bath and use the cold large bowl to toss the shrimp, onion, fennel slices, and fennel fronds. Pour the cooled brine over the shrimp. Cover with plastic wrap and refrigerate for about 1 hour, tossing once, until chilled and ready to serve. (Pickled shrimp will keep in the refrigerator for about 2 days.)

CHARLESTON RECEIPTS

WE WERE SITTING IN VEREEN COEN'S formal dining room in a single house on Meeting Street, under a portrait of her grandmother in a white dress, in the very place at the table where, in 1949, Coen's mother, Mary Vereen Huguenin, compiled *Charleston Receipts,* one of the country's first and most successful spiral-bound community cookbooks. Recipes were solicited from Junior League members and from others in the community, and as the recipes came in, Huguenin and a committee of the League's sustaining members conferred here on the mahogany, appraising the recipe's usefulness to the manuscript, testing occasionally, making a few adjustments.

"*Charleston Receipts* left the most wonderful sense of camaraderie among the women who worked on it, and cooked together," Coen said, acknowledging all the effort her mother and others put into creating the book. Coen maintains three large scrapbooks her mother had begun of press clippings and memorabilia related to the cookbook, and we pored over them for several hours, gleaning six decades' worth of Charleston food stories and odd footnotes. "I've been lucky to be a cheerleader for the book," Coen said.

Published as a fund-raising venture by the Junior League of Charleston to support a local charity, the Charleston Speech and Hearing Center, the cookbook grew in sales and reputation to become the definitive twentieth-century cookbook for the region. It got that way largely through the sheer determination, hard work, and marketing savvy of Mrs. Huguenin, who made the book her life's mission—and through the recipe contributions of hundreds of Charlestonians. But it is the book's inherent value that makes it exceptional: compared to the typical community cookbook, *Charleston Receipts* is ten times as rich—in recipes

and in the other details about life in Charleston around the time of the Second World War. There are more than four hundred "receipts"—the archaic term for recipe—and their diversity and breadth are impressive. The many threads of English, African, Huguenot, Portuguese, German, Polish, and other ethnic influences on Charleston are palpable in its pages (even if chapter headings and headnotes register as lily white in perspective), everything from eighteenth-century punches and elaborate poultry dishes, to opossum, to the quotidian staples of Lowcountry tables, like greens and grits. There are a few—a precious few—cans of soup.

Despite the book's limitations (which are not unique: the "cook til done" vagueness of any 1950s cookbook hinders its viability in today's kitchens), as cooks we return to *Charleston Receipts* again and again to remind ourselves just how broad and exciting the range of ingredients and preparations used to be, and also to marvel at how far we've come in many respects. Coen prefers to see the open-endedness—the cook till doneness—of the recipes as the key to the book's longevity: "It's left to the eye of the beholder!"

The attributions printed with each recipe include the contributor's maiden moniker, when appropriate, so reading *Charleston Receipts* is a dive into a torrent of local names, giving a real sense of regional character. The poetry here is distinctive, and somewhat haunting. Take, for example, the credit on "Brown Oyster Stew with Benne Seed": "Mrs. Augustine T. S. Stoney (Louisa Jenkins)."

It's a very Charlestonian name: both "Stoneys" and "Jenkinses," whether black or white, are associated with Edisto Island and with the country. Incidentally, it's a very cool recipe.

Fans of *Charleston Receipts* may be surprised to discover, as

A MODEL POSES, CIRCA 1951, WITH THE SAME CHARLESTON
SEAFOOD VENDOR WHO APPEARS ON THE COVER OF *CHARLESTON
RECEIPTS*, IN AN ILLUSTRATION BY MARGARET B. WALKER.
(B. ANTHONY STEWART/NATIONAL GEOGRAPHIC STOCK)

we did recently, that the familiar green-covered cookbook had a precursor, titled *Charleston Recipes,* assembled by two young members of the League and published in 1948, in a run of 2,000 copies. Martha Lynch Humphreys and a cousin, Margaret B. Walker, compiled this earlier version, slightly smaller in size and scope, which depicted on its candy-apple red cover a woodcut image of the "crab man," an iconic Charleston seafood vendor, rendered by Walker. Contained in its pages are 403 recipes, 77 of which were republished in *Charleston Receipts.* The existence of *Charleston Recipes* somewhat disturbs the genesis story of *Charleston Receipts,* as presented in the introduction to that book and told around town for the last few decades.

Fans of the novelist and historian Josephine Humphreys, whose mother was Martha Humphreys, will also be interested to learn that *Charleston Recipes* is fundamentally a Walker-Humphreys and Huguenin family cookbook, with close to 100 recipes contributed by members of those two families. (They used alternate renderings of their names to make the pool of contributors seem more widespread.) Mary Huguenin was a contributor to *Charleston Recipes,* and was on the committee that put it together. Her "Crabmeat au Gratin" appears on page 42 of *Charleston Recipes*; in *Charleston Receipts,* it became "Meeting Street Crab Meat," page 84. It's the inspiration for our Wentworth Street Crab Meat (page 127).

Both Josephine Humphreys and Vereen Coen suspect that this early iteration of the book became successful quickly enough that it attracted the attention of the older sustaining members of the League, who took over the project from the Humphreys-Walker duo, bulked up the project, and professionalized it to a degree.

Ironically (for a couple reasons!), Ernest Mickler's best-selling *White Trash Cooking,* published in 1986, included seven recipes lifted whole from *Charleston Receipts,* and the League (implications be damned) sued for plagiarism, later settling the case. Among the recipes plagiarized were those for opossum and broiled squirrel, both of which were originally contributed by Martha Lynch Humphreys, who was—lest you get the wrong impression—an elegant lady, a Vassar graduate, a hilarious conversationalist, and by her daughter Josephine's account, a terrible cook.

PECAN CHEESE WAFERS

MAKES: 56 WAFERS, ENOUGH FOR 8 FOR SNACKING

TIME: 35 MINUTES, INCLUDING BAKING TIME

Imagine a cheese straw in-the-round with a pecan half on top and you're most of the way to the glory of a pecan cheese wafer. Now, all you have to do is make them. Fortunately, it's easy—even simpler than cheese straws because the dough doesn't have a tendency to pull apart and break when you move the straws from the cutting board to the baking sheet—or, for that matter, from the baking sheet to the cookie jar.

We often serve these together with Savory Benne Wafers (page 49) at a cocktail party because, like those savory sesame cookies, these are addictive, but very different: slightly spicy and cheesy, and perfect with a cold Hugo (page 23) or a Moonshine Martini (page 25).

Since ovens can be variable and you want these to turn out perfectly, check them after 15 minutes, in case your oven runs hot or cold.

¾ cup all-purpose flour, plus more for rolling

½ teaspoon kosher salt

¼ teaspoon red pepper flakes

4 tablespoons (½ stick) unsalted butter, cut into 4 pieces and softened

4 ounces extra-sharp Cheddar cheese, preferably orange, grated (about 1½ cups)

2 tablespoons heavy cream, whole milk, or buttermilk

1 scant cup pecan halves

1 Preheat the oven to 325°F.

2 Put the flour, salt, and red pepper flakes in the bowl of a food processor and process a few times until well combined. Add the butter and cheese, and process continually until the mixture resembles coarse crumbs that are beginning to clump together, about a minute. Add the cream or milk, and continue to process until the mixture comes together in a ball, about 10 seconds.

3 On a lightly floured surface, roll the dough into an 8 by 10-inch rectangle that is ⅛ inch thick. With a small round or oblong cookie cutter, cut the dough into wafers. With a spatula, transfer the wafers to an ungreased baking sheet. Press one pecan half gently into the center of each wafer. Bake until firm and gently browned, 15 to 20 minutes.

4 Remove from the oven and set the sheet on a rack or trivet. Either serve warm or let cool to room temperature, and then place in a container with a tight-fitting lid. (Pecan cheese wafers will keep for about 4 days. You may bring them back to life after that with a short, 2- to 3-minute ride in a toaster oven set to light toast.)

SHRIMP POPOVERS

SERVES: 6   TIME: 45 MINUTES, INCLUDING BAKING TIME

These steamy, crusty popovers with a subtle shrimp perfume are our new star on the bread plate. They're good enough that if you don't have a popover rack (a metal frame of deep nonstick cups), it may be worth investing in one. The batter pops over vigorously enough that a teaspoon of shrimp butter (or any other type of compound butter or cheese) laid on top becomes nicely incorporated into the middle of the bread by the time the popover finishes baking.

The shrimp butter below is worth its own recipe. It's basically a Charleston shrimp paste, a compound of quick-cooked shrimp and butter, and a few tablespoons are delicious spread on toast or biscuits, stirred into grits (see Charleston Hominy, page 172) for breakfast, or tossed with pasta. It's more shrimp than butter, so you can even form it into tiny patties, about an inch in diameter, brown both sides in a skillet, and create mini shrimp burgers, for hors d'oeuvres. Feel free to season your shrimp butter with a splash of sherry, if desired. Whenever possible, we purchase shrimp with shells on, as we find the effort of shelling them is rewarded with firmer, fresher-tasting shrimp. Because the shrimp butter is so versatile, we've scaled it here to yield more than the popovers require.

1 cup all-purpose flour

½ teaspoon kosher salt

½ teaspoon sugar

1 cup whole milk

2 tablespoons unsalted butter, melted

2 large eggs, lightly beaten

Scant ¾ cup Shrimp Butter, chilled (recipe follows)

1 Position a rack in the middle of the oven and preheat the oven to 450°F.

2 Sift the flour, salt, and sugar into a medium bowl and then add the milk, 2 teaspoons of the melted butter, and the eggs, whisking to combine until the batter is smooth and noticeably thickened, about 3 minutes.

3 Heat a 6-cell popover tray or muffin pan in the oven for 5 minutes. Remove and brush the insides of the cups with the remaining melted butter. Fill each cup just one-fourth full of batter, then place a heaping teaspoon of the cold shrimp butter into each. Pour in more batter, until each mold is two-thirds full.

4 Bake for 20 to 22 minutes, until the risen tops are golden brown and don't appear damp. Remove the popovers from their cups, using a butter knife to pry any sticky ones out, and serve immediately.

SHRIMP BUTTER

MAKES: 2 CUPS, OR ENOUGH FOR 20 POPOVERS
TIME: 30 MINUTES, PLUS 1 HOUR COOLING

1 teaspoon kosher salt

1 pound medium (26 to 30 count) shell-on shrimp

½ cup (1 stick) unsalted butter, at room temperature

½ teaspoon sugar

1 Pour 2 cups of water into a small saucepan, add ½ teaspoon of the salt, and bring to a boil over medium-high heat. Add the shrimp and cook for about 2 minutes, stirring, until the shrimp are uniformly pink and firm. With a slotted spoon, transfer the shrimp to a bowl to cool. When they are cool enough to handle, peel the shrimp. (You should have about 2 cups.)

2 Put the shrimp, butter, remaining ½ teaspoon salt, and the sugar in the bowl of a food processor and pulse until it has a uniform felty appearance and no lumps of butter are visible, about 1 minute. Transfer to a small vessel with a tight-fitting lid and chill in the refrigerator for 1 hour before using. (Shrimp butter will keep for up to 4 days in the refrigerator.)

CRAB SALAD   SERVES: 4 AS AN HORS D'OEUVRE, OR ENOUGH FOR 2 LARGE CRAB ROLLS

TIME: 8 MINUTES PREPARATION, 1 HOUR 30 MINUTES CHILLING

If you've read one of our previous books, you know that we have an aversion to heavy, processed crab dips made with cream cheese and Cheddar. That's because blue crab, *Callinectes sapidus,* certainly one of the iconic foods of Charleston, has such a delicate sweet-salty-scallopy flavor that a light touch is key. You want to avoid masking the deliciousness of the crab meat (and laying waste to all that effort you spent picking the meat from the shell). No matter how delectable, you may yearn to pair fresh crab with some flavorful textural companions.

This crab salad, which we serve often on ribs of romaine and endive, on crackers, and also on toasted, buttered top-loading hot dog buns for a terrific crab roll, is a new favorite. The key here is the pickled celery, which has just the right crunch, acidity, and spice to enhance the crab's flavor without masking it; the two ingredients are bound by a light dressing of sour cream, mayonnaise, and pickled-celery brine.

¼ cup fresh lemon juice

2 tablespoons white wine vinegar

Kosher salt

½ teaspoon sugar

2 pinches of celery seeds, finely ground in a mortar and pestle

1 large rib of celery, halved lengthwise and sliced very thinly on the bias (¾ cup)

2 tablespoons sour cream

1 tablespoon high-quality mayonnaise

8 ounces fresh (nonpasteurized) blue crab meat (lump, backfin, or claw, or combination thereof)

1 tablespoon finely chopped fresh chives

Freshly ground black pepper

Paprika, for garnish (optional)

1 In a small bowl, whisk together the lemon juice, vinegar, 2 tablespoons of cold water, 1 teaspoon salt, the sugar, and celery seeds. Add the celery; the liquid should completely cover the sliced celery. Cover the bowl and refrigerate for 30 minutes.

2 Drain the celery, reserving the liquid. In a medium bowl, whisk the sour cream and mayonnaise with 1 tablespoon of the celery liquid until thoroughly combined. Flake the crab meat into the dressing, add the celery and the chives, and stir to combine. Season to taste with salt, black pepper, and reserved celery liquid. The salad tastes best when given time for the flavors to meld; refrigerate for at least 1 hour—though not more than 24 hours—and remove from the refrigerator 30 minutes before serving to bring to room temperature. Garnish with paprika, if desired.

SMOKED EGG SALAD TOASTS

SERVES: 8 AS AN HORS D'OEUVRE, OR MAKES 4 OPEN-FACED SANDWICHES   TIME: 1 HOUR

In the 1980s, you had to drive deep into the country to get farm-fresh eggs—the kind with marigold-orange yolks; shells in the spectrum spanning blue, green, white, and brown; and intense buttery-creamy flavor. Everything changed when, in the mid-1990s, Celeste Albers moved to the area where her father had grown up, and started Green Grocer, a poultry and dairy farm on Wadmalaw Island, about eighteen miles south of town. She soon became a local-food legend and a raw-milk firebrand, her cell number on every serious chef's speed dial.

We're grateful that we can now buy her eggs almost every Saturday at the Farmer's Market on Marion Square. And if you're wondering why we would take a beautiful farm-fresh egg and subject it to hard-boiling and smoking in this recipe, we have an answer: this recipe is insanely delicious! And furthermore, "smoky" is a distinctive Lowcountry flavor profile—think hardwood-roasted oysters. So why not liven up an egg salad with smoke? This is a fun recipe to roll out on friends; serve it as an hors d'oeuvre, on toasted baguette slices, or as we more often do, as an open-faced sandwich for an afternoon snack.

8 large eggs

1 tablespoon apple wood chips designed for stovetop smokers

3 tablespoons high-quality mayonnaise

2 tablespoons buttermilk, preferably whole

2 teaspoons hot sauce, such as Tabasco or Crystal

¼ teaspoon kosher salt

4 slices whole wheat bread, toasted

Freshly ground black pepper

About 2 ounces arugula or baby lettuces

1 Bring 6 quarts of water to a rolling boil in a large stockpot. Turn the heat down so the water settles to the barest simmer, and lower the eggs into the pot gently with a skimmer or ladle. Cook for exactly 14 minutes.

2 While the eggs cook, get the smoker ready: put the wood chips in the center of your stovetop smoker pan or, if using a conventional roasting pan and rack as a smoker, in the center of a 9 by 13-inch steel or aluminum roasting pan. Wrap the roasting rack in aluminum foil, then place it in the pan.

3 Transfer the eggs to a strainer and run a spray of cold water over them until the shells are cool enough to peel, about 3 minutes. Peel the eggs and halve them lengthwise. Separate the yolks from the whites, putting the yolks in a medium bowl.

4 Set the whites on the rack of the stovetop smoker. Cover the smoker only partly; if using a roasting pan, cover with aluminum foil, crimping the edges tightly, but leaving one corner uncrimped. Set the smoker over medium-high heat, and when you see the first wisp of smoke rise from the pan, cover it completely and smoke the egg whites for 6 minutes. Transfer the pan to a cool burner on the stove and let the eggs sit in the pan with the lid closed for another minute or two. Remove the egg whites and chop coarsely.

5 Sieve the yolks through a medium-fine strainer into a fluffy pile in the bowl. Add the mayonnaise, buttermilk, hot sauce, and salt and stir until the mixture is smooth and resembles cake batter. Fold the chopped egg whites into the yolk mixture.

6 Divide the egg salad among the toasts, grind a bit of black pepper over each, and top with the arugula. Slice each toast on the diagonal, and serve.

GUINEA SQUASH DIP

MAKES: ABOUT 2 CUPS DIP, ENOUGH FOR 8 FOR SNACKING   TIME: 35 MINUTES

When *Solanum melongena*, the member of the nightshade family commonly known as eggplant, arrived on North American shores with the Spanish colonists, it was a white-skinned variety, ovoid and about the size of a guinea hen's egg. We find recipes for "guinea squash" (roasted and fried) in *The Carolina Housewife*, circa 1847, but interestingly, no recipes for the vegetable appear in the 1934 edition of *200 Years of Charleston Cooking*. Guinea squash returns in the midcentury's *Charleston Receipts*, in the curious recipe for "Clams and Guinea Squash (Eggplant)," in which the peeled vegetable is boiled, then mashed and layered in a casserole with canned chopped clams and cracker crumbs and baked in an oven.

Try as we might, we couldn't make that concept delicious, but we were inspired enough by the vegetable to make something else quite fantastic—namely, a dip of charred guinea squash, lemon juice, and mayonnaise buzzed in a food processor. Call it a Southern cousin of the smoky Middle Eastern eggplant purée baba ganoush, if you like; it's scrumptious on everything from crackers to all manner of raw vegetables. The surprise: when we tried dabbing it on raw clams on the half-shell, we found that the lemon in the dip created an affinity between eggplant and clam we hadn't anticipated. It's an unconventional pairing, but a tasty one!

1½ pounds eggplants, preferably smaller white or purple varieties, halved lengthwise

About 3 tablespoons extra-virgin olive oil

Kosher salt and freshly ground black pepper

1 tablespoon fresh lemon juice, or more to taste

1 tablespoon high-quality mayonnaise, or more to taste

1 Preheat the broiler. Pour 1 tablespoon of the olive oil into a pie plate, and turn each piece in the oil to thoroughly coat—adding more oil, 1 tablespoon at a time, as necessary.

2 Lay the eggplants cut side up on a rimmed baking pan and season with salt and black pepper. Broil the eggplants with their surfaces 2 to 3 inches from the heat, until they are thoroughly browned, about 10 minutes. Turn the eggplants so their skins face up, and continue to broil until the skins are thoroughly blackened, about 6 minutes more.

3 Transfer the eggplants to a bowl, cover, and let rest 10 minutes, until completely cooked through and soft. Peel off the skins, and put the eggplant pulp in the bowl of a food processor, add the lemon juice and mayonnaise, and process until the mixture is smooth and spreadable. Season to taste with lemon juice, salt, and black pepper.

4 Transfer to a small bowl and serve. (Or cover and refrigerate for up to 3 days.)

RICE AND HAM CROQUETTES WITH TOMATO SAUCE

SERVES: 4   TIME: 1 HOUR 30 MINUTES

The old Lowcountry cookbooks have dozens of recipes for different ways you can make rice a base for sauces and stews. There are rice waffles and rice breads, rice cakes and rice croquettes. When we ran across the croquettes in Mrs. Samuel G. Stoney's *Carolina Rice Cookbook* (1901), we immediately thought of *arancini*—addictive fried rice balls often served with tomato sauce as an appetizer or a snack in Italy. We don't know for sure whether rice croquettes ever came into contact with the tomato sauce from an earlier Lowcountry cookbook, Sarah Rutledge's 1847 *The Carolina Housewife*.

What? You're thinking, *Italian tomato sauce in the South*? In the nineteenth century?

Sì, sì. In fact, the archives at Middleton Place has the very copy of *The Carolina Housewife* owned by Paolina Bentivoglio Middleton, the Italian woman who married Sarah Rutledge's cousin, Arthur Middleton (grandson of the Arthur who signed the Declaration of Independence), in Rome in 1841. The book contains annotations throughout, written in Paolina Middleton's own hand, and in the margin of the recipe on page 90 for "Tomato Sauce" are the words, *Mio recetto*. We—and more important, Barbara Doyle, the archivist at Middleton Place—are fairly certain that this means the recipe was contributed to Sarah Rutledge's cookbook by her cousin.

In any event, the rice croquettes found in the old books tend to be rather monastic affairs of egg and milk and not much else, so we find they take well to the cross-cultural dressing up. Here, we've torqued the seasoning of the rice balls themselves with country ham and scallions; and the garlicky, spicy sauce (which cooks in the time it takes to form and fry the rice croquettes) is the perfect dunk for the croquettes. Or, if you prefer, you can pour the sauce over them the way you would meatballs. Leave out the country ham, and you have a knockout vegetarian dish.

Buon appetito, y'all!

TOMATO SAUCE

¼ cup olive oil

1 cup diced sweet onion (1 medium onion)

4 large garlic cloves, thinly sliced

Kosher salt and freshly ground black pepper

1 (28-ounce) can crushed San Marzano tomatoes

¼ teaspoon red pepper flakes

CROQUETTES

2 large eggs

3 cups cooked rice, lightly seasoned with salt and freshly ground black pepper

½ cup plus 2 tablespoons finely diced country ham or prosciutto

½ cup finely chopped scallions (white part and 2 inches into green)

3 ounces cream cheese, very soft

2 tablespoons whole milk

1¼ cups panko bread crumbs

4 to 6 cups canola or other frying oil

1   Make the tomato sauce: Heat the olive oil in a heavy-bottomed pot over medium heat. Add the onion, garlic, ½ teaspoon salt, and ¼ teaspoon black pepper, and cook until fragrant and soft but not browned, about 6 minutes. Add the tomatoes and the red pepper flakes and cover. When the sauce comes to a simmer, turn the heat to low and continue to simmer partially uncovered, stirring occasionally, for about 1 hour, until the sauce is thick.

2   Make the croquettes: Preheat the oven to 225°F.

3   In a large bowl, mix the rice, ham, scallions, and cream cheese until thoroughly combined. Season the mixture to taste with salt and black pepper. Beat one of the eggs well, add it to the bowl, and stir gently with a spatula until evenly coated.

(recipe continues)

A CONCH SHELL–ADORNED PALM—A BACKYARD ORNAMENT AND
CONVERSATION PIECE.

4 Using wet hands, form the rice mixture into Ping-Pong-size balls. Beat the remaining egg in a small bowl with the milk. Put the bread crumbs in a shallow bowl. Dip the balls in the egg and then roll in the crumbs until evenly coated.

5 Pour the oil into a 4-quart (or larger) Dutch oven or heavy-bottomed pot to a depth of about 1½ inches. Turn the heat to medium high, and when the oil reaches 350°F on a frying thermometer, fry the rice balls in batches, about six at a time, turning them in the oil as they brown, for about 3 minutes total. Transfer as finished to the oven, placed on a heat-proof plate lined with a paper towel. When all the rice balls have been fried, serve with the warm tomato sauce.

CLEMENTINE PADDLEFORD'S VISIT TO CHARLESTON

NOTHING DID more to whip up locals' pride in *Charleston Receipts* (see page 52) and to cement the reputation of the book for readers outside the city than the article Clementine Paddleford wrote, illustrated with recipes, for the *New York Herald Tribune*. Paddleford, a Kansas-born Columbia Journalism School graduate, was well on her way to becoming America's first celebrity food writer for her regional home-cooking column "How America Eats." This column combined the features of a food-oriented travel piece with firsthand accounts of what was actually happening in American home kitchens. In the Charleston papers, coverage of her two-day visit to the Holy City in February 1951 was extensive, with the *Evening Post* publishing two stories. "New York Herald Editor Arrives for Brief Visit Here," one headline read, and included her itinerary, down to every dinner and tea date. Paddleford was

described in an article by Sarah Brewton in the *Evening Post* as "a charming New Yorker." Another headline: "Food Expert Adds Charleston to List of Cities Famous for Good Eating."

What we love most, in all the hullabaloo that surrounded Paddleford's time in Charleston, is almost a footnote to the story, relayed in the last paragraph of Brewton's article: "When she boards a plane Monday for New York, Miss Paddleford will take along a jar of palmetto palm pickle. . . . Mrs. E. M. Seabrook went this week to the Isle of Palms. There she extracted the heart of a palmetto palm tree to make up this memento."

To writers like us, who seek gold in the story of a food's procurement, it seems that the most exciting—and most quintessentially Charleston—episode of Paddleford's trip may have taken place a few days before she arrived.

SHAD ROE SPREAD

MAKES: 1 QUART, ENOUGH FOR 10 TO 16 FOR SNACKING   TIME: 1 HOUR

The return of the American shad (*Alosa sapidissima*) from the North Atlantic to the rivers of the Lowcountry every February and March is celebrated by those of us who enjoy the roe—in fact it's often heralded as the arrival of "shad roe season," even though the meat of the fish (in the same family as herring, and just as rich in omega-3s) is also prized in Charleston (see Broiled Shad, page 140, and Smoked Shad, page 139). The typical roe treatment, whether at home or in a restaurant, is to sauté them in butter or bacon drippings, and to serve them whole, with a squeeze of lemon juice on top. It's a delicious way to eat shad roe for brunch or lunch, but one that will eventually wear you down with its predictability.

Fortunately, there are other ways to frame the delectably mild, fishy flavor of shad roe that makes it more shareable and attractive, like this spread infused with wine, shallots, and herbs, for hot buttered crackers, toast, or endive leaves. The spread is also delicious stirred into grits. When buying, look for vibrant yellow-orange to burgundy-colored roe in a nearly translucent membrane with a healthy network of veins. Each set has two torpedo-shaped lobes. The roe should have almost no odor.

1 cup dry red wine

½ cup red or white wine vinegar

1 (8-inch) sprig rosemary

2 shallots (about 6 ounces), thinly sliced into half-moons

1 tablespoon plus 1½ teaspoons kosher salt, plus more to taste

2 complete shad roe (18 to 20 ounces total)

4 ounces cream cheese, at room temperature

6 tablespoons crème fraîche or sour cream

1 teaspoon freshly ground black pepper

⅓ to ½ cup finely chopped chives, parsley, basil, cilantro, or dill (or a combination), plus a few whole sprigs for garnish

Lemon wedges for garnish

Buttered toast, crackers, or endive leaves, for dipping

1 Combine 6 cups of water with the wine, vinegar, rosemary, shallots, and 1 tablespoon plus 1 teaspoon salt in a medium saucepan, and bring to a vigorous boil over high heat. Poke each of the roes with a skewer in three or four places, and add to the boiling brine. Cook for 4 minutes and then turn off the heat but leave the pan on the stove, allowing the roe to cool for 20 minutes in the brine. (If the roes burst their membranes, that is fine.) With a medium-fine mesh strainer, drain the roes and shallots over a bowl, reserving ¼ cup of the brine (discard the rosemary).

2 With a hand-mixer or a rubber spatula, combine the cream cheese, crème fraîche, black pepper, chopped herbs, and ½ teaspoon salt in a bowl, mixing just until the herbs are evenly incorporated. Once they are cool enough to handle, add the shallots to the bowl, and then the roes, pushing them through the strainer. Put 2 tablespoons of the reserved brine into the bowl and then fold the mixture with a rubber spatula until the spread is evenly blended, with a lavender hue, and no clumps of cream cheese remain (a few clumps of roe are okay). Season to taste with salt and more brine, if desired. Serve at room temperature in a bowl garnished with the lemon wedges and reserved herb sprigs. (The spread will keep, covered, in the fridge for about 2 days.)

SOUPS

THE BISQUE—PALE, DELICATE, AND CREAMY, SCENTED WITH THE SEA
(and often a dash of sherry)—would seem the archetypal Charleston soup course, and yet, afflicted as we are by the city/country mind-set, we crave rustic pleasures nearly as much as we do the finer ones. For example, we thrill to a long-cooked, murky gumbo studded with okra—or truly to any soup that pairs okra with beef—and also to the messiness of a Frogmore Stew, more solid than liquid, with whole crab shells, corn cobs, and sausage links. Look out for bay leaves!

The Frogmore Soup—note "soup," not stew—we include at the top of this chapter shows our hand, however, in that, for the kind of multi-generational entertaining we do most often these days, a proper soup makes the most sense, serves the most people, and allows us to focus on building interesting layers of flavor. So we took the profile of a Frogmore Stew and tamed it for the table. Sure, we'll take some heat from the hardened traditionalists, for making a Lowcountry boil (another term for it) friendly and approachable, but if you truly enjoy the flavors of this dish, you're going to love being able to drink it without having to take a break every few seconds to pick shrimp legs from between your teeth.

There are flourishes here that reflect our interest in employing Southern ingredients in fresh ways—in the Tomato and Watermelon Gazpacho (page 80), and in Red Pea Soup (page 87)—and our abiding curiosity with peanuts and everything they can do in the kitchen (in this case, a pairing with oysters, in Peanut and Oyster Stew, page 85).

And for everyone who hankers for the cream and sweet shellfish—and the sherry—we've presented here a range of elegant things to sip before the main course, like She-Crab Soup (page 77) and Celery and Crab Soup (page 86), that harness those classic nuances and step them up with a few key techniques and supporting vegetables.

FROGMORE SOUP SERVES: 6 TIME: 1 HOUR 15 MINUTES

The epic Lowcountry boil or Frogmore Stew, combining shell-on shrimp and whole blue crabs with corn on the cob, new potatoes, and smoked sausage (and occasionally other vegetables), is a rustic, outdoor dish—often served without plates or bowls, on a newspaper-covered plywood table. The "stew" requires diners to get in elbows deep, to grab the corn in two hands, crack the crab to get at the meat, and shell the shrimp as you work your way through the pile. A stack of dishtowels is a necessity.

We love the combination of flavors in the classic stew—especially when well seasoned with bay and cayenne. We don't always love the mess, nor the fact that it's too easy outdoors, in a distracting setting (the dogs underfoot, new guests arriving), to overcook the shrimp and crab as you wait for the potato to soften up. So we got the idea to create a Frogmore Soup, tamed for an elegant dinner table, that preserves the flavors of the original along with its beautiful fall colors, while subtracting the various inedibles (the shells, the corn cobs). We couldn't resist a few minor tweaks, like slicing the shrimp into nuggets, to lend the soup some satisfying textural contrasts. It's a terrific starter course for the Thanksgiving meal, or for any formal dinner headed into meaty territory.

Try to seek out only U.S.-harvested wild blue crab, occasionally marked *Callinectes sapidus,* for this soup, whose delicacy will expose all the faults in tinny imported crab.

¾ pound medium (26 to 30 count) wild-caught U.S. shell-on shrimp

1 small bay leaf

Kosher salt

1 dash of cayenne or paprika

3 tablespoons unsalted butter

3 ounces smoked pork sausage, Cajun andouille, or kielbasa, minced

1 cup minced onion (about 1 medium)

⅓ cup minced celery, leaves reserved for garnish

1 ear sweet corn

½ cup dry white wine

4 ounces fresh U.S. blue crab meat, picked clean of shell fragments

½ cup heavy cream

Freshly ground black pepper

(recipe continues)

1 Peel and devein the shrimp, reserving the shells in a small saucepan. Chop each shrimp crosswise into 3 or 4 pieces and reserve. To the saucepan with the shrimp shells add 2 cups of water, the bay leaf, ½ teaspoon salt, and the paprika, and bring to a simmer over high heat. Simmer on medium-low heat until reduced by half, about 20 minutes. Strain the broth and discard the shells.

2 Melt the butter in a medium saucepan, add the sausage, and gently cook over medium-low heat, stirring occasionally, until the sausage has visibly shrunk, about 5 minutes. Tip the pan and with a slotted spoon, transfer all but 1 to 2 tablespoons of the sausage to a small bowl, and reserve for garnish.

3 Add the onion and celery and ½ teaspoon of salt to the pan, and cook over low heat until soft and translucent but not browning, 8 to 10 minutes.

4 Meanwhile, cut the kernels from the corn cob. You should have about ⅔ cup. Scrape the cob with the back of a spoon and add the juice to the pan along with the corn kernels. Cook for 4 minutes, then turn the heat to medium and add 1½ cups of the shrimp broth, 1½ cups of water, and the white wine, and simmer for 5 minutes. Season the soup to taste with salt.

5 Let the soup cool for about 10 minutes, and then process the soup carefully, in batches if necessary, in a food processor until mostly smooth (some corn kernels may remain recognizable), 1 to 2 minutes. Return the soup to the saucepan, and bring to a simmer over medium-low heat. Add the crab and shrimp, and simmer until the shrimp are firm and just cooked through, about 2 minutes.

6 Stir in the cream, season with salt and freshly ground black pepper, and serve immediately, ladling the soup into serving bowls. Make sure to include some crab and shrimp in each bowl, and garnish with a pinch or two of reserved sausage bits and some torn celery leaves.

LOWCOUNTRY GUMBO   SERVES: 6 TO 8   TIME: 1 HOUR 45 MINUTES

Okra is the centerpiece of any good Lowcountry gumbo (filé has its partisans farther west). The one we like these days, made with sweet shrimp and briny oysters, uses okra in two ways: one portion is cooked to disintegration, to thicken the stew; the other is added closer to finishing time, for flavor and a firmer texture. We use a blend of chiles, if available, to provide the sizzle, and we support the fishy flavors of the gumbo by using a high-quality fish broth as the main liquid—either homemade or purchased from a fishmonger, who will use bones and fresh fish to create the stock. We like to serve this with Charleston Rice (page 133) or Skillet Cornbread (page 213).

8 tablespoons (1 stick) unsalted butter

3 tablespoons all-purpose flour

3 tablespoons tomato paste

¼ teaspoon cayenne

Kosher salt and freshly ground black pepper

2 bay leaves

4 ounces spicy sausage, cut from the casing

2 cups chopped yellow onion (about 1 large)

1 cup finely chopped jalapeño pepper, or poblano or serrano chiles, or a combination

2 quarts high-quality fish or shellfish broth

1½ cups shucked oysters (18 to 24) and their liquor, separated

4 cups chopped (cross-cut) okra (about 1 pound)

1 pound medium (26 to 30 count) shell-on shrimp, peeled

1 Melt 6 tablespoons of the butter in a 6-quart pot and add the flour, stirring over low heat to make a paste, and continuing to stir for about 8 minutes, until it turns a toasty, golden brown, releasing a nutty aroma. Add the remaining 2 tablespoons butter and the tomato paste, and stir until the butter has melted and the tomato is evenly incorporated. Add the cayenne, ½ teaspoon salt, 1 teaspoon black pepper, and the bay leaves along with the sausage, and stir until the sausage has begun to render some fat, about 5 minutes. Then add the onion and chile, stirring often, until they soften but do not brown, 4 to 5 minutes.

2 Add the broth, the oyster liquor, and 2 cups of the okra and bring to a boil, stirring and scraping the bottom initially to suspend the flour, vegetables, and sausage. Turn the heat down so that the mixture simmers and cook for 30 minutes with the cover on, but ajar. Add the remaining 2 cups okra and simmer, again with the lid ajar, until the gumbo has thickened noticeably, about 30 minutes.

3 Add the shrimp and oysters, turn off the heat, and cover, allowing the pot to sit for 2 minutes. Discard the bay leaves and serve immediately. (Leftover gumbo will keep refrigerated for approximately 2 days.)

CHARLESTON OKRA SOUP
SERVES: 4 AS A MAIN COURSE WITH RICE, OR 6 AS AN APPETIZER   TIME: 2 HOURS 30 MINUTES, 1 HOUR SEASONING TIME

She-Crab Soup (page 77) is the heroine of Charleston soup courses, and you'll find it on the menu at most restaurants channeling Lowcountry cuisine. But Charleston Okra Soup is every bit as important in the tradition and lore of the Holy City. In fact, when Clementine Paddleford, the famed food writer for the *New York Herald Tribune*, visited Charleston in 1952 (see Clementine Paddleford's Visit to Charleston, page 66), it was the okra soup recipe from *Charleston Receipts* that Mary Vereen Huguenin demonstrated for Paddleford in her kitchen at 64 Meeting Street—a moment photographed for the *Evening Post*.

Okra soup is resolutely old school. It shows up on the menus in the tea rooms that open every spring in church parish halls in the Lowcountry, and is often paired with a pimento cheese sandwich. It's a deeply flavored, tomato-based, meaty soup that always has as its foundation a delicious beef bone. Pork, although much beloved in Charleston, is rarely found in conjunction with okra; this preference for beef with okra is seldom articulated, yet innate to the culture, etched into the kitchen practice of Charleston home cooks over the last couple of centuries. We've asked hundreds of cooks about this pairing, but no one can explain why it is so. Our best hunch is it's aesthetic—simply that the flavors pair well together. In our version of this soup, we use a sliced beef shank, so that every portion has a few morsels of meat in it. Choose a shank with a generous plug of marrow, which dissolves into the soup, giving it an even more silky texture and beefy flavor.

1½ pounds beef shank, cut into ¾-inch cubes, marrow bone reserved

Kosher salt and freshly ground black pepper

1 tablespoon canola oil, plus more if needed

2 cups chopped yellow onion (about 2 medium)

3 bay leaves

½ teaspoon red pepper flakes

¼ teaspoon smoked paprika

1 (28-ounce) can crushed tomatoes

1 pound okra, trimmed, cut on the bias into ½-inch-thick ovals

Fresh parsley for garnish (optional)

1 Season the beef and marrow bone with ¾ teaspoon salt and ½ teaspoon black pepper. Put in a shallow dish, covered, and bring to room temperature, about 1 hour. Pat the pieces dry with a paper towel.

2 Pour the oil into a large Dutch oven or heavy-bottomed pot over medium-high heat, and when it shimmers, brown the beef and marrow bone in batches, if necessary, taking care not to crowd the pan and adding oil by teaspoonfuls if the pan becomes too dry. With a slotted spoon, transfer the browned beef and bone to a bowl, and turn the heat to medium. Add the onion, bay leaves, red pepper flakes, paprika, and 1¼ teaspoons salt. Cook, scraping up any browned bits on the bottom of the pan and adding a teaspoon of water or oil if the pan becomes dry, until the onion softens, about 6 minutes; you don't want the onion itself to char.

3 Add 1 quart of water and the tomatoes, return the beef and marrow bone to the pan, and cover. When the soup simmers gently, uncover and reduce the heat to low. Let cook, stirring occasionally, until the meat is just tender, about 1 hour. Add the okra, and continue cooking until the okra is just tender, about 25 minutes.

4 Discard the bay leaves, and season to taste with salt and freshly ground black pepper. Divide among bowls, garnish with parsley, if desired, and serve.

SHE-CRAB SOUP   SERVES: 4   TIME: 1 HOUR

She-crab soup might just be this city's most over-worked culinary icon—so much so that in restaurants of quality in Charleston, you can detect more than a few chefs assiduously avoiding it. But an expertly made she-crab soup is a rare pleasure at home, and should be a part of every cook's repertoire. When we were in our teenage years, the soup seemed extra special because it's seasoned with sherry and traditionally served with a cruet of the fortified wine, the latter to pass around the table in case you wanted to add an extra jolt.

But she-crab soup isn't about the sherry (and in fact, we've come to realize that too often the sherry overpowers the crab), it's about the roe; and we don't think we'd ever truly reckoned with how important that roe is—coupled with the freshest crab meat you can find, of course—until the recent spring day we picked and cleaned an entire bushel of crabs (eighty, give or take) in a sitting. Since female crabs with roe inside are most prevalent in the spring, we found crab roe inside many of the adult females, called "sooks," as we cleaned them, after cooking. When you remove the carapace (or top shell) from the body of the crab, the crab roe—if it's there—will appear as a mass of bright orange in the middle of the body, and sometimes you may also find more roe tucked in the sharp left and right points of the carapace. The roe has an earthy-briny flavor, and adds a pale orange color to this soup. In our recipe, we blend it into the soup itself and also use a portion to garnish each bowl.

Is it possible to buy crab roe alone? Unfortunately, no. So when we make this soup now, we buy picked crab meat and a half-dozen female crabs with roe from our local market. Any fish market that takes the time to sell hard-shell blue crabs will know how to spot a female with crab roe, because the roe makes the underside of the carapace appear light orange. It really is worth going to the trouble to find the real deal; you won't be disappointed!

Regarding the sherry: recently we've taken to giving each guest his or her own shot glass full of fino sherry (one of the most delicate expressions of the fortified wine) to drink as a paired beverage, instead of sending a cruet around the table.

6 live hard-shell sooks (female blue crabs with roe)	1 tablespoon plus 4 teaspoons dry sherry, preferably fino, plus more for serving
1 tablespoon all-purpose flour	
2 tablespoons unsalted butter	
1 cup finely minced shallots (2 to 3 large)	1½ cups picked lump, backfin, or jumbo lump crab meat
Kosher salt and freshly ground black pepper	Chopped fresh chives (optional)
1 quart half-and-half	

1 Bring a large pasta pot two-thirds full of water to a boil, and using tongs, transfer 2 of the crabs to the pot. Cook until their shells turn bright orange, about 3 minutes, then transfer the cooked crabs to a colander set in the sink and run cold water over them. Add the next 2 crabs to the pot and repeat until all the crabs have been cooked.

2 As each cooked crab becomes cool enough to handle, slip your thumb beneath the place on its underside where the cape of shell tapers to a point, and lift the bottom shell up, pulling the entire carapace off the body of the crab. Clean out and discard the spongy-feathery gills on the body. Carefully pick out any orange roe you may see inside the body, and reserve. Then snap one of the smaller legs off the body of the crab to use as a pick, to tease out any roe in the hollows of the carapace that taper to a sharp point, and reserve. Repeat with the remaining crabs until all the roe has been picked. Then split the crab bodies and legs, pick the meat from them, and add it to the rest of the picked crab meat.

(recipe continues)

3 Pour off all but 3 cups of the cooking water, and add the picked crab bodies, legs, and carapaces, then return to a boil. Let boil until reduced by a third, about 10 minutes, and strain the crab broth into a 4-quart saucepan or Dutch oven.

4 Heat the broth over high heat until it simmers. Put the flour in a small bowl or ramekin, spoon 3 tablespoons of the hot broth into it, and whisk it to a smooth paste with a fork. Pour the remaining broth into a blender, add ¼ cup of the crab roe, and liquefy until the roe is completely dissolved in the broth. With the blender running, add the flour paste to the broth.

5 Return the Dutch oven to the heat and melt the butter over medium-low heat until it's frothy. Add the shallot, ½ teaspoon salt, and ¼ teaspoon black pepper. Cook, stirring occasionally, until the shallot is soft, fragrant, and translucent, but not brown, about 4 minutes. Add the half-and-half, the broth mixture, and 1 tablespoon of the sherry, and cover. When the soup comes to a simmer, turn the heat to low, uncover, and simmer gently, stirring occasionally, until the soup has reduced by about one-sixth, 12 to 15 minutes.

6 Add the crab meat and cook for 2 minutes over low heat, stirring to combine. Season the soup with salt and black pepper.

7 Pour a teaspoon of sherry into each bowl before serving, and garnish each bowl with about 1½ teaspoons roe and chives, if using. Serve with additional sherry—in a shot glass for each guest, or in a cruet for passing around the table—for those who might want more.

SPRINGTIME TREAT: PARISH HALL TEA ROOMS

SOMETHING WE ALWAYS LOOK forward to in the spring—in addition to the balmy weather and the magnolia blooms—is the reopening of church tea rooms, a tradition that dates back to the 1940s.

The "tea rooms" in fact serve lunch (with proceeds going to the church missions, choirs, and youth groups) from roughly 11:30 A.M. to 2 P.M., give or take. All the parishioners pitch in, doing the cooking, serving, and cleaning up. As such, it's a great opportunity to taste authentic Charleston home cooking, as most of the recipes prepared are old family treasures, along with a few from local cookbooks. In many tea rooms, like that of the Old St. Andrew Episcopal Church (believed to be the longest-running tea room in the area), homemade preserves, jams, and jellies made by parishioners are available for sale. The rooms typically open around the first week of May and, depending on the church, may run for a week up to a month. In mid-March, Teresa Taylor, long-time food editor of the *Post and Courier,* and an excellent chronicler of Charleston's food scene, publishes a tea room calendar.

The tea room we especially look forward to visiting every spring is St. Philips's, and that's because, beyond serving a stellar okra soup and Huguenot torte, the church's parish hall was where Ted's middle-school rock band, Modern Art, often rehearsed. The church donated the space after the band had been successively kicked out of the Wyricks' attic on Legare Street, the Geers' back bedroom on Atlantic Street, and then the Middletons' garage on South Battery.

TOMATO AND WATERMELON GAZPACHO WITH SHRIMP

SERVES: 8   TIME: 20 MINUTES, PLUS 1 HOUR CHILLING

Thirty years ago, two French conceptual artists, Jean-Marie Mauclet and Ghislaine Gallimard, rumbled into town in a black-green 1940s Dodge and opened Gaulart et Maliclet Café Restaurant with the tagline "Fast and French." G&M (as locals immediately took to calling the place) was a brand-new thing for the ol' town: a bar-height communal table running the length of the narrow ground floor of an early nineteenth-century row house on Broad Street. And the food they served was not the cream-laden, fancified French of nearby Perdita's and Marianne's, but snackier, more workaday fare: a slice of pâté on toast with cornichons and a bowl of soup. At night there were simple tagines and bouillabaisses.

Our mom loved the place instantly, but we were in that adolescent phase where our own preferred lunches were two Big Macs (Ted) or two Filet-o-Fish (Matt) from the drive-thru of the McDonald's on Spring Street, inhaled before we had time to exit the parking lot. What eventually won us over to G&M was its gazpacho. Spicy and garlicky and cold, with a dollop of sour cream and a dusting of cumin, it's a piquant pizza in liquid form.

For most of our teenage years, we thought Jean-Marie and Ghislaine had invented the soup; when we were in our thirties, we learned a surprising bit of history about the classic Spanish cold soup as it relates to the foodways of the American South. Early Spanish settlers in present-day Florida brought the preparation with them in the sixteenth century (one of Pensacola's most prominent regional dishes is "Gazpachi," a salad-like form of the soup). And the recipe must have made its way up to Virginia at some point, too, because Mary Randolph's 1824 *The Virginia Housewife* includes a recipe for "Gaspacha."

We're not sure whether gazpacho ever made landfall in South Carolina before G&M, but we've taken the liberty of spinning our own gazpacho in a Palmetto State direction, cutting the tomato with the cucumbery sweetness of watermelon and garnishing it with chilled fresh shrimp. It's a spicy, icy-cool soup, the perfect savory refreshment for a sweltering summer day.

In 2010 Jean-Marie and Ghislaine announced they would soon retire, and we were distraught, as their café—just a block from our office—is our lunchtime go-to most days of the week. Fortunately, instead of closing the restaurant, they sold the business to three longtime café employees (Jennifer Bremer, Marc Jenkins, and Latonnya Wallace), who have ensured its menu of affordable, tasty French lunch specials and collegial atmosphere endure. Gazpacho is served daily.

(recipe continues)

1 jalapeño pepper, preferably red

4 cups seedless watermelon chunks (about 1½ pounds)

1 large garlic clove, mashed to a paste

2 pounds ripe plum, beefsteak, or heirloom tomatoes, cored and cut into quarters

2 tablespoons red wine vinegar, plus more to taste

Kosher salt

8 cooked large shrimp, peeled and sliced in half lengthwise, for garnish (optional)

1 green jalapeño pepper, finely diced, for garnish (optional)

Freshly ground black pepper

1 Roast the red jalapeño over a gas flame (or beneath the broiling element of an electric range), turning with tongs every minute or so, until lightly charred all over. Using a paper towel, rub off as much of the blistered skin as possible. Trim the stem, remove the seeds, and transfer the chile to a blender or food processor. Add the watermelon and garlic. Purée, then transfer to a bowl and refrigerate.

2 Add the tomatoes to the blender or food processor (you need not rinse it first), and process to a smooth purée. Strain the purée through a fine sieve to strain out the skin and seeds, pressing on them to extract as much of their juice as possible.

3 Stir the tomato purée into the watermelon purée along with the vinegar and season the gazpacho with salt and more vinegar, if desired. Cover with plastic wrap, and chill for 1 hour in the refrigerator.

4 When ready to serve, taste for seasoning again, as the soup will be colder. Garnish each bowl with a couple of chilled shrimp halves and/or the diced fresh jalapeño, if desired, and freshly ground black pepper.

SOUP BUNCHES

Soup bunches" were sold throughout the twentieth century in the vegetable markets of Charleston, and often by vendors on the streets, as a convenience for starting a pot of soup or stew. Conceptually, it takes the bouquet garni of mixed herbs a step further; all that remains is to top a pot with water and salt, add a chicken carcass or a smoked seasoning meat, or perhaps some additional vegetables (a stray bell pepper, a few chard leaves), and you're well on your way to dinner. The typical soup bunch includes carrot, celery, and thyme for their aromatic qualities, and turnips, rutabagas, sweet potatoes, and cabbage for savor and sweetness. To this day, the Piggly Wiggly grocery stores in the Charleston area will occasionally put together some soup bunches in the fall, or will make up one by request. A well-tied soup bunch makes a nice house present, with Charleston flavor, so prepare a few at a time.

CHARLESTON SOUP-BUNCH VENDOR AND MODEL CIRCA 1951. (B. ANTHONY STEWART/NATIONAL GEOGRAPHIC STOCK)

FOR 4 BUNCHES

1 green cabbage, outer few leaves removed, cut into quarters through the root end

8 ribs of celery

8 medium carrots, split in half lengthwise

8 large turnips with greens (if available), washed, peeled, and split in half

4 sweet potatoes, peeled and cut in half

24 sprigs thyme

Divide the ingredients into four equal portions and bind each bundle together as best you can with butcher's twine, using the longer carrots and celery ribs and the turnip greens to corral the other ingredients. (Or use a mesh bag, of the type in which some roasted peanuts and onions are packed.)

PEANUT AND OYSTER STEW SERVES: 6 TIME: 1 HOUR

The lovely notion of combining oysters with nutty flavors has been a steady current through Charleston cookbooks, a relatively recent example being the oyster and benne (sesame) soup in *Charleston Receipts*. One of the earlier examples, however, appeared in Sarah Rutledge's 1847 *The Carolina Housewife*, in a recipe for "Ground-Nut Soup," where the oysters played second fiddle to the groundnuts—the peanuts:

> *To half a pint shelled ground-nuts, well beaten up, add two spoonsful of flour, and mix well. Put to them a pint of oysters, and a pint and a half of water. While boiling, throw on a seed-pepper or two, if small.*

We adore the simplicity and efficiency of her recipe and language: it plays out so plainly in the mind that you can almost see the stoneware bowl and apron strings. And yet it's difficult to make the flavors sing, following the recipe as written. We began with her basic formula, but introduced a few ingredients that embolden the flavors while keeping the peanuts and the oysters—both—at top billing. We wrestled with the idea of adding other ingredients (like paprika, sherry, lemon peel) to jazz up the soup, but in the end decided that the minimalist approach suits the spirit of the peanut-oyster combination best. It's a perfect stew for the first chilly days of fall, or for the last ones in the spring.

1 Process the peanuts in a food processor to coarse crumbs and reserve.

2 Melt the butter in a medium saucepan over medium-high heat. When the bubbles subside, add the celery, jalapeño, 1½ teaspoons salt, and the flour and stir with a wooden spoon until the flour is evenly incorporated. Cook for about 2 minutes, stirring occasionally, until it looks like it is drying out. Add the peanuts, stirring for a minute, then the broth, wine, 1 cup of water, and the oyster liquor. Bring to a simmer, turn the heat down to medium, and simmer covered, stirring occasionally, until the soup has reduced by about a third, about 40 minutes. Season to taste with salt and black pepper.

3 Turn off the heat and add the oysters, stirring gently twice, and allow to sit for a minute. Serve immediately, garnishing each bowl with the sliced scallions and a lemon wedge, and including a few oysters in every portion.

1 cup roasted unsalted skinned peanuts

4 tablespoons (½ stick) unsalted butter

¾ cup very finely chopped celery (about 2 smaller ribs)

4 tablespoons minced, seeded jalapeño pepper (about 2 small)

Kosher salt

1 tablespoon all-purpose flour

2 cups fish or shellfish broth

1 cup dry white wine

1 pint shucked oysters and their liquor (about 24 to 32 oysters), separated

Freshly ground black pepper

2 finely sliced scallions (white and green parts)

1 lemon, cut into wedges

CELERY AND CRAB SOUP   SERVES: 4   TIME: 50 MINUTES

As late summer turns to fall, finding she-crabs with roe—the key ingredient for a She-Crab Soup (page 77)—in the markets becomes increasingly difficult. We developed this recipe so we'd have a delicious crab soup option year-round—or simply for when we didn't have the time or patience to pick roe from half a dozen crabs!

This soup marries the almost anise-like, herbal flavor of celery with delicate, briny-sweet crab. Both ingredients operate on the same calming, soothing plane as the potato and cream that serve to thicken this soup.

1 cup heavy cream

2 pinches of celery seeds, ground in a mortar and pestle

2 tablespoons unsalted butter

3 cups chopped celery (6 to 8 ribs), plus yellow leaves, for garnish

1 cup chopped yellow onion (about 1 medium)

½ teaspoon kosher salt

½ cup dry white wine, such as pinot grigio or sauvignon blanc

1 large Yukon Gold potato, peeled and finely diced (about 1½ cups)

2 cups fish or shellfish broth, or bottled clam juice

1 cup lump fresh (nonpasteurized) blue crab meat (lump, backfin, or claw, or any combination thereof)

Freshly ground black pepper

1   Pour the cream into a small saucepan, add the celery seeds, bring to a simmer, and cut the heat. Cover and reserve.

2   Melt the butter in a large sauté pan over medium heat, add the celery, onion, and salt, and sauté, covered, stirring occasionally, until the onion is translucent and softened, about 7 minutes. Add the wine and continue to cook until the pan is almost dry, about 7 minutes. Add the potato and the broth, and bring to a simmer. Lower the heat and continue to cook, uncovered, until the potato is completely soft, about 15 minutes. Transfer, in batches if necessary, to a food processor and process until completely smooth.

3   Wash the sauté pan and dry it. Pour the soup back into the pan over lowest heat. Add the cream and the crab meat to the stew, and whisk gently to combine completely. Cook until the crab and cream are just warmed through to serving temperature, about 3 minutes. Season with salt and freshly ground black pepper.

4   Divide the soup among four bowls, and garnish each with celery leaves.

RED PEA SOUP SERVES: 8 TIME: 2 HOURS

Dried "red" field peas—they're actually a beige to mahogany color—are a treasured ingredient in the Charleston area and considered the truly correct legume to combine with rice in a traditional Hoppin' John (page 91); using black-eyed peas in Hoppin' John is common, but the flavor of red field peas is earthier, and perhaps a shade beanier, than that of other peas. They grow well in the Lowcountry, where they are also called cow peas, finding favor among that animal group as well.

We chose to highlight the meaty flavor of red field peas in this rustic soup, and to lighten the puréed peas (which can feel heavy by themselves) with spicy turnip and onion.

2 ounces bacon (about 2 slices)

1 teaspoon vegetable, canola, olive, or peanut oil

1 medium yellow onion, chopped (1 cup)

5 sprigs thyme

2 sprigs rosemary

¼ teaspoon turmeric

1 tablespoon minced garlic (about 3 large cloves)

2 splashes of dry white wine

2 cups chicken or vegetable broth

1¾ cups dried red field peas (cow peas), picked clean and rinsed

Kosher salt and freshly ground black pepper

4 cups peeled, diced turnip or rutabaga (about 2 turnips)

3 tablespoons heavy cream

1 tablespoon distilled white or white wine vinegar

1 In a large stockpot, fry the bacon slices over medium heat, flipping occasionally, until most of the fat has rendered out and the bacon is crisp, about 8 minutes. Eat the bacon on the spot or reserve for another use. Add the oil, onion, thyme, rosemary, and turmeric to the pot and stir often, until the ingredients are well combined and the onion has softened and become translucent, 4 to 5 minutes. Add the garlic and sauté for a minute more, stirring to avoid browning.

2 Add the white wine to calm the pan, then add 7 cups of water, the broth, field peas, and 2½ teaspoons salt. Bring to a boil, partially covered, and cook for 30 minutes. Add the diced turnip, and boil, partially covered, for another 30 minutes, until the turnip and peas are both tender. Allow to cool for 20 minutes or more. Remove the thyme and rosemary sprigs (and discard), and process the soup, in batches, in a food processor.

3 Using a mesh strainer, strain the soup to smooth it (strain twice if you have the patience; we don't). Return the soup to the pot and reheat over medium-low heat. If the soup is overly thick, add more broth by the half cup. Add the cream and vinegar to finish the soup, stirring well to incorporate. Season to taste with salt and black pepper and serve.

VEGETABLES

IT'S FINALLY BEGINNING TO SINK IN! A MORE NUANCED UNDER-standing of the prominent role vegetables play in the Southern diet is gradually displacing the assumption that Southern cooking is all about pork barbecue and fried chicken. It's high time folks discovered the true diversity of vegetables that grow—and have always grown!—in the South. To read visitors' accounts of the Charleston Market in the early 1800s is to be astonished by the sheer variety: asparagus, beans, beets, cabbage, cucumbers, cymling (pattypan) squash, eggplant, kale, lettuce, onions, peas, potatoes, salsify, squash, and turnips, to name a few.

We hope this chapter pushes the veggie love even further forward. Here are some classic comfort foods—Long-Cooked Green Beans (page 106), collards Matt torqued with four kinds of capsicum (Four-Pepper Collards, page 100), and Stewed Cabbage (page 109)—mixed in with some preparations you might not have encountered before. Take, for example, Fried Salsify "Oysters" (page 97), which may sound contemporary, but the idea is 1847, through and through. And we've nudged the classic Pan-Roasted Okra, Corn, and Tomatoes (page 116) out of the stewed realm, giving it a pan-roasted treatment that deepens the flavor and deliciousness. And lest you believe that old saw about all Southern vegetables being long-simmered or fried "'til the life's cooked out of them," check into our Skillet Asparagus with Grapefruit (page 93) and—perhaps the easiest recipe in the entire book—Butter Beans with Butter, Mint, and Lime (page 100). Their freshness and simplicity is uplifting.

HOPPIN' JOHN

SERVES: 6   TIME: 1 HOUR 10 MINUTES, PLUS SOAKING TIME

The classic Charleston hoppin' John is a blend of cooked rice and red field peas, aka cow peas, with perhaps just a slight inflection of bacon and black pepper. It's more often a background starch than the star of the show, but it does become the favored guest at New Year's meals, along with collard greens (the hoppin' John for good luck and the collards for money). In Charleston, it's important to go to the extra step of sourcing field peas, which are smaller (integrating better with the rice) and more flavor packed than black-eyed peas. We admit to using black-eyed peas on occasion, but whenever we can find the field peas, we prefer to show off their superiority in this version. The ultimate hoppin' John would employ field peas and the Carolina Gold variety of rice, once grown in the Charleston area, that has recently been restored to commercial production.

The combination of legume, rice, and animal fat is an ancient one, and historians have traced the lineage of this dish back through the Caribbean, western Africa, northern Africa, and into the Middle East, to the region now called Iraq. Nutritionally, the combination is a nearly perfect vegetable protein, and you could do a whole lot worse than to eat nothing but hoppin' John and vitamin-packed collard greens the remainder of your life. Variations on the formula—like adding tomato or, god forbid, lemongrass—are scorned by the strictest traditionalists (one of whom, a friend of ours and a talented cookbook author who goes by the name of Hoppin' John Martin Taylor, scolded us for including tomato in our recipe in our first cookbook!). So if you do get an urge to tweak, we encourage you to act on it in the privacy of your own home. You can even use black-eyed peas if you prefer, without harming the spirit of the dish.

1 cup dried red field peas (cow peas), picked clean	5 cups chicken or vegetable broth
3 ounces bacon (2 to 3 thick slices)	Kosher salt and freshly ground black pepper
1 teaspoon vegetable oil	½ teaspoon red pepper flakes
1 medium yellow onion, coarsely chopped (¾ cup)	1½ cups long-grain rice

1 Rinse the dried peas in a strainer, then put them in a medium bowl. Pour in enough fresh water to cover by an inch or more, and soak for 3 hours.

2 In a 4-quart pot, fry the bacon slices over medium heat, flipping occasionally, until most of the fat has rendered out and the bacon is beginning to crisp, 6 to 8 minutes. Eat the bacon on the spot or reserve for another use. Add the oil and onion, and cook until the onion is softening and translucent, 3 to 4 minutes. Add the broth, 1 teaspoon salt, ½ teaspoon black pepper, and the red pepper flakes and bring to a boil.

3 Drain the peas, add them to the pot, and boil gently over medium to medium-high heat, uncovered, until they are tender but still have some bite, 25 to 30 minutes. Add the rice to the pot, stir once, cover, reduce the heat to low, and simmer for about 20 minutes, until most of the broth has been absorbed but the rice and peas appear very moist.

4 Remove the pot from the heat and allow the hoppin' John to steam, covered, until all the liquid appears to have been absorbed, about 8 minutes. Season with salt and black pepper.

5 Fluff the hoppin' John with a fork, transfer to a serving dish, and serve immediately.

SKILLET ASPARAGUS WITH GRAPEFRUIT

SERVES: 4   TIME: 25 MINUTES

This recipe romances March in Charleston, a stellar month: the asparagus we get from Johns Island is at its slenderest, tenderest peak; the grapefruits are just falling off trees downtown, on their way out of season. The house and garden tour season is in full swing with azaleas, dogwoods, and lilies in full bloom; the camellias are just over the hill, going out with a bang, dropping explosions of petals on the flagstone.

In the Charleston vegetable pantheon, asparagus typically takes a back seat to the collards, shelled peas, and squashes, but it shouldn't. In the 1880s, a settlement of French immigrants in Mount Pleasant, just across the Cooper River from Charleston, established a commercial asparagus farm whose harvest became in short order the priciest, most sought-after asparagus available in the urban markets of the North. We're guessing the reason for its popularity was that it was grown close to the Cooper River; our own favorite local asparagus comes from the vegetable garden of friends of ours, about 300 yards from the creek bank, and we swear that the salty air gives the stalks a quality that makes them tastier than most Central American or California-grown grocery-store spears.

This recipe will make your asparagus shine wherever it hails from. We simply char the asparagus to smoky lusciousness in a large skillet, then strew grapefruit segments over it with a vinaigrette made with the sweet-and-sour juice left over from segmenting the fruit.

1 grapefruit, preferably a ruby variety

Kosher salt

2 tablespoons white wine vinegar

1 teaspoon Dijon mustard

2 tablespoons extra-virgin olive oil

1 teaspoon canola, vegetable, or grapeseed oil, plus more if necessary

1 pound medium asparagus, trimmed of any woody ends

Freshly ground black pepper

1 With a zester or Microplane grater, scrape some grapefruit zest from the skin of the fruit for garnish, and reserve. Segment the grapefruit: trim off the bottom and top of the fruit with a knife so that you have a flat surface upon which to rest it as you peel it. Peel the fruit by placing the tip of a sharp knife just inside the border where the pith meets the pulp, and slicing down with firm, clean strokes following the curvature of the fruit. Repeat until the entire fruit has been peeled. Then, over a bowl or wide board to catch all of the juice, gently cut the segments of pulp with a sharp knife by slicing toward the core as close as possible to the membranes that separate the segments. Once you've extracted all the citrus segments, squeeze the membranes to release any remaining juice and then discard the membranes. Gently strain the segments, reserving segments and juice in separate bowls. Add ¼ teaspoon salt, the vinegar, 1 tablespoon of water, and the mustard to the bowl with the grapefruit juice and whisk to combine. Pour in the olive oil, whisking to emulsify.

2 Pour the canola oil into a large skillet over high heat, and when it smokes, add half of the asparagus and ¼ teaspoon salt, and cover. Cook, partly covered, until the asparagus is blackened on one side, 3 to 4 minutes. Turn the asparagus in the pan, cover, and cook until the asparagus is thoroughly blackened, 3 minutes more; transfer to a serving platter. Repeat with the remaining asparagus, adding another teaspoon of oil to the pan (if it's become too dry) and seasoning with salt.

3 When all the asparagus is on the platter, scatter the grapefruit segments evenly over the asparagus. If the dressing has broken, whisk to re-emulsify, pour it over the asparagus, and grind some black pepper over the top. Garnish the platter with the reserved zest, and serve.

TRUCK FARMING

SIDI LIMEHOUSE, who cultivates a mix of vegetables on Johns Island, a crescent-shaped sea island not far from the Charleston peninsula, boasts 300 subscribers to his Rosebank Farms CSA. His long perspective on truck farming in the area is shared by few others in town. As a hands-on farmer, Limehouse (he's "SIGH-die" to most everyone) is famously hard to reach, which is why we interviewed him recently on his moving tractor—Ted on the left running board and Matt on the right.

Sidi is a prominent character, as much for his salty opinions and spicy backstory (busted in the late 1970s for an incident involving 13,000 pounds of marijuana, on hunting property co-owned by South Carolina governor James Edwards) as for his fine produce. Born and raised at the family's Mullet Hall Plantation nearby, Limehouse runs an approximately 100-acre operation today, one that is becoming more diverse daily, growing corn, figs, collard greens, eggplant, asparagus, tomatoes, pears, pomegranates, Meyer lemons, and virtually any other fruit or vegetable that will take root in the sandy soil at his farm. (A few times in the last century, the cultivator has turned up an unexploded shell in these fields, lobbed at Mullet Hall by the USS *Marblehead,* anchored on the Stono River.)

From the Civil War, when the local market for vegetables crashed, until just after the Vietnam War, the pattern for farmers on the sea islands was to chase the big agricultural money. They would upstage farms in Virginia and New Jersey by sending prettier vegetables to market in New York City several weeks earlier in the season—cabbages, asparagus, strawberries, and new potatoes all generated fortunes in the Charleston area at one time or another from this technique—only to be superseded eventually by growers in Georgia and Florida, or points west.

Rock-solid industrial tomatoes are still grown on Johns Island, especially around the settlement of Legareville, and on other islands in the area, but Limehouse is glad to be done with that. On this particular spring day, he was dismayed at the damage a hailstorm had inflicted on his beets and tomatoes, and at the sight of two whole rows of Vidalia onions, wilting with a disease he doesn't recognize.

"Jimmy Shaffer over there has three hundred acres of tomatoes; I don't know how he sleeps at night," said Limehouse, referring to his second cousin (their common ancestor a German "carpetbagger" who arrived after the Civil War). "Like those Vidalia onions," he continued. "If I had twenty-five acres planted in them, I'd be tearing my hair out."

In an effort to keep his hair (Limehouse's curly, more salt-than-pepper mop sticks out under his hat and includes a full beard), he continues to experiment each season, to explore what might grow well—a globe artichoke row was neither a slam dunk nor a total failure—and, perhaps more important for him, what sells well to the evolving tastes of Charlestonians. As popular as boiled peanuts are in the area, the peanuts he grew a few seasons ago were decidedly not a hit with his CSA clients. Neither were butter beans, which we always assumed were indelibly Charleston and among the healthiest options out there: "They used to be popular," Limehouse said, "but now those people are just dead."

A LEGAREVILLE TOMATO FIELD IN APRIL.

GRILLED CHAINEY BRIAR   SERVES: 6   TIME: 30 MINUTES

Chainey briar is what Charlestonians of a certain age call the tender shoots of the smilax (aka cat briar) vine, which can be found growing in the dunes and along sandy fence lines throughout the area. The distinctive spade-shaped leaves distinguish smilax from other vines growing in the same terrain. When raw, chainey briar has a delicious asparagus-and-olive-oil flavor that is fresh and green; lightly cooked, it is even more appetizing and tender. Chainey briar appears most often in community cookbooks of the rural sea islands, like Edisto and Yonge's.

Most chainey briar found among the dunes or in metropolitan Charleston are thin, curly tendrils, although our friend Tom, who gentleman-farms on Johns Island, recently introduced us to "bull briar," the thicker sprouts of mature smilax vines that grow in the forested areas of the sea islands. Bull briar, which truly resembles large asparagus, would seem to represent more vegetable for one's effort, but it is found so high in the trees that a pole pruner is usually required to harvest it. We're just as happy to spend the afternoon on a path to the beach, eating every third tendril we pick, until the basket is full.

Chainey briar almost never appears in the farmer's markets, so you must forage for it yourself (or ingratiate yourself to farmer Sidi Limehouse, page 94, who will occasionally indulge good friends with a basketful). Its flavor is robust enough that it grills well, wilting and charring in places. Dressed with oil and lemon, it makes for an exciting side dish with pre-colonial roots.

1 pound chainey briar

1 tablespoon extra-virgin olive oil, plus more for the pan

Kosher salt and freshly ground black pepper

2 teaspoons fresh lemon juice

1 Thoroughly wash the chainey briar, removing any ants or foreign matter and pinching off the stem ends (which will toughen as they age) so only the tender parts remain. Toss the chainey briar in a large bowl with the olive oil to coat, scatter ½ teaspoon salt over the bowl, and toss again.

2 Lightly oil a grill pan, and place it over high heat. When a drop of water sizzles when dropped on the pan, spread the chainey briar in an even layer about ½ inch high (you may have to grill multiple batches, depending on the size of your pan). Allow the chainey briar to sizzle and pop for a minute or two, until the tips of some begin to blacken. Use tongs to shuffle the chainey briar on the grill pan and allow them to cook a minute or two more, until almost all the fronds show signs of wilting. Reserve the chainey briar in a large covered bowl as you move on to grill another batch.

3 When all the chainey briar is wilted and charred, dress it with the lemon juice, toss lightly, and season to taste with salt and black pepper. Serve warm or at room temperature.

FRIED SALSIFY "OYSTERS"

We think of avant-garde chefs as masters of the trickery of serving food that appears to be one thing but is actually another: it looks like a mandarin orange, but in fact—it's chicken-liver pâté! (Heston Blumenthal, dinner, London, 2010) It looks like an "everything" bagel, but in fact—it's ice cream! (Wylie Dufresne, WD-50, New York City, 2009) If cookbooks by South Carolina authors, such as Phineas Thornton's 1845 *The Southern Gardener and Receipt Book*, and Sarah Rutledge's 1847 *The Carolina Housewife*, are any indication, this sort of culinary sleight-of-hand has been going on for years.

Both of these volumes feature recipes for dishes that present themselves as fried oysters, but in fact—it's the carrot-like root salsify. Sarah Rutledge's recipe, titled "To Dress Salsify in Imitation of Oysters," reads:

> *Scrape and boil the salsify; then beat them fine in a mortar. Season with salt and pepper, and mix them in a batter of eggs, and a very little flour. Drop the size of an oyster, and fry of a light brown.*

The recipe that follows here is a rather more detailed road map to making flavorful fried salsify "oysters." And do they ever look like fried oysters! They're like light-as-air hushpuppies, or a less weighty falafel substitute. In fact, they make a knockout po-boy, with tartar sauce. But they're a fun and fascinating, crispified side dish to serve whenever you'd instinctively turn to a savory purée like mashed potatoes, sweet potatoes, or parsnips.

Wedge of lemon

1 pound salsify

½ cup half-and-half

Kosher salt and freshly ground black pepper

3 tablespoons finely chopped scallions (white and green parts)

1 large egg, beaten

3 tablespoons bread crumbs

4 to 5 cups peanut or canola oil

1 Fill a medium bowl half full with water and squeeze the wedge of lemon into it. Peel the salsify, and put it in the bowl of water to keep it from browning. When all the salsify is peeled, cut the salsify into small dice, returning the dice to the lemon water.

2 Pour the half-and-half and ½ cup of water into a 2-quart saucepan over high heat, add 1 teaspoon salt, and bring to a boil. Reduce the heat to low, strain the salsify, and add it to the pan. Simmer until very tender, about 15 minutes.

3 Strain the salsify and transfer it to a large bowl. Mash to a purée with a fork, potato masher, or whisk, and then fold in the scallions. Let cool slightly so as not to cook the egg, and season to taste with salt and black pepper. Add the egg and the bread crumbs and mix thoroughly to combine.

4 Pour the peanut oil into a deep skillet or 4-quart Dutch oven to a depth of about 2 inches, and heat to 350°F. Form the salsify mixture into heaping tablespoon-size football shapes by rolling it between two teaspoons, then dropping them into the oil, taking care not to crowd the pan. Turn them in the oil as they brown, about 2 minutes per side. Reserve fried salsify "oysters" on a plate lined with a paper towel.

5 When all the "oysters" are fried, serve immediately. Alternatively, transfer to a low oven to keep warm until serving time.

BUTTER LETTUCE WITH TOASTED PECANS AND PICKLED FIGS

SERVES: 6   TIME: 40 MINUTES, INCLUDING MACERATING TIME

Traditional Southern pickled fig recipes call for green, underripe figs bathed in a vinegar-and-sugar syrup. They emerge crunchy, with a bread-and-butter-pickle sweetness. By contrast, the quick-pickled figs in this salad—a favorite of ours in late July, when ripe figs begin to appear on trees throughout downtown Charleston—use only the figs' own soft, understated sweetness, and their gentle sourness comes from giving them a quick dunk in a gently acetic brine (which, if your fig variety has purple-black skin, will lend the pellucid vinegar a pretty pink hue). We use some of that figgy vinegar in a simple dressing with Dijon and honey, and we drizzle it over a salad composed of butter lettuce with a scattering of toasted pecans and tender, quick-pickled figs over the top.

This salad is a delicious appetizer, and makes a perfect side salad to Smothered Pork Chops (page 182), or a light supper with Wentworth Street Crab Meat (page 127). When we go the latter route, we typically crumble into it a few ounces of a South Carolina cheese, such as Clemson blue cheese or Split Creek Farms' goat cheese.

¼ cup plus 1 tablespoon white wine vinegar

Kosher salt

1 teaspoon honey

6 ounces fresh figs, quartered, or cut into eighths if they are very large

½ cup pecan halves

Freshly ground black pepper

2 teaspoons Dijon mustard

6 tablespoons mild-tasting olive oil

2 large heads butter, romaine, or mixed lettuces, torn

4 ounces blue cheese or goat cheese (optional)

1 Pour ¾ cup of water, ¼ cup of the vinegar, and ¼ teaspoon salt into a bowl. Add the honey and whisk until the salt dissolves and the honey is incorporated. Add the figs to the bowl, and let stand for 30 minutes.

2 Preheat the oven to 250°F.

3 Spread the pecans on a rimmed baking pan and toast for 15 minutes until fragrant. Set aside to cool.

4 Strain the figs, reserving the figs and 2 tablespoons of the brine. Season the figs with salt and black pepper. Add the remaining tablespoon vinegar and the Dijon mustard to the reserved brine and whisk together. Add the oil, pouring in a thin stream and whisking until the dressing is emulsified.

5 Divide the lettuces among six bowls or plates. Scatter some figs, pecans, and cheese (if desired) over each portion, and drizzle with the vinaigrette.

MATT'S FOUR-PEPPER COLLARDS

SERVES: 8   TIME: 1 HOUR 35 MINUTES

The pairing of the bright green flavor of chiles and the earthy character of collard greens is what's exciting about this pepperiffic recipe for collards, which celebrates both vegetables and requires no seasoning meat. The greens absorb the mellow, warming effect of long-cooked hot peppers, without the electricity of the raw article.

This dish also packs a jolt of color—not typically a hallmark of collards—if you use red jalapeños (which are simply green jalapeños that have remained on the plant into late-summer maturity). But if you can't find red ones, not to worry: step this dish up to five-pepper collards by adding a chopped red, yellow, or orange bell pepper and a green jalapeño for chile heat. This collards dish makes a terrific starting point for a Collards Sandwich (recipe follows) prepared with good Cheddar.

¼ cup peanut or canola oil

3 jalapeño peppers, preferably red, seeded and chopped

1 large poblano chile, seeded and chopped

1 cup chopped yellow or white onion (about 1 medium)

1 tablespoon kosher salt

1 teaspoon freshly ground black pepper

1 tablespoon cider vinegar

1½ teaspoons smoked paprika

4 pounds collard greens (about 3 bunches), stems trimmed, leaves rolled and sliced into ¾-inch-thick ribbons (about 5 quarts)

1 Pour the oil into a large stockpot over medium-high heat, and when it shimmers, add all of the remaining ingredients except the collards. Cook, stirring occasionally with a wooden spoon, until the peppers appear dry, 6 to 8 minutes.

2 Add the collards to the pot by handfuls, moving them around with a wooden spoon, and folding them into the peppers in the bottom of the pan, until the greens appear wilted, slick, and slightly darkened, about 5 minutes.

3 Add 6 cups of water and cover. When the liquid first begins to simmer, stir once, turn the heat to medium low, and cover. Simmer for 1 hour and stir again. Serve drained, but still wet with the broth.

COLLARDS SANDWICH

SERVES: 4   TIME: 10 MINUTES

Our friend Capers White, a Rock Hill, South Carolina, native now residing in Charleston, once asked us over the dinner table, "Y'all ever made a collards sandwich? It's the best thing to do with leftover collards."

This brilliant idea had never occurred to us, and as minor experts in things to do with leftover collards, the news was bittersweet—we'd missed out on thirty-plus years of the most amazing sandwiches. If you've never had one, then this recipe may change your life.

Hundreds of delicious collards sandwiches later, we can tell you the key is to use really well-seasoned greens with an extra splash or two of vinegar in them (salt them before step 2, opposite, if they're underseasoned), and the freshest bread available. Once you've tried this version, let your imagination roam in leftovers mode—a wildcard ingredient, like a slice of bologna, or thinly sliced country ham, or a smear of mayo and relish, or thin slices of Jerusalem Artichoke Pickles (page 136) will endear these sandwiches to you even more.

Butter or mayonnaise

8 slices fresh bread, toasted

1 heaping pint Matt's Four-Pepper Collards (page 100)

6 ounces Cheddar cheese, sliced

Thinly sliced ham or pickles, or relish (all optional)

1 Preheat the broiler.

2 Spread a thin layer of butter or mayonnaise on one side of each slice of toast. Put 4 of the slices on a baking sheet.

3 Drain the collards in a colander set in the sink, pressing with a spatula to chase off some liquid. For each sandwich, take ½ cup tightly packed collards into your hand and squeeze once again to remove excess liquid, then form the greens into a squarish patty and lay it down on one of the slices of toast on the baking sheet. Repeat three times, once for each of the 4 sandwiches.

4 Apply the cheese to the surface of each of the open-faced collards sandwiches, and broil for 3 minutes, until the cheese begins to melt into the greens (keep the broiler door open and don't let your eyes off them for even a second).

5 Add either ham, pickle, or relish, if desired, on top of the cheese, cover each sandwich with the remaining sliced bread (butter or mayonnaise side down), and serve immediately.

HOLY CITY FORAGING

CONSIDER THE LOQUAT, *Eriobotrya japonica,* a humble yellow fruit slightly smaller than a golf ball and native to China. Loquats emerge on trees throughout the Lowcountry in April (March, if it's been a warm winter), with furry skin enveloping a shallow layer of yellow-orange flesh. A loquat has large seeds, and even at the peak of ripeness, its sweet-sour apple flavor is no more mind-blowing than, say, that of a Granny Smith apple, of which it is a distant relative.

So why bother? Because like mulberries, figs, chicken mushrooms, persimmons, plums, kumquats, citrus fruits, and rosemary and many other herbs, loquats are ingredients in a Lowcountry life. Foraging for them is part of an underground economy that's as much about the knowledge of a food's where-abouts as it is about actually harvesting them (plus, loquats make a terrific cordial when steeped in vodka, see page 33). We trade sources with friends—*I'll tell you where a huge fig tree is if you tell me where you found your persimmons!* The mind-set of extreme self-reliance, of finding fruit outside the ration book, ran so strong here that it outlasted the Great Depression and all the twentieth-century wars, to influence subsequent generations. The newest wave of cooks in Charleston's restaurant kitchens is open to the novelty and freshness of foraged plants and fungi, and so the knowledge bank is being slowly rebuilt.

Near the beaches we find prickly pear cactus, whose magenta-colored pulp is a challenge to extract (but wonderful in margaritas when you do), and—perhaps the most plentiful of all the wild edibles in the region—chaney briar, which grows along the paths to the beach on barrier islands like Isle of Palms and Folly Beach. Chaney briar's appealing tender shoots taste slightly asparagus-like, and a bit salty since it often grows near the ocean (page 96).

We know just one reliable spot for foraging chicken mushrooms (*Laetiporus sulphureus*), and it happens to be at the base of a live oak tree alongside River Road on Johns Island—a shoulderless, narrow two-lane blacktop that's been the scene of dozens of car-tree fatalities in our lifetimes. We court death in more ways than one when we forage for mushrooms there, but have to admit it gives us triple thrills to do it.

SWEET POTATOES WITH SORGHUM MARSHMALLOWS

SERVES: 8   TIME: 1 HOUR 35 MINUTES

Sweet potatoes are ideal for a minimalist presentation: baked and puréed, they have more natural sweetness, inherent spice, and butteriness than any other vegetable we know. They're close to perfect all by themselves, and yet people (throughout the South, it's not just Charleston) insist on heaping additional "Christmas" on them—the brown sugar, the cinnamon, nutmeg. The marshmallows on top, though, a grace note of even softer candy (and smoke, if they're nicely charred), suddenly make a world of sense when paired with the gently seasoned—not too sweet!—sweet potato purée, slightly tart from a jolt of lemon juice. This iconic Southern comfort food is scrumptious with store-bought marshmallows, and hits the stratosphere with homemade Sorghum Marshmallows.

Serve with Smothered Pork Chops (page 182) and alongside Long-Cooked Green Beans (page 106) or Matt's Four-Pepper Collards (page 100).

4 pounds sweet potatoes, pricked twice with a fork

4 tablespoons (½ stick) unsalted butter, softened, plus more for the pan

3 tablespoons fresh lemon juice (from 1 large)

Kosher salt and freshly ground black pepper

3 (12-inch) batons of Sorghum Marshmallows (page 217), or approximately 24 store-bought marshmallows

Paprika or smoked paprika, for dusting (optional)

½ cup chopped toasted pecans, for garnish (optional)

1 Preheat the oven to 400°F.

2 Put the sweet potatoes on a baking sheet lined with foil and bake for 1 hour, until fragrant and soft. Remove from the oven and cut the potatoes lengthwise. Decrease the oven temperature to 350°F.

3 When the potatoes have cooled, peel them and add the flesh to a large bowl. Top with the butter, pour the lemon juice over the potatoes, and mash well until smooth. Season with 1 teaspoon salt and some freshly ground black pepper. (The purée will keep for 2 days in the fridge.)

4 Turn the purée into a buttered 9 by 13-inch heatproof pan and smooth into an even layer. When nearly ready to serve, bake for about 20 minutes to warm the dish, then remove from the oven. Lay the marshmallows in rows on the surface of the purée, pressing them in slightly. Return the pan to the oven and bake for 5 minutes, until the marshmallows are beginning to droop. Remove from the oven.

5 Set the oven to broil and place the potatoes within a couple inches of the heat just until the marshmallows begin to blacken in places but do not go up in flames, 45 seconds. (Keep the oven door open and don't take your eyes off them!)

6 Serve immediately with a light dusting of paprika and chopped toasted pecans, if using. Make sure there is some marshmallow in every serving.

LONG-COOKED GREEN BEANS

The essence of "soul" in Southern food, much mythologized in film and print, is illuminated in a few choice examples, like the secret to these long-cooked green beans.

Modern culinary logic—and everything we've learned from top restaurant chefs—suggests that for optimum flavor, vegetables should be cooked a bare minimum, to toothsomeness and no further, lest the more fragile aromatic components of the produce's flavor be driven away. We use this insight to great effect when we stumble across the perfect pod of okra or a baby pattypan squash in the garden. We eat them raw, or blanch them for a few minutes in salted water, or cook them only briefly in a hot pan.

There are monumental exceptions to this premise in Southern cooking. In the cafeterias, boardinghouses, and home kitchens that accounted for the majority of meals consumed in Charleston before the dawn of the restaurant era, dishes like long-cooked green beans weren't even considered worthy of a recipe—they were just vegetables, and this is how you cook them: fill a pot with water and the trimmed vegetables, add your favorite seasoning meat, season with salt and pepper, and cook at a low simmer on the back of the stove until serving time. These green beans are found today at restaurants like Martha Lou's Kitchen, where classic Southern dishes are prepared, homemade style, in large aluminum pots on a stove.

True, the color will have long gone by the time these beans hit the table, but the concentrated bean flavor that results when they tumble in the broth for more than an hour is revelatory. The method highlights an aspect of the beans' character that isn't revealed with the snap-and-crunch of a blanched or raw bean. That peeling away of the more obvious outer layers of flavor to reach, in due time, the heart of the vegetable's character—that is soulful cooking. This technique works well with most legumes and with collards, cabbage, and other brassicas. Our recipe here hits the classic notes (we use bacon as our seasoning meat, dried red pepper flakes, and black pepper) and is precise with the liquid, so the broth emerges so tasty you'll want to drink it straight.

Serve the beans warm and slightly soupy, with Skillet Cornbread (page 213), Cornmeal-Crusted Mahi (page 135), or Smothered Pork Chops (page 182).

¼ pound smoked slab bacon or smoked sausage, sliced

2 pounds green beans, stems trimmed, cut into 2- to 3-inch lengths

Kosher salt and freshly ground black pepper

¼ to ½ teaspoon red pepper flakes

1 tablespoon cider vinegar

2 tablespoons unsalted butter

1 Bring 2 quarts of water to a simmer with the bacon in a 6-quart stockpot over high heat. Add the beans, and when the liquid returns to a simmer, turn the heat to low, and cook uncovered for 30 minutes.

2 Add 1 tablespoon salt, 1 teaspoon black pepper, the red pepper flakes, and vinegar. Cover and simmer on low for 45 minutes (you should be left with just 1½ to 2 cups broth; if the beans appear to be boiling dry, add water as necessary by half cups).

3 Season to taste with salt, and add the butter, stirring to melt, before serving.

STEWED CABBAGE   SERVES: 6 TO 8   TIME: 2 HOURS

Martha Lou Gadsden opened Martha Lou's Kitchen in 1983, in a small pink cinderblock building on Morrison Drive, a four-lane thoroughfare that rumbles with tractor-trailers hauling off Interstate 26 on their way to the Charleston docks. Back then, Morrison Drive was thick with businesses: car dealerships, paint wholesalers, and rug specialists spread out along the avenue, as well as a prominent blacksmith's shop. By the early nineties, the dealerships had departed and the town's clangorous recycling center moved in, but these days the neighborhood's getting its groove back, with a distinctly culinary tune: there's the new local-produce depot, GrowFood Carolina; the hipster diner The Tattooed Moose, serving duck confit banh-mi; and the Mexican favorite, Santi's. We mostly credit Martha Lou for the neighborhood's current verve (real estate agents are calling the area "NoMo" for North Morrison) because, for three decades, Martha Lou's Kitchen has shined as a beacon of excellent Southern food prepared with love.

Step through the screen door and you are standing in her kitchen. There are a few banquettes to the right, beneath a mural that depicts the St. Philips Church spire downtown, as well as a scene of Mosquito Beach, a summer enclave on the Folly River (and just down the road from Backman Seafood, page 150), popular for over a century with the county's African American population—in fact, the Kittiwah Island scene in *Porgy and Bess* is likely based on Mosquito Beach. All the proteins at Martha Lou's—fried whiting, fried pork chops, fried chicken—are stunningly fresh and cooked to order, but we're equally smitten with her vegetables, loosely topped with foil for a long, gentle simmer at the back of the stove. We recently had the privilege of cooking alongside Mrs. Gadsden at a luncheon during the Charleston Wine and Food Festival. She made her okra soup; we prepared our own spin on one of her favorite side dishes, stewed cabbage with meaty pork neck bones. For our cabbage dish, we enlisted chef Craig Diehl of Cypress Restaurant—a guy with a gift for cured and smoked meats of any kind—to smoke us some neck bones from South Carolina–raised hogs. It was a real honor to spend the afternoon serving alongside Martha Lou, taking care of a hungry crowd and basking in her aura, if only for a few hours.

In this recipe you may use purple or green cabbage; both vegetables take on a whitish gray hue once cooked, but the purple cabbage will leave your broth an electric magenta color. That's cool, but we prefer to use green because we find the contrast of the luscious pearly-green broth and the pinkish hues of the seared neck bones to be more appealing at the table. Be sure to serve each portion with a meaty neck bone.

1 large head green cabbage (3 pounds)

1 tablespoon canola oil

1 pound smoked pork neck bones

½ teaspoon red pepper flakes

⅓ cup distilled white or white wine vinegar

2 teaspoons kosher salt

1 With your largest chef's knife, slice the cabbage into quarters lengthwise. Trim out the core from each quarter and discard the cores.

2 Pour the oil into a large Dutch oven or stew pot set over medium-high heat and when it shimmers, tilt the pan around so the oil covers the bottom in a thin sheen. Add the neck bones, taking care not to crowd them in the pan, and brown them on all sides, about a minute per side. Gather the neck bones toward one side of the pan and add the red pepper flakes to the empty part, toasting them in the oil, just until fragrant, about 15 to 20 seconds. Immediately add 6 cups of water, the vinegar, and salt and bring to a boil over high heat.

3 Once the potlikker is boiling, pull the cabbage leaves apart and add them in handfuls, sinking them beneath the surface of the liquid with a wooden spoon, until all the cabbage has been added. When the broth returns to a simmer, turn the heat to low and continue to simmer, partially covered, until the meat falls from the bone and the cabbage is completely tender, about 1½ hours. Serve.

BUTTER BEANS WITH BUTTER, MINT, AND LIME

SERVES: 8   TIME: 20 MINUTES

Along with muscadine grapes, butter beans are among the farmer's market treasures of late summer in Charleston—reason to wake up with gusto to another day of stultifying heat and oxford-soaking humidity. We do all kinds of things with butter beans: we make a hummus-like spread for the cocktail hour, we simmer them with seasoning meats of all sorts, and we compose marinated salads aplenty. But this may be our most simple treatment yet, and one of the most satisfying.

Butter beans come in many varieties, and at stands like Joseph Fields Farm at the Saturday Farmer's Market in Marion Square, shelled beans are kept in large tailgating coolers. Some beans are green with purple speckles, some are reddish brown, a few are ivory colored, and there's every shade of green besides. For this simple side dish, we like to use the small green ones (though you may use frozen baby lima beans if butter beans aren't in season).

Kosher salt

6 cups fresh shelled butter beans or frozen baby lima beans

3 tablespoons unsalted butter, cut into small pieces

Juice of 2 large limes

1 cup loosely packed mint leaves, chopped

Freshly ground black pepper

1 teaspoon grated lime zest, for garnish

1 In a medium saucepan, bring 6 cups of water and 1 tablespoon salt to a boil over high heat. Add the butter beans and cook until tender, 9 to 12 minutes, depending on the size of the beans. Drain in a colander, and shake the colander several times to shed as much water from the beans as possible.

2 Put the butter in a large serving bowl, and pour the warm butter beans on top. Toss the beans with the butter until all the butter is melted. Add the lime juice and toss again to distribute. Fold in the mint, season with salt and black pepper, and scatter lime zest over the top. Serve immediately.

GIAN CARLO'S PASTA   SERVES: 4   TIME: 20 MINUTES

The composer Gian Carlo Menotti (1911–2007) left his mark on Charleston by bringing the festival he had created in Spoleto, Italy, to the city in 1977. In this highly principled, cultured, and mercurial man (who collaborated with and lived much of his life with the composer Samuel Barber), Charleston had met its late-twentieth-century match. Spoleto Festival USA flourished, galvanizing the cultural yearnings of the populace, while Charleston provided Menotti with the most ravishing set this side of La Scala.

True, the first years of the festival brought a few dramatic clashes, at least concerning the food: Jane Ries, who had founded one of Charleston's first formal culinary classes in her kitchen on Queen Street, received an urgent call one day.

"You must help me," said the Italian-accented gentleman on the line. "I heard you know how to cook. They're poisoning me; they're trying to kill me. The man they sent to cook for me only prepares burnt pork chops and instant chocolate pudding."

Ries (who later, in the 1990s, became the *Post & Courier* restaurant critic) became Menotti's private chef, preparing dinners on a shoestring for the visiting divas, ballet companies, musicians, performers, and local dignitaries whom Menotti entertained. She baked baguettes from scratch and tossed giant bowls of pasta and salads. As the city embraced him, Menotti's dance card gradually filled, and downtown hosts and hostesses would eagerly loan out their mansions for his stay every May and June. Ries continued to cook for him for eight years, preparing for his annual visit by stockpiling her freezer with country pâté.

This pasta recipe, for al dente capellini, is one that Menotti taught Ries when he stayed a season at 1 East Battery (a magnificent edifice of brick and stucco at the very tip of the peninsula). The recipe is specifically for early-summer dining, when Charleston's first crop of tomatoes reaches its peak. It combines two pounds of the finest quality garden-ripe tomatoes with a full bunch of parsley, and with plenty of salt, pepper, and finishing-quality extra-virgin olive oil (just becoming available at that time in Charleston).

Kosher salt

2 pounds best-quality heirloom summer tomatoes, preferably red and yellow

2 cups firmly packed flat-leaf parsley leaves (1 large bunch), washed and well dried

1 teaspoon freshly ground black pepper

¼ cup plus 1 tablespoon finest extra-virgin olive oil, with grassy flavors

12 ounces (¾ pound) dried capellini (angel hair) pasta

¼ teaspoon flaky sea salt, such as Maldon

1 Fill a pasta pot with 1 gallon of water, add 3 tablespoons kosher salt, and bring to a boil.

2 Meanwhile, core the tomatoes and chop them and the parsley, both medium fine, no piece more spacious than a dime. Combine them in a large serving bowl along with any tomato water. Sprinkle ½ teaspoon kosher salt and ½ teaspoon of the black pepper over the top. Drizzle 1 tablespoon of the olive oil into the bowl, but do not toss yet.

3 Add the pasta to the boiling water and stir once or twice to keep the pasta from sticking to itself. After 2 full minutes, turn off the heat, and pull the pasta from the pot immediately using tongs, allowing excess water to drip back into the pot before heaping it into the bowl on top of the tomatoes.

4 Drizzle the remaining ¼ cup olive oil over the pasta, and then add the remaining ½ teaspoon black pepper and the flaky sea salt. Toss at the table if serving immediately; toss in the kitchen if serving at room temperature, or as a side dish.

DIRTY RICE AND GREENS   SERVES: 6   TIME: 45 MINUTES

Dirty rice is rice that is the opposite of bland: it has been oiled up, smudged with meaty things, and seasoned with red and black pepper until it makes you pay attention. It's a popular side dish at buffets throughout the Charleston area for the way it pairs with poultry, seafood, and long-cooked vegetables. It was that affinity that led us to combine collard greens with dirty rice in a single recipe.

This is basically a collards pilau, but we combine the greens with the rice after they both are cooked independently. To make it more of a true pilau, use 4 cups collards potlikker instead of the water called for in this recipe, and omit the salt.

1 tablespoon peanut, canola, or olive oil

⅓ pound sweet or hot Italian sausage (about 1 link), cut from the casing and crumbled

1 slice thick-cut bacon

5 ounces chicken livers (about 3 large)

½ teaspoon red pepper flakes

2 cups chopped yellow onion (about 1 large)

1 tablespoon minced garlic (about 3 large cloves)

1 teaspoon minced fresh thyme

1½ teaspoons kosher salt

½ teaspoon freshly ground black pepper

2 cups long-grain white rice

2 cups cooked seasoned greens (such as Matt's Four-Pepper Collards, page 100), roughly chopped

1 Pour the oil into a 6- to 8-quart cast-iron pot or Dutch oven over medium-high heat and add the sausage and the bacon slice, flipping the bacon a few times to render its grease while pushing the sausage around with a wooden spoon to brown evenly. After 2 to 3 minutes, when the sausage is not visibly raw, add the chicken livers, pushing them around and mashing them with the spoon to break them down as they cook, about 2 minutes.

2 Add the red pepper flakes, onion, garlic, thyme, salt, and black pepper and stir to mix evenly. Cook for about 2 minutes, stirring occasionally, until the onion begins to give up some moisture. Add the rice and stir until the grains are glazed with oil.

3 Add 4 cups of water, stir until evenly distributed, and cover. When the liquid comes to a boil, turn the heat down to medium low and simmer, covered, for 15 minutes, until the rice is tender and the liquid is nearly gone.

4 Turn off the heat and add the cooked collard greens, stirring just enough to combine. Cover again and allow to steam for 5 minutes before serving. Season with salt and freshly ground black pepper to taste. (Dirty Rice and Greens will keep about 4 days in the refrigerator in a covered container.)

BRUSSELS SPROUTS WITH BENNE AND BACON

SERVES: 6   TIME: 30 MINUTES

For recipe developers/food writers like us, Thanksgiving is our birthday, Chanukah, Christmas, New Year's Eve, and Fourth of July all rolled into one. We tend to pull out all the stops at Thanksgiving, splurging on a $200 heirloom turkey, testing out new recipes we've been working on, and in general showing off (pies *and* layer cake, anyone?). On turkey day, we adopt the oft-repeated ethos of Ted's mother-in-law, Lucy Day: "If it's worth doing, it's worth overdoing."

This recipe is a balance for all that excess, an easy Thanksgiving sleeper dish that's a joy to prepare at the eleventh hour, when everything's gone to hell: the layer cakes are threatening to overflow their pans, the turkey's not even in the oven yet, and Great-Aunt Doris keeps interrupting you to ask, for the twelfth time, where you said the vodka was.

This is also one of our favorite ways to eat Brussels sprouts, one that transforms them into a light, easy-to-eat side dish. The dash of sesame oil and scattering of toasted sesame seeds may seem to be inspired by Japanese or Chinese cooking, but in fact sesame seeds arrived in the Lowcountry from Africa during the slave trade. Benne seeds still find their way into dishes both sweet and savory in Charleston, and the toasted seeds are almost bacony in flavor, simpatico with the smoked bacon in this dish.

2 pounds Brussels sprouts, root ends trimmed and any discolored leaves discarded

4 ounces slab bacon, cut into large dice

¼ cup extra-virgin olive oil

¼ cup canola or grapeseed oil

½ teaspoon toasted sesame oil

¼ cup champagne vinegar

½ teaspoon red pepper flakes

½ teaspoon sugar

Kosher salt

2 teaspoons toasted sesame seeds

Freshly ground black pepper

1 Fill a large pot fitted with a steamer basket about 1 inch deep with water and bring to a boil.

2 Meanwhile, shred the Brussels sprouts in a food processor using a 2- to 4-mm slicing disk (alternatively, you can cut the sprouts in half lengthwise and slice them ¹⁄₁₆ to ⅛ inch thick). Add the Brussels sprouts to the steamer and steam until the firmest pieces of the shredded sprouts are soft and pliant, but the sprouts are still bright green in color, 6 to 8 minutes. Transfer to a large bowl.

3 Scatter the bacon in a large skillet or sauté pan over medium-high heat, and cook, stirring occasionally, until the bacon is firm and just golden brown, about 4 minutes. Transfer the bacon to a paper-towel-lined plate. Pour off all but a tablespoon of the bacon fat from the pan and add the three oils, the vinegar, red pepper flakes, sugar, and ¾ teaspoon salt. Stir the dressing in the pan with a wooden spoon, scraping up any browned bits from the bottom of the pan.

4 Pour the warm dressing over the Brussels sprouts, add the sesame seeds and reserved bacon, and toss thoroughly with tongs to combine. Season with salt and black pepper and serve immediately. (Store any leftovers in the refrigerator in a container with a tight-fitting lid no more than 4 days.)

PAN-ROASTED OKRA, CORN, AND TOMATOES

SERVES: 6   TIME: 45 MINUTES

We bring high-summer cookout spirit to the classic Lowcountry vegetable trinity by charring the okra and corn in a cast-iron skillet. The resulting caramelized, sweet vegetable flavor is the perfect complement to the acidity of fresh tomatoes that have been gently stewed with some onion, garlic, and bacon. You can turn this into a vegetarian dish in a snap by substituting a healthy pinch of smoked sweet paprika for the bacon, adding it to the pan along with the onion and garlic. Since you'll lose the fat rendered by the bacon, you should add up to a tablespoon more vegetable oil to make sure the onions and garlic don't brown.

3 tablespoons vegetable oil, plus more for brushing

8 ounces fresh okra, halved lengthwise

Kosher salt

1½ cups corn kernels (from 2 large ears)

2 pounds fresh tomatoes

2 ounces slab bacon, cut into large dice

1 medium white onion, chopped (¾ cup)

1 large garlic clove, mashed to a paste

1 to 2 teaspoons vinegar, either red wine, white wine, or distilled white (optional)

Freshly ground black pepper

1 Heat a large cast-iron skillet over high heat until very hot and brush lightly with vegetable oil. In a bowl, toss the okra with 1 tablespoon of the oil and season with ¼ teaspoon salt. Cook the okra in the pan in two batches, turning once, until charred and tender, 3 to 4 minutes per batch depending on the size and freshness of your okra. Reserve in a bowl so you can reuse the cast-iron skillet.

2 Add 1 tablespoon of the oil to the corn and season with ¼ teaspoon of the salt. Add the corn to the skillet and cook over high heat, stirring occasionally, until lightly charred in spots, about 3 minutes. Reserve the corn in a bowl, separate from the okra.

3 Bring a large saucepan of water to a boil and fill a bowl with ice water. Score the tomato bottoms with an X. Add the tomatoes to the boiling water and blanch for 10 seconds to loosen their skins. Transfer the tomatoes to the ice water to cool. Core and peel the tomatoes, and halve them crosswise. Working over a sieve set in a bowl, tease out the seeds with your fingers. Press on the seeds to extract the juice, then discard them. Chop the tomatoes and reserve them in the bowl of their juice.

4 Pour the remaining tablespoon oil into the skillet over medium-high heat, and when it shimmers, add the bacon. Sauté the bacon until it just begins to brown, about 4 minutes, then add the onion and ½ teaspoon salt. Stir continuously for about 2 minutes, allowing the onion to release some moisture, but not letting it brown. Add the garlic and cook for about a minute to let its flavor bloom (do not brown the garlic). Then add the tomatoes, and stir to combine. Cover the pot, reduce the heat to medium, and cook for about 4 minutes until the tomatoes have mostly collapsed.

5 Add the corn, stir to combine, and cook for 3 more minutes. Add the okra, stir, and cook just until the okra is heated through, about 2 minutes. Season to taste with the vinegar (which you may or may not need, depending upon the acidity of the tomatoes), salt, and black pepper; serve.

FISH *and* SHELLFISH

IF WE LEAVE YOU WITH ONLY ONE IMPRESSION FROM THIS BOOK, let it be the following: the cuisine of Charleston is intertwined with the sea. You'll notice that this chapter is the largest in the book, and that's because there's so much sparklingly fresh raw material to inspire us here.

Charleston's coastal orientation isn't unique among cities along the eastern seaboard, but what does seem special is the community of people here devoted to finding the freshest fish they can. It means that in 2013, we can be on a first-name basis with the shrimpers, oystermen, crabbers, fish cutters, wholesalers, and retailers (the fish scientists and game wardens, too). Our late grandmother would think nothing of driving half an hour to Rockville, on Wadmalaw Island, to purchase shrimp fresh off the boat—"her" boat. (We prefer the convenience of the trawlers on Shem Creek in Mount Pleasant, just a short drive from downtown.)

Even if you're not among the multitudes here who love to catch their own fish, or to net for shrimp and crabs, there are countless options for purchasing local and imported fish and shellfish. We know of few other towns in this country with a sustainable seafood CSF—community supported fishery.

The recipes in the chapter range from rustic, simple preparations of the local bounty, like Skillet Whiting (page 121), to more baroque recipes, such as Broiled Shad with Shad Roe Mousse (page 140), that would be most at home on a silver platter on a Federal sideboard. You'll have all the know-how you need to put on an outdoor Crab Crack (page 148) once you've read this chapter, and of course you'll have our own updated riff on the ubiquitous Shrimp and Grits (page 169).

SKILLET WHITING

SERVES: 2 TIME: 45 MINUTES

Elsewhere on the eastern seaboard, whiting (*Menticirrhus americanus*, or kingfish) is considered a staple fish—food for the fryer, nothing much to get excited about. But a Charleston fish market without whiting is a rarity, because we adore this tasty fish, which consumes a diverse diet of tiny tender proteins tossed about in the surf breaks, its preferred habitat. Consequently, whiting can be as sweet and pleasant as shrimp. It's gently priced too, and often an excellent fish value. Fresh examples smell minerally, like ocean water, and not fishy.

We like this super-simple skillet preparation of the whole whiting, which is rustic in appearance, but allows the pure flavor of fresh whiting, cooked on the bone, to come through clearly. The fillets pull easily away, but we still use our fingers to dig in and strip the skeleton clean.

¼ cup canola or peanut oil

2 (12- to 14-ounce) whole whiting, scaled and gutted, head on

Kosher salt and freshly ground black pepper

1 tablespoon plus 1 teaspoon fine- or medium-fine cornmeal

Lemon wedges, hot sauce, or pepper vinegar, for serving

1 With a rack set in the upper third of the oven, preheat the oven to 350°F.

2 Pour the oil into a large ovenproof skillet over medium-high heat. Turn the whiting belly up, and sprinkle all over, inside and out, with 1 teaspoon salt, ½ teaspoon black pepper, and the cornmeal. When the oil begins to smoke, put the whiting upright—belly side down—as if they were swimming, bending them slightly to fit the curvature of the skillet (if they won't remain upright, leave them on the side they prefer). Fry the fish until the bellies are browning and the visibly cooked area of skin is beginning to creep up the side of the fish, 8 to 10 minutes (flip once at 5 minutes if they are resting on their side).

3 Carefully transfer the skillet to a rack in the upper third of the oven, and bake for about 20 minutes, until the fish are cooked through and firm on top. Dust each fish with a few pinches of salt and pepper before serving, one fish per person on a plate, with a stack of napkins, fingerbowls, and lemon wedges, hot sauce, or pepper vinegar.

RETIRED TRAWLER, ROCKVILLE, SC.

WHOLE FLOUNDER WITH SUNCHOKE AND SHRIMP STUFFING

SERVES: 2   TIME: 50 MINUTES

Henry Shaffer is the last direct link to a number of Charleston kitchen traditions that came into being at Henry's Restaurant (see Henry's Cheese Spread, page 47, and Deviled Crab, page 153). Perhaps the most richly decadent of these were the whole stuffed fish dishes with fancy, Frenchy names like seafood à la Wando (lobster, shrimp, crab, and oysters simmered in a casserole with butter, button mushrooms, scallions, and sherry), and pompano à la Gherardi. This latter dish was a whole pompano that had been sliced down the side and boned whole to create a fish pocket that then was stuffed with sherried shrimp and crab meat, topped with strips of bacon and chopped green olives, and baked in a covered dish.

In his home kitchen, Shaffer patiently taught us this technique, which he learned at his father's restaurant, and which could be applied to a whole pompano or flounder. This is our tribute, using Shaffer's method, to those dishes. We've tweaked our stuffing to be somewhat lighter than the original—it's a simple, flavorful hash of steamed shrimp and Jerusalem artichokes tossed with lemon, dill, finely diced toast, and a bit of butter.

1 (1¼-pound) flounder, scaled, gutted, and head removed

1 slice thick-cut bacon

4 ounces Jerusalem artichokes (sunchokes), peeled and finely diced (about 1 cup)

¼ pound large (21 to 25 count) shrimp, peeled and deveined

2 very thin slices white bread, such as Pepperidge Farm, toasted and diced (about ½ cup)

Pinch of grated lemon zest

1 tablespoon fresh lemon juice

3 tablespoons unsalted butter, melted

2 tablespoons chopped fresh dill

¼ teaspoon kosher salt

1 Bone the whole flounder, Shafferstyle (see box).

2 Preheat the oven to 375°F. While the oven heats, throw the bacon into a large skillet and put it in the oven.

3 Pour 2 inches of water into a steamer fitted with a steamer basket and set it over high heat. Add the Jerusalem artichokes, lay the shrimp on top of them, and steam, covered, until the shrimp are just done, about 5 minutes. Remove the shrimp from the steamer and transfer to a cutting board to cool. Continue to steam the artichokes until they're just tender, about 5 more minutes.

4 When the shrimp are cool enough to handle, chop them roughly and transfer to a large bowl. When the artichokes are ready, add them to the bowl with the shrimp, along with the diced toast, zest, lemon juice, 2 tablespoons of the melted butter, the dill, and salt and toss until well combined. Gently spoon the stuffing into the cavity of the flounder. The flounder will appear overstuffed; that is fine!

5 Once the bacon has rendered its fat and the skillet is hot, remove from the oven and lay the flounder in it (the fish will sizzle in the fat). Brush the skin of the fish with the remaining tablespoon melted butter. Roast in the oven until the fish is cooked through, about 18 minutes. (Discard the bacon, or if you prefer, crisp it further in a small skillet, chop it, and use as a garnish.)

6 Lift a portion of the fillet from each side of the fish onto two plates, and top with spoonfuls of the stuffing and the crisped bacon, if using.

HENRY SHAFFER'S FLOUNDER DEBONING TECHNIQUE

A plane of rib bones runs through the center of the pancake-flat flounder; we're going to open up the top side of the fish like a book, cut through the bones at their very edges, around the perimeter of the fish, and remove them, leaving behind a fish pocket.

1 Begin with a scaled, gutted flounder, head off.

2 Trim away any collarbones that remain from the edge where the head was detached.

3 Lay the flounder with its gently rounded top side up on a cutting board, and find the center line that runs from the tail to the head (it should be obvious in the skin markings of the fish). With a thin sharp knife, cut down through the flesh along the center line just as deep as the plane of bones.

4 Scraping with the knife along the plane of bones, release the upper flesh, left fillet and then right, just as far as the edge of the fish, so the fillets remain attached at their outer edge.

5 Pry up a fillet with one hand so you can see where it is connected to the fish, and cut down through the thin bone tips at the fish perimeter with the knife (or with fish scissors), trying as best as possible to cut only bone, and not to cut all the way through the fish. Repeat on the other side.

6 Slip the tip of the knife between the bone plane and the bottom fillet on one side and cut with a scraping motion along the bone plane toward the outer edge of the fillet without cutting through the outer edge. Repeat with the other side.

7 Pull up the spine—and with it the plane of bones—beginning at the head end of the fish. It should pull up and away from the fish pocket until you reach the tail (if any rib bones remain connected, snip them with fish scissors or cut with a knife). Cut the spine at the tail to release all the bones.

"In charleston, it's *Henry's* for foods"

48-54 MARKET STREET

FAMOUS · FOR · SEA · FOODS

WENTWORTH STREET CRAB MEAT

SERVES: 2   TIME: 20 MINUTES

There was a time not too long ago when, from the stoop of our office on Broad Street, we could have witnessed every weekday the 2 P.M. exodus of lawyers, bankers, architects, and insurance and real estate agents, ambling their way south from the business district to their homes for "dinner." Dinner, for traditional Southern families, was the hearty midday meal, served in the dining room with linens on the table—and often with mother's silver. "Supper" was the lighter evening meal, usually a casserole or baked savory item that the hired cook might cover and stash in the fridge before leaving for the day. The dish would then be reheated and served with a soup or salad, and with a simple sweet for dessert. This arrangement of the day's meals has gone the way of the three-martini lunch, with dinner out at a restaurant finding favor as a way to entertain, leaving the workday uninterrupted (and the kitchen clean).

Though we are far from traditional in our habits, we find there are many evenings when we're yearning for a light supper to serve our families with toast and a salad. On those days this creamy, cheesy crab casserole is a favorite with our wives. It is adapted from a popular recipe called "Meeting Street Crab Meat" contributed to *Charleston Receipts* by Mary Huguenin, the cookbook's co-editor, and presumably named for the street the family lived on, an important north-south corridor on the peninsula. (Mrs. Huguenin's recipe for "Crabmeat au Gratin" appeared in the 1948 *Charleston Recipes,* a precursor to the later cookbook; see *Charleston Receipts,* page 52).

The earlier recipe offers a variation in which shrimp is partnered with the crab; the later recipe suggests a substitution of crab for shrimp. We took a few liberties with our own crab gratin recipe—which we've named, in turn, for the location of our sometime test kitchen—such as dialing back the amount of flour in the dish, and lightening the cream base with shellfish broth, which simultaneously amps up the flavor. And we sauté shallots with a few pinches of nutmeg in making the creamy sauce because, in concert with the zip of the sherry, it creates some intrigue. It's also quite easy to do.

Outside of the supper realm, Wentworth Street Crab Meat makes a great self-serve hors d'oeuvre at a cocktail party, to be spooned by guests onto thin baguette slices or crackers. If you choose that route, prepare this dish in a larger, crocklike vessel (instead of the shallow gratin dishes).

¾ cup fish or shellfish broth

1 tablespoon plus
1 teaspoon all-purpose flour

2 tablespoons unsalted butter

2 tablespoons finely diced
shallot (about 1 medium)

¼ teaspoon kosher salt

¼ teaspoon freshly ground
black pepper

3 pinches of ground nutmeg

¾ cup heavy cream

2 tablespoons dry sherry

8 ounces picked U.S. blue
crab meat, preferably jumbo
lump

2 ounces extra-sharp white
Cheddar cheese, grated
(¾ cup)

Paprika or cayenne, for
dusting (optional)

Toast or grilled bread, for
serving

---

1 Preheat the broiler.

2 In a small saucepan, heat the broth over high heat until it simmers. Put the flour in a small bowl or ramekin, spoon 3 tablespoons of the broth into it, and whisk it to a smooth paste with a fork. Pour the rest of the hot broth into a bowl and reserve both broth and paste.

(recipe continues)

HOW TO PICK A CRAB

1 Begin by removing the two large claws, setting them aside for later.

2 Peel up the rounded (female) or pointed (male) plate on the underside of the crab with one thumb, and then insert the other thumb in the gap that is exposed between the orange top shell and the underside. Pull your thumbs apart to split the top shell off the crab; discard the top shell.

3 Pinch off and discard the spongy-feathery gills revealed on top of the crab and snap the crab body in half down the middle, separating the two sets of legs.

4 Crack each body half with your hands to reveal the meat inside and pluck, suck, and prod the white meat out of the cartilaginous framework, using the pointed end of a leg or claw as a picking tool.

5 When you've picked the crab body clean, crack open the claws. Experts let little go to waste: break open one end of each slender leg and chew on the opposite end of it to chase the meat out. Then it's on to the next crab!

3 Return the saucepan to the heat and melt the butter over medium-low heat until it's frothy and add the shallot, salt, black pepper, and nutmeg. Cook, stirring occasionally, until the shallot is fragrant and translucent, but not brown, about 3 minutes. Add the cream, sherry, the reserved broth, and reserved flour paste mixture, and whisk to combine. Bring to the gentlest simmer and cook, stirring occasionally, until the cream sends up thick bubbles and is thickened to the consistency of a gravy, 6 to 8 minutes. Add the crab meat and cook just until it is heated through and the sauce coats the crab meat thickly, about 4 minutes.

4 With a slotted spoon, divide the crab meat between two 6- to 8-ounce gratin or brûlée dishes and put them on a rimmed baking sheet. Spoon the crab gravy over the crab meat just shy of covering the meat (you may have some left over for sopping with bread; lucky you!). Sprinkle the cheese over the top of the casseroles, and broil about 2 inches from the heat, until the cheese is gently browned and bubbling, about 3 minutes. Remove the casseroles from the oven and dust with paprika, if using.

5 Serve with spoons for scooping the casserole onto the toast.

SHARK SANDWICH SERVES: 4 TIME: 15 MINUTES

I f you're a nerd of a certain age—we are!—you may snicker at this concept on first impression. (For the rest of you, *Shark Sandwich* was the title of the fictional heavy metal band Spinal Tap's fourth album, which received a very bad, two-word review in the 1984 mockumentary *This Is Spinal Tap*.)

Entirely coincidentally, the thin slices of shark sold in Charleston fish stores like Backman's, Marvin's, or Crosby's fry up beautifully in a skillet with a light dredge of flour and they make a delicious sandwich. Black-tipped and Mako sharks, caught in the creeks and estuaries and just offshore, are the most common species sold in the area, and they are small enough that the fishmongers often slice the tail portion into ¼-inch-thick, pearly-pink disks or U-shapes rather than the thicker steaks of a larger shark species.

The single bone in the center is easily removed after frying, and the thinness of the slices makes them perfect for loading a sandwich, to which we lend some excitement with tangy green tomato relish spread on one slice of bread and mayonnaise on the other. A leaf of lettuce and a grind of black pepper are the finishing touches that take this sandwich to 11 (on a scale of 1 to 10). Serve with glasses of beer or fino sherry.

⅓ cup all-purpose flour

Kosher salt and freshly ground black pepper

1 pound black-tipped or Mako shark steaks, each ¼ to ½ inch thick

2 tablespoons unsalted butter

3 tablespoons peanut or vegetable oil

¼ cup high-quality mayonnaise

8 slices bread, lightly toasted

¼ cup green tomato or sweet onion relish, or another sweet-and-sour relish

4 lettuce leaves, for garnish

1 Blend the flour, 1 teaspoon of the salt, and 1 teaspoon of the black pepper and spread in an even layer on a plate. Lightly dredge each slice of shark by laying it down in the flour, pressing lightly, flipping it over, and pressing once more.

2 Melt the butter with the oil in a 10-inch skillet over medium-high heat, and when the butter is frothy, add 4 shark slices to the skillet, frying on both sides and flipping as necessary until lightly browned, about 3 minutes per side. Transfer the cooked slices to a plate lined with a paper towel and fry the remaining slices, moderating the heat if the skillet becomes too hot.

3 Spread the mayonnaise on 4 slices of bread and relish on the other 4. Lay the mayo side face up on a cutting board. Season the shark to taste with salt and pepper and remove the central bone, where present, from each shark slice. Distribute the shark slices equally among the 4 breads, breaking the slices into pieces if necessary to cover the sandwiches evenly. Apply a leaf of lettuce to each sandwich along with a grind of black pepper. Finally, lay the relish sides of the bread down on top, and serve.

SHRIMP SUPREME   SERVES: 6   TIME: 20 MINUTES

Certain recipes in the definitive mid-century cookbook *Charleston Receipts* (see page 52) took on a life of their own in the decades that followed the book's publication in 1950. "Shrimp Supreme," a ketchup-tinted and bay leaf–infused shrimp creole, is one of those. "Meeting Street Crab Meat" (see page 127), and "Faber's Pilau" (see page 177), are others. They tend to be dishes worthy of serving your most exalted stranger-guests, but simple enough for anyone to pull off, even in a state of disarray. Your wife brought friends home from yoga class? College roommate dropped in unannounced? Hurricane David bearing down? Think Shrimp Supreme, served over Charleston Rice.

We were never actually served Shrimp Supreme while growing up at 83 East Bay Street, but we recently discovered that the dish had been served in our very dining room, as documented by *National Geographic* photographer Robert Sisson for a 1953 feature about South Carolina. Several years ago, Matt was trolling the Smithsonian archives for Charleston photos when he came upon an arresting image of a trio at the dinner table, in a dining room decorated with distinctive Chinoiserie wallpaper—yellow sky, pine trees, gold accents and peacocks. The wallpaper registered immediately—it appeared exactly as it was in 1979, when we first moved to 83 East Bay Street. (Mom hated the "scaly-legged" peacocks, but tolerated the wallpaper.) The four people in the image remained mysteries until a few years later, when Vereen Coen introduced herself at our "Throwdown! With Bobby Flay: Country Captain." The binder she brought of *Charleston Receipts* memorabilia contained the same image, clipped from the same magazine. She was the young woman facing the camera; the seated man was named David Maybank. Shrimp Supreme over bright, white rice was on each plate.

Later, we made a few more connections that tied the entire group and the dish together. David Maybank's wife contributed the recipe for Shrimp Supreme to *Charleston Receipts*; that book was edited and promoted by Coen's mother, Mary Huguenin. By happenstance, our friend and colleague, the barbecue star Jimmy Hagood, is the grandson of David Maybank. When we showed Jimmy the photo recently (he'd never seen it) and asked him about his grandmother's Shrimp Supreme, he dismissed it as an old-fashioned dish.

Jimmy may not be wrong about that, but it's unquestionably delicious and our version (we dialed back the ketchup and boosted the bay, lemon juice, and peppery heat) tastes great. With a dash of fish sauce, kaffir lime, and lemongrass, this would approach something very close to Thai cooking. Feel free to head in that direction, if you wish, and let the peacocks lead the way.

4 tablespoons (½ stick) unsalted butter	¼ teaspoon red pepper flakes
4 tablespoons all-purpose flour	¼ teaspoon kosher salt, plus more to taste
1½ cups half-and-half	2 bay leaves
⅓ cup ketchup	2 pounds cooked peeled shrimp, rinsed, preferably with tails still on
¼ cup Worcestershire sauce	
1 tablespoon fresh lemon juice	Charleston Rice (recipe follows)
½ teaspoon freshly ground black pepper, plus more to taste	

1   Melt the butter in a 10-inch skillet over medium-high heat until it's frothy, and whisk in the flour until it becomes a smooth paste. Turn the heat down to medium, add the half-and-half, and whisk until it bubbles.

2   Add the ketchup, Worcestershire, lemon juice, black pepper, red pepper flakes, salt, and bay leaves, and whisk until smooth. Add the shrimp and ¼ cup of water, and stir with a wooden spoon to blend. Cook, stirring, over medium for 5 to 10 minutes, until very hot. Season with salt and freshly ground black pepper. Discard the bay leaves and serve immediately over Charleston Rice. (Shrimp Supreme will keep about 2 days in the refrigerator in a covered container.)

CHARLESTON RICE

MAKES: 2 CUPS RICE   TIME: 40 MINUTES

The classic Charleston rice of the twentieth century (as rice enthusiasts are quick to point out) is rinsed so thoroughly of its starch and cooked so gently that each grain remains distinct even after being fully cooked. It's the opposite of sticky, overcooked take-out restaurant rice. In the ideal telling, each grain of Charleston rice, when dropped on a plate, bounces independently of its brethren. Rice like this (if it existed) would, in theory, absorb more delicious gravies and liquids, pound for pound, than gluey rice, because there would be more interstitial space between the grains to soak them up.

The hallmark of classic Charleston rice of the nineteenth century was its flavor, since the older long-grain varieties of rice grown in the region, like Carolina Gold, were much more aromatic, with that nutty, beguiling aroma similar to that of the American-grown jasmine or basmati we enjoy today. Rice was grown for nearly three centuries in the brackish tidal marshes of the upper Lowcountry, using the natural rise and fall of the tides to flood and drain impounded fields, and with the supply of slave labor to carve, maintain, and tend them. The advent of large mechanical pumps would allow rice to be grown on dry land adjacent to the Mississippi River and eventually in California, where most American rice is now grown.

We enjoy combining the flavor of the nineteenth century with the technique of the twentieth century. Key to the textural effect is cooking one's rice in a rice steamer, which is a double boiler with vents cut into the insert at its upper rim. This allows the rice to cook gently, instead of in the tumult of a rolling boil. In the steamer method, one uses a 1:1 ratio of rice to liquid. True Charleston rice, for accompanying gravies or Shrimp Supreme, is finished plain, without using broth, but perhaps with a tablespoon of butter and a pinch of salt.

1 cup Carolina Gold, basmati, or jasmine rice, rinsed well in cold water and drained

1 tablespoon unsalted butter

2 pinches of kosher salt

1 Add an inch and a half of water to the bottom of a rice steamer and put the rice, 1 cup of water, the butter, and salt in the steamer basin. Cook the rice at medium-high heat for 30 minutes, then turn off the heat and allow the rice to sit in the pot, covered, for another 5 minutes.

2 With pot holders, remove the lid and carefully remove the basin of rice from the steamer, and serve immediately with a broad rice spoon. (Leaving the rice in the steamer will cause it to crispify slightly on the bottom, which is desirable if you like it that way.)

SHRIMP SUPREME BEING SERVED BY WILLIAM MOTT AT 83 EAST BAY STREET IN THE EARLY 1950S. (ROBERT SISSON/NATIONAL GEOGRAPHIC STOCK)

CAPTAIN JUNIOR MAGWOOD

"AS THE STORY GOES, Junior's daddy, Captain Clarence, shanghaied his mother by offering her a bag of candy, and took her to Little Bull Island," said Andrew Savage, attorney to the late Captain Clarence "Junior" Magwood (1922–2001). The Magwood captains—shrimpers, oyster harvesters, clammers, and fishermen for more than three generations running—occupy an important place in Charleston's seafaring history. For a century or more they have resided in Mount Pleasant, a fishing village across Charleston Harbor, and on Little Bull Island, an island of an acre or two that the Magwood family owns about fourteen miles north of the entrance to the harbor.

Virtually everyone in Charleston has reaped the benefits of the Magwoods' heroic labors—we do so today, as Captain Wayne, Junior's son, continues to take the trawler *Winds of Fortune* to sea from Shem Creek, bringing back the freshest shrimp we can buy.

It only heightens the mythic qualities of the Magwood family to know that their house on Little Bull Island was fashioned from timber salvaged from shipwrecks. And yet with no bridge to the island, few had ever been there to see for themselves.

(SOURCE UNKNOWN)

One person who had, in the days before Hurricane Hugo swept Little Bull Island clean (see Rock and Rye, page 27), is former game warden Benjamin Moise, who maintained a cordial— but necessarily businesslike—relationship with the Magwoods and, like many people telling Junior Magwood stories, relished the Captain's gift with the bottom end of the English language.

"He could take the paint off a wall with his cussin'," said Moise in a recent interview. "He could do it for five minutes straight and not use the same word twice." Many of Moise's acrimonious encounters with Junior were offshore, during conch season, in the cold months immediately following the shrimp season. The Captain didn't hold the new size limits, designed to protect the sustainability of the conch harvest, in much regard. Savage would often have to get in an open launch and motor out

to the Captain's trawler to try to calm the situation between Magwood and the authorities—usually Moise.

Shrimp boat captains must be both brutes and ballerinas, with the heavy equipment and with finely detailed regulations. The rigging of the enormous pocket-shaped shrimp net is incredibly complex, with aprons, trapdoor-excluder devices (for sea turtles), and tickler chains. (A single net may weigh over a ton.) Junior took pride in his net work, and when he was not at sea he could be found in the shed, tying knots and making repairs with a thimble and needle, behind the C.A. Magwood & Sons ice house.

Junior enjoyed drawing, and would often scribble a shrimp trawler on the back of a paper plate to give to a visitor as a souvenir (his son Wayne continues the tradition). In fact, his generosity impressed people as much as his foul mouth. Savage, for all the court appearances he made to answer to Magwood's trawling violations, never charged his client a fee, explaining, "He fed my family two hundred days out of the year."

Henry Shaffer (see page 122) recalls that when he worked at his family's restaurant, Henry's, in the 1940s, Captain Magwood would deliver shrimp directly to the door on Market Street in a pickup truck, its tailgate rusted through from the salty, fishy water sloshing around in the bed. Though a Captain at sea, on the streets of Charleston, Junior relinquished the wheel to an employee, since he didn't own a driver's license.

Moise remembers Magwood being nimble at the stove on Little Bull Island, preparing collard greens, fried pork chops, and chicken (along with the ever-present shrimp and oysters). Diabetes slowed the Captain down a little later in life but never quite quenched the fire.

"He told me if he caught cancer, he was going to go out and kill every game warden he could find," said Moise. "Junior was always a contradiction: he could go from that formidable temper to being very gracious and with a gentlemanly deportment. You just had to be there at the right time."

SMOKED SHAD   SERVES: 4 TO 6   TIME: 20 MINUTES

Billy McCord, a fisheries biologist for the South Carolina Department of Natural Resources, based in the department's headquarters on the south side of Charleston Harbor, is today an expert on the ecology of small coastal islands in the Lowcountry, but for most of the 1980s and 1990s, he studied anadromous fishes—like shad, striped bass, and sturgeon—which use freshwater rivers as seasonal spawning grounds while spending most of their lives in the salty Atlantic.

In the late 1970s, McCord worked closely with shad fishermen on the Savannah River, and while there he studied with a fishmonger who had mastered the challenge of boning shad. When he returned to Charleston, McCord practiced the technique to improve his speed, but has never cracked the ten-minute mark (see Peter Alexandre, page 140).

"It's not worth the effort to me. It's a rich fish and the bones pull easily, so I prefer to pull the bones out of it as I eat it," he said, adding, "It's the best smoked fish I've ever tasted; it has plenty of natural flavor and doesn't need spices."

We concur with the latter sentiment: if you like smoked salmon, you will love the simple decadence of smoked shad, which is quick and easy to hot-smoke on the stovetop. Serve this with plenty of lemon, perhaps a drizzle of finishing-quality extra-virgin olive oil, and with a tonic salad of parsley, arugula, or watercress.

1 tablespoon hickory, apple, or mesquite wood chips for stovetop smokers

2 (14-ounce) shad fillets, skin on and preferably boned

½ teaspoon kosher salt

½ teaspoon freshly ground black pepper

Lemon wedges, for garnish

1 Put the wood chips in the center of the stovetop smoker or, if using a conventional roasting pan and rack as a smoker, a 9 by 13-inch steel or aluminum roasting pan; wrap the roasting-pan rack with aluminum foil.

2 Season both sides of the shad fillets and set skin side down on the rack inside the smoker. Cover the smoker only partly; if using a roasting pan, cover with aluminum foil, crimping the edges tightly, but leaving one corner uncrimped. Set the smoker over medium-low heat, and when you see the first wisp of smoke rise from the pan, cover it completely. Smoke the shad for 10 minutes, and then remove from the heat. Allow the fillets to sit in the smoker for another 5 minutes (don't peek). They should be beige-brown and cooked through but damp on top.

3 Serve immediately with the lemon wedges.

BROILED SHAD WITH SHAD ROE MOUSSE

SERVES: 6   TIME: 1 HOUR 30 MINUTES

Charlestonians are fortunate to have the option of purchasing in a local fish market shad fillets, which are rare in other places because the fish is famously bony, and few fishmongers have the patience, knowledge, or time to fillet it. In fact, there may be only a handful of individuals who have mastered the technique of boning shad to create fillets.

For the last several springs, when the shad return to Charleston Harbor and swim up the rivers to their spawning grounds, Peter Alexandre sharpens his fillet knife and checks in with Dan Long, of Crosby's Seafood Wholesale, the largest locally owned fish distributor in the area. Alexandre, who emigrated from Haiti in 1981 on a soccer scholarship to the College of Charleston, is one of the known masters of the shad-boning art, quick enough at the complicated task that shad fillets at Crosby's are an affordable option, at least as long as they are available during the relatively brief, eight-week season.

Crosby's also sells the whole fish, which can be baked for several hours, or pickled, to dissolve the bones.

American shad—the largest member of the herring family on the Atlantic coast—has a high oil content, like its smaller cousins, and the fillets are beautifully veined with fat, resembling farmed salmon, so the fish stands up well to long cooking times. Still, if we purchase fillets, we prefer to subject them to a brisk, smoky broil, until the skin crisps delectably, or to smoke them on the stovetop (see Smoked Shad, page 139).

The decadent shad presentation here, favored by our friend Sallie Duell, layers the broiled fillets with an herb-seasoned mousse made from the roe, and the combination is so rich and delicious that a 1-inch-wide slice will suffice for most adults—a single fish may serve six or more. It slices nicely with a serrated bread knife and looks terrific as a trophy presentation, surrounded on an oblong platter with crisp spring greens and lemon wedges.

1 tablespoon sweet white wine, like muscadine, sauternes, or oloroso sherry

⅓ cup cider vinegar

Kosher salt

¼ teaspoon turmeric

1 shad roe (2 lobes, 10 to 12 ounces total), each lobe split down the middle

1½ teaspoons honey

2 tablespoons finely chopped bright, tender herbs, like dill, basil, and mint

2 teaspoons freshly ground black pepper, plus more to taste

2 teaspoons fresh lemon juice (about 1 small), plus
2 lemons, cut into wedges, for garnish

⅓ cup heavy cream

3 large egg whites

Unsalted butter for greasing the bowl

1½ teaspoons flaky sea salt, such as Maldon

2 (14-ounce) skin-on shad fillets, scaled, at room temperature

2 teaspoons peanut or vegetable oil

2 bunches watercress or pea shoots, for garnish

1 Set a rack in the middle of the oven and preheat the oven to 350°F.

2 In a medium saucepan over high heat, bring the wine, 1 cup of water, the vinegar, 1 teaspoon salt, and the turmeric to a boil. Turn the heat to medium, add the split roes, and simmer for 6 minutes, flipping them over halfway through, until the roes are just cooked through.

3 Drain the roes with a mesh strainer and, when cool enough to handle, break them up into a large bowl, discarding any large bits of membrane. With a rubber spatula, blend in the honey, the herbs, ½ teaspoon

salt, ½ teaspoon black pepper, and the lemon juice until thoroughly combined. Season to taste with additional salt and black pepper, if needed.

4 Whip the cream in a medium bowl until soft peaks form and fold it into the roe mixture with a rubber spatula. Whip the egg whites until nearly stiff in a separate bowl and fold into the roe mixture with a rubber spatula until fully incorporated. Transfer the roe mixture to a buttered stainless steel mixing bowl and put the bowl in a deep roasting pan filled with about 2 inches of hot tap water. Transfer the roasting pan to the oven and cook for about 30 minutes, until the mousse has firmed and slightly darkened on top (the surface will appear dry and toasty brown). Remove the bowl from the water bath to a warm place on the kitchen counter, near the stove.

5 Turn on the broiler, making sure there is a rack positioned about 4 inches from the heat.

6 Sprinkle the flaky sea salt and the remaining 1½ teaspoons black pepper evenly over both sides of the fillets, with slightly more of the seasoning applied to the skin sides. Pour the oil into a large cast-iron skillet and coat the entire surface with the oil. Lay the shad fillets in the pan side by side, skin side up, and center the skillet under the broiler, allowing the fish to cook until the skin is well blistered and blackened all over, 5 to 6 minutes. Remove the skillet from the oven to the stovetop while you ready an oval serving platter.

7 Using two spatulas, remove from the pan and center the least attractive fillet, skin side up, on the platter. Then spoon a layer of mousse, slightly thicker than the fillet itself, over the fillet. Transfer the most attractive fillet, also skin side up, on top of the mousse layer to create a sandwich. The mousse will begin to spread out under the weight of the top fillet, which is fine. Apply a final dollop of mousse on top as garnish and decorate the perimeter of the platter with watercress and lemon wedges.

8 After presenting the platter, cut the sandwich crosswise into six portions with a large serrated knife. With a pie server or spatula, transfer each portion to a serving plate, and garnish with a tuft of watercress and a couple lemon wedges.

THIS PAGE FROM
TOP LEFT:

PETER ALEXANDRE
REMOVES THE ROE
FROM A FEMALE SHAD.

REMOVING WHOLE
LINES OF BONES
AT ONCE, LEAVING
BEHIND A FILLET
WITH RIBBONS
OF MEAT.

SHAD CONTAINS
750–1000 BONES.

STONE CRAB CLAWS WITH BAY BUTTER

SERVES: 2 AS A MAIN COURSE, 4 AS AN APPETIZER   TIME: 45 MINUTES

Many Charlestonians will be surprised to learn that stone crabs (*Menippe mercenaria*) are harvested regularly out of the Stono River just south of Charleston Harbor, and in other neighboring waterways. The crabs are almost entirely absent from regional cookbooks, and only recently did the claws begin to appear on restaurant menus.

We've spent quite a bit of time on the estuaries around Johns and Kiawah Islands with Fred Dockery, a multidisciplinary waterman with more than two hundred crab traps in the Stono River, and watched as he demonstrated one of the few sustainable wild harvests. Thanks to the crab's miraculous ability to grow back a missing limb, the fishermen may harvest the largest claw, no smaller than 2¾ inches long (7 cm), and must return the crab to the water with the other claw intact, so it can continue to live and to regrow the claw (according to some studies, within 12 to 24 months; other studies have estimated that only two-thirds of crabs survive to regenerate the claw). "When you're good at it, you use a gentle grace," says Dockery.

Now that stone crabs are officially part of the Charleston cornucopia, we couldn't resist this simple pairing of the sweet claw meat with a clarified butter, seasoned with the eucalyptus-like spice of fresh bay leaves. Bay laurel trees of all types, including culinary varieties (*Laurus nobilis*), grow well in the sandy and humid atmosphere of the sea islands, and in more than a few backyards downtown. Imported dried bay leaves will do the trick in this recipe, but the fresh have an intensity and a vibrance that's worth seeking out.

Like the bay leaves, the stone crab claws are best when boiled fresh, without being refrigerated in between the ocean and your pot. Chilling them first will cause the meat to stick to the shell, and this is why most crab claws available from retailers will have already been boiled. Feel free to use precooked claws; they will simplify your life and turn this recipe into an exercise in butter seasoning.

Kosher salt

24 raw stone crab claws, harvested the same day

12 tablespoons (1½ sticks) unsalted butter

4 bay leaves, preferably fresh

1 lemon, cut into wedges, plus lemon slices for finger bowls

1 Bring 2 quarts of water to a boil in a stockpot with 1 tablespoon salt. Add the claws, return to a boil, and cook until they change color from their uncooked greenish hue to a creamy ivory and vibrant red, 6 to 8 minutes. Drain and plunge the claws into a bowl of ice water to cool. Drain after 5 minutes. (Cooked fresh claws will keep for up to 4 days in the refrigerator.)

2 Crack each claw across its broadest part with a nutcracker or with a quick blow with a hammer or the blunt side of a cleaver. Leave the shells otherwise intact, to be peeled at the table, but supply ample napkins or hand towels and a finger bowl with lemon slices floating in it. Another option—the way you're likely to be served the claws in a restaurant—is for the chef to remove enough shell to reveal the nugget of claw meat, leaving just the two pincers intact as a handle. The knuckles are delicious, too, but require another crack and some effort to extract them.

3 Heat the butter, 2 pinches of salt, and the bay leaves in a small saucepan over medium heat, moving the butter around with a wooden spoon until it's virtually all melted and the white curdsy solids have settled. Turn off the heat and skim off the most obvious clumps of the solids with a soup spoon. Pour the seasoned butter into warm ramekins and serve immediately with the cracked claws and wedges of lemon.

CREEK SHRIMP   SERVES: 4   TIME: 10 MINUTES

The immature white and brown shrimp that are netted fresh from the many creeks around the Lowcountry in the summer and into fall aren't vaunted on restaurant menus, and they rarely make it to market (larger shrimp are considered much more valuable). But for those lucky enough to be raised near a creek, they supply the most exquisite, concentrated shrimp flavor experience possible—and form the basis for some Charlestonians' most dearly held childhood food memories.

Fresh, small, and sweet, they're often served in the shell—and even head on—for the quickest path to the table, leaving it up to the individual to pinch off the head and peel them before popping them in his or her mouth. (Even better, if your shrimp happen to be tiny and tender enough, they may be eaten shell and all.) They're occasionally called breakfast shrimp, as their sweetness makes them the perfect complement to the starches (grits, potatoes), eggs, and ham of a breakfast. Shrimp and Grits (page 169) is an elaboration of this basic premise.

But nearly anything will do for a modest gravy: a generous knob of butter, a few splashes of vinegar, broth, or beer on top of that—the real point is the shrimp itself. If you don't have a cast net and a saltwater license, check out a local seafood purveyor, like Backman Seafood (see Conch Fritters, page 150), and purchase only local shrimp, the smallest available.

3 tablespoons peanut or vegetable oil

2 tablespoons unsalted butter

2 pounds headless small (40 count or more) shell-on shrimp

4 teaspoons kosher salt

1 tablespoon freshly ground black pepper

¼ cup fish broth, Tarragon Vinegar (recipe follows), or beer

1 Add the oil and butter to a very large skillet set over medium-high heat, stirring the butter around to melt. When the butter has stopped foaming, add the shrimp in an even layer and season with 2 teaspoons of the salt and 1½ teaspoons of the black pepper. Cook for about 4 minutes, stirring twice, until the shrimp shells begin to turn opaque and smell toasty.

2 Add the broth, and then use a slotted spoon or spatula to turn over the shrimp. Season with the remaining salt and black pepper, and cook for a minute or two more, until the largest shrimp in your skillet is evenly cooked on both sides. Serve immediately with Charleston Hominy (page 172), paper napkins, and a bowl for the shells.

FRED DOCKERY, AKA "ALL-DAY FRED"

TARRAGON VINEGAR
MAKES: 1 QUART
TIME: 5 MINUTES, PLUS 1 DAY OF STEEPING

Tarragon vinegar, the key ingredient in a béarnaise sauce (an herbed variation of hollandaise), also appears as an ingredient in several Southern cookbooks (perhaps because Charleston has a huge population of French Huguenot descent?). Making tarragon vinegar—or any flavored vinegar from an appealingly scented, sturdy herb—couldn't be easier and it's a versatile, flavor-packed ingredient to have on hand: for seasoning collards or green beans, for making salad dressings and marinades, and for shaking from a cruet onto oysters and clams on the half-shell. A glass milk bottle with a few leafy stalks of tarragon inside it can often be seen in our kitchen window.

4 to 6 stems fresh tarragon

3 pinches of kosher salt

1 quart distilled white or unflavored white wine vinegar

1 Wash and dry the tarragon, discarding any blemished or darkened leaves. Push the stems into a quart-size bottle and sprinkle the salt into the mouth of the bottle (depending on the width of the bottle's mouth, you may need to put the salt on a small piece of paper and fold it into a V-shaped trough to pour it in).

2 Using a funnel, if necessary, pour the vinegar into the bottle. Cap the bottle, or seal with a piece of plastic wrap or aluminum foil, and swirl the vinegar around until the salt mostly dissolves, about 1 minute. Steep for a day at room temperature, and then store in the refrigerator for optimum freshness.

CRAB CRACK   SERVES: 24   TIME: 1 HOUR

A "crab crack" in the Lowcountry is much like an oyster roast, a rustic outdoors event where the sea creatures being consumed are the only luxuries around. One has to stand as there are typically no chairs, the table is a piece of plywood set on sawhorses, and there are no utensils. Clean-up after a crab crack is usually a hose-down. For those of us who love freshly boiled blue crabs, this scene is heavenly; nothing stands in the way of our digging in, and the lack of creature comforts reduces competition at the table from prissier gourmands.

Eating crab picked fresh from the shell, though, is quite rare—almost all restaurants prefer to get their crab pre-picked for them, rather than to bring in whole crabs and spend the effort extracting the meat and cleaning up. In fact, Fred Dockery, a professional waterman who specializes in crabs and shrimp, sells virtually all his blue crabs to one or two retail fish markets (Marvin's, on Dorchester Road, and Crosby's, downtown on Spring Street), and has learned over the years that demand trails off on a predictable monthly cycle that tracks with the delivery of Social Security checks.

A day spent on Fred Dockery's crabbing boat on the Kiawah River is an education in all the quirks, both annoying and sublime, of the crab business, among them the beauty of a brown pelican alighting on the boat's stern and the scourge of "pot-snot," a seaweed that clogs up the traps in certain seasons.

"Crabbers like solitude, but we all learn to live around each other," he said, of the approximately 150 other active crabbers in the state. "Each has his own dynamic: I'm known as 'All-Day Fred'; Willie will never get his traps up in the deep of the channel; Wes never at the edge of it," Dockery told us. His floats are identified by a pale lavender color (a risible detail, to the other crabbers) because he's a Minnesota Vikings fan.

North Carolina, being closer to northern markets, hauls in about ten times more crab, according to Dockery, than does South Carolina. Moreover, South Carolina no longer has a picking plant for processing the crab into the restaurant- and supermarket-friendly pint containers. Crab harvesters like Dockery aren't permitted to pick their own crabs for sale.

Here is a point or two that will make you an expert in the purchase of blue crabs before your next crab crack. Although some people prefer the flavor of female crabs ("sooks"), the males ("jimmies") will typically be bigger and are more sought after by the most ardent crab lovers. Males and females are distinguished by the plate on their underside: a female has a rounded plate; the male has one shaped like the Washington Monument. In either case, look for "rusty" patches on the white undersides of the shells, indicating that a shell hasn't molted for a long while; crabs just about to molt their shells are heavier and more packed with meat than those that have already expended all the energy required to rebuild a new shell (which leaves them lighter and water-logged).

½ cup kosher salt	1 lemon, cut in half
6 bay leaves, shredded	72 live large blue crabs (about a bushel)
3 tablespoons cayenne	
1 tablespoon black peppercorns	Hot sauce, for serving
	Beer
1 tablespoon celery seeds	

1 Pour 4 gallons of water into a large (at least 6-gallon) pot and bring to a vigorous boil on the stove or on a propane-fueled trestle cooker outdoors. Add all the ingredients except the crabs, hot sauce, and beer.

2 Add about 15 crabs at once to the pot and boil for 3 minutes, until their shells turn a deep orange. With long-handled tongs, transfer the crabs to a table spread with newspaper. Repeat with the next batch of crabs. Serve with nutcrackers (for the claws), plenty of hand towels, a shaker bottle of hot sauce, and oceans of beer.

CONCH FRITTERS

MAKES: ABOUT 50 FRITTERS, ENOUGH FOR 4 TO 6 PEOPLE

TIME: 1 HOUR

The Backman Seafood of today, in the Sol Legare community on James Island, about twenty minutes from downtown Charleston, is a roadside seafood store with the freshest local fish and oysters available; nearly fifty years ago, it was merely one facet of a thriving shrimping and fishing operation helmed by Susie Backman, a widow and mother of eight, including her son Thomas Backman, Jr., a present-day owner (see Shrimping, page 162). Mrs. Backman was a brilliant entrepreneur and captain who could guide a ship to the Florida Keys, mend nets, lead a group of fishermen, and make big money—around $3,000 a week, in 1965 dollars—on the shrimp that abounded on the south Atlantic coast. She owned three 45-foot-long trawlers, the *Porgy,* the *Ruby-W,* and the *Scotch & Soda.* In the summer seasons, she caught white and then brown shrimp, and in the winter, a brief season of conch (which in the Lowcountry is primarily two different species of whelk, knobbed *Busycon carica* and channeled *Busycotypus canaliculatus*).

Mrs. Backman's business prowess led to a six-page profile in *Ebony* magazine in November 1965, titled "Queen of Shrimpers," which quoted her as saying "Fishing is what I live for. I love it. Out there, on the ocean, it's a dream. I'm in my world."

These days, Backman Seafood, a white block building with red trim and a large ship's anchor out front, is a hub of the community and a must-visit for seafood lovers in the Lowcountry. It features just the staple creatures that inhabit the marshes, creeks, and channels nearby: flounder, croaker, whiting, skate, black-tipped shark, sheepshead, shrimp, crab, squid, and whelk. All the offerings are neatly laid out on ice, the finfish displayed whole, ready to be cleaned to your specification at the scaling station. It's so spotless, and the turnover so brisk, that you could be led blindfolded into the store and your nose wouldn't provide a clue as to what is sold there. And there are sacks of oysters, too, in season; just walk back along a sandy path to a refrigerated trailer by the creekside pier where Mrs. Backman's trawlers were once tied up.

Recently, after an unsuccessful free-jam with conch meat we harvested from a friend's crab trap and cooked ourselves in the test kitchen (tough, flavorless, quite stinky), we sought out Mr. Backman for advice. Dressed in dark green work pants and matching shirt, he offered us his family recipe for conch fritters: "We grind them up as small as two grains of rice, with celery, onion, and green bell pepper, egg to bind, and a little flour. It'll be like potato chips—your hand keeps moving for more and you don't know why."

We resolved to try again, with the one conch preparation that truly makes sense: granulating the meat to make it tender, and frying it, to make it crave-worthy. We even adapted the recipe for cherrystone clams (as tough as conch, more plentiful, and, to our taste, more delicious; squid works, too). Cooked canned shellfish is acceptable, but keep in mind that due to all the water in a can, it may take five 6.5-ounce cans to produce what you need for this recipe. These fritters are every bit as addictive as Mr. Backman claims.

10 ounces drained, cooked chopped conch, clams, or squid (2 cups)	¾ cup all-purpose flour
	1½ teaspoons kosher salt
⅔ cup chopped celery	1½ teaspoons freshly ground black pepper
⅔ cup chopped yellow onion	
⅔ cup chopped green bell pepper	½ teaspoon baking powder
	2 cups peanut or canola oil
2 large eggs	1 lemon, cut into wedges

1 Process the chopped conch, celery, onion, and bell pepper in a food processor, pulsing about 8 times for a total of 30 seconds, scraping down the sides once or twice with a rubber spatula, until the mixture begins to roll over on itself and no piece is bigger than a couple grains of rice.

2 In a large bowl, beat the eggs until frothy. Add the flour, salt, black pepper, and baking powder. Fold the conch and vegetable mixture into the eggs with a spatula until well incorporated.

3 Preheat the oven to 200°F.

4 Heat the oil in an 8-inch saucepot over medium-high heat until it reaches 350°F on a deep-fry thermometer. Prepare a heatproof platter lined with a double thickness of paper towel.

5 Working in batches of about 12, form and fry slightly heaping teaspoonfuls of batter, turning every minute or two, until they are toffee-brown all over, about 5 minutes total. Remove with a slotted spoon to the towel-lined platter. Note: the quickest, easiest technique for portioning the fritters is to use a measuring teaspoon, packed slightly overfull with dough, and to dip your index finger into the bowl of the spoon to push out the dough, dropping it into the oil from about 8 inches height with a quick flick.

6 Store the platter in the warm oven as you fry subsequent batches. Stir the batter bowl periodically if the batter begins to separate. When all the fritters have been fried, serve immediately with lemon wedges.

SHRIMPER SUSIE BACKMAN, MENDING A NET, CIRCA 1965.
(VERNON MERRITT III/BLACK STAR)

OYSTER PAN ROAST

SERVES: 2   TIME: 15 MINUTES

Beautiful, fresh oysters served raw and cold are hard to improve upon, but if you truly love the flavor of oysters, then you know that sometimes you crave the intensity of a warm oyster—especially when it's cooked in the company of complementary ingredients like cream, lemon, and shallot, as in this simple pan roast. It's a spontaneous, immediate-gratification method for celebrating our favorite bivalve, and it brings together elements of a Lowcountry oyster roast with the qualities of a fine soup. The liquids reduce to a silky gravy and the toasted red pepper flakes contribute a smoky, outdoorsy note. Served over slices of toast (or even better, grilled bread), an oyster pan roast makes an outstanding brunch or lunch.

Since brisk evaporation is so vital to this recipe, a 10-inch skillet should only accommodate two servings at once. If you'd like to prepare multiple batches, this recipe scales up in a snap for a small crowd: keep the multiplied liquid ingredients in a pitcher by the stove to streamline the operation, pouring out about a cup of liquid for each batch of oysters.

¼ cup fish or shellfish broth, if available, or water

½ cup heavy cream

1 tablespoon dry sherry

1 tablespoon fresh lemon juice

1 cup room-temperature shucked oysters (12 to 16) and their liquor, separated

¼ teaspoon red pepper flakes

2 tablespoons unsalted butter

2 tablespoons finely chopped shallot (about 1 medium)

Kosher salt and freshly ground black pepper

Toast

2 teaspoons minced chives or thinly sliced scallion (green part only), for garnish

1 Mix the broth, heavy cream, sherry, lemon juice, and oyster liquor together in a medium bowl.

2 Add the red pepper flakes to a dry skillet over medium-high heat and stir the flakes until they begin to darken and become fragrant, about a minute. Add the butter, shallot, and salt and black pepper to taste. Sauté the shallot, stirring with a wooden spoon, for about half a minute, until fragrant.

3 Add the liquids, reduce the heat to medium, and bring to a bare simmer. Add the oysters and continue to simmer for about 4 minutes, moving them around gently, until they've firmed up. Season to taste with salt and black pepper. Serve immediately over toast and garnish with chives or scallion.

DEVILED CRAB   MAKES: 10 DEVILED CRABS   TIME: 45 MINUTES

Many individuals and businesses in Charleston once claimed to have the best deviled—or "devil"—crab in town, often baked and served in a crab shell. Until it closed in the 1980s, the iconic Edisto Motel Restaurant, on the old U.S. coastal Highway 17 in Jacksonboro, about thirty miles south of Charleston, was a popular destination restaurant for carloads of Charlestonians eager to feed a craving for the best fried oyster and shrimp platters—and deviled crabs, naturally—in the region. The late Henry's Restaurant, on Market Street downtown (see page 47), once claimed the mantle, too, but nowadays it is Henry Shaffer, grandson of the Henry's founder, who makes the most acclaimed restaurant version of deviled crabs in town, blending crab, stale bread, egg, and spices, and packing shells to order every Friday morning as a celebrated subcontractor in the kitchen of The Wreck, a seafood restaurant that does a fantastic job of frying almost anything fresh off a fishing boat.

Shaffer, a gifted storyteller, remembers first seeing and smelling deviled crab baking in the kitchen of his Grandma Hasselmeyer in 1938, in her home on Ashley Avenue. She packed the crab shells, placed them in the oven on a large cookie sheet, and later transported them in an old black Packard to Market Street so Grandpa Hasselmeyer could serve them with beer—Henry's was a beer parlor then, and hadn't added a full menu.

Our version of deviled crab borrows a few of the insights Shaffer taught us—the minimalism of the egg-and-butter binder, the cayenne, and the anatomically proportionate blend of claw and lump crab meat. We also turned up the Edisto Motel recipe for deviled crab published in a 1970 Adams Run, South Carolina, cookbook, *Cooking for That Man,* and loved how the grated hard-boiled egg in that version lightened the texture without dampening the flavor of crab.

We go to the trouble of saving crab shells and baking them in a hot oven to clean them, for later use in deviled crab. We pack them with the mixture for the classic presentation of the dish (modern restaurants must use a metal effigy of a shell, for sanitary reasons). Truly, though, the shell is not necessary; this formula also makes a perfectly delicious deviled crab cake.

5 tablespoons unsalted butter

2 tablespoons dry sherry

1 tablespoon fresh lemon juice, plus 2 lemons cut into wedges for garnish

½ teaspoon cayenne, plus more if desired for garnish

1 teaspoon freshly ground black pepper

1 teaspoon kosher salt

1 large egg

1 pound U.S. blue crab meat (ideally, 2 parts jumbo lump and 1 part claw meat, about 2 cups)

2 large hard-boiled eggs, peeled and grated into crumbles

3 scallions, finely chopped (white part and 2 inches into green)

2 small jalapeño peppers, seeded and finely chopped

½ cup panko bread crumbs, plus ¼ cup more for garnish

10 cleaned crab shells (optional)

Chopped fresh parsley, for garnish (optional)

1   Preheat the oven to 425°F.

2   Melt 3 tablespoons of the butter, pour into a mixing bowl, and whisk in the sherry, lemon juice, cayenne, black pepper, and salt. Add the egg, break it up with the whisk, and whisk to combine.

3   In a large mixing bowl, toss the crab with your hands (feel for any missed shell remnants and remove) with the grated egg, scallions, jalapeños, and ½ cup bread crumbs. Add the butter mixture to the crab, tossing with your hands to evenly and gently combine. The mixture will be halfway between sticky and crumbly, but easy enough to compress into a cake. (Microwave or fry a small sample to check for spiciness. If planning to make crab cakes, form the cakes and refrigerate the

(recipe continues)

mixture for about 30 minutes, or longer if wrapped in plastic wrap.)

4   Using a ⅓-cup measure as a mold, pack the crab mixture into 10 portions, then either press the patties into cleaned crab shells or turn out onto a greased baking sheet if you intend to make crab cakes. Arrange the filled crab shells, if using, on a baking sheet. Top each portion with a sprinkling of the remaining ¼ cup bread crumbs. Cut the remaining 2 tablespoons butter into 10 thin pats and set on top of each portion of crab.

5   Bake in the oven on the middle rack for about 20 minutes, until the crab is slightly browned and drying on top. Remove, garnish each with a pinch of cayenne and some parsley, if using, and serve immediately with lemon wedges. (If making cakes, flip each cake once before garnishing and serving, as the bottom side will have browned more alluringly.)

FRIED SHRIMP

SERVES: 6   TIME: 40 MINUTES

Fresh shrimp are practically a currency in Charleston, they're so plentiful and well regarded, and one of the pleasures of living in Charleston is being able to mint your own, to haul them ashore using a circular cast net (it takes some practice, but it's a fun skill to develop), or, next best, to select your shrimp right off the boat.

Wayne Magwood, son of the late Junior Magwood (see page 138), is the current Captain of the Magwood fleet, headquartered on Shem Creek, and a truly amiable guy. If you find him just back from a trawl to sea (and if his outing was successful), you can watch as the catch is loaded into the icehouse for chilling, heading, and packing. You may even be able, if you're nimble enough, to pick from the hamper baskets of shrimp, whiting, crab, and flounder on the back deck of the trawler, as his crew finishes their work sorting the various creatures dumped from the nets.

Truly fresh shrimp, even for epicures who think they've tasted it all, is a revelation in its flavor and texture.

3 pounds headless large (21 to 25 count) shell-on shrimp

1 cup all-purpose flour

6 tablespoons fine or medium-fine cornmeal

4 teaspoons kosher salt

4 teaspoons freshly ground black pepper

4 teaspoons panko bread crumbs (optional)

3 to 4 cups peanut or canola oil, or a blend thereof

Lemon wedges

Cocktail sauce

1 Peel the shrimp, leaving the tails on. Devein if you wish (in this recipe, deveining has the benefit of revealing more surface area for the dredge to cling to). Discard the shells or reserve them for broth.

2 Preheat the oven to 225°F.

3 Sift the flour, cornmeal, and salt together into a bowl, and turn out onto a large plate. Sprinkle the black pepper and bread crumbs, if using, evenly over the dredge. Using your hands or two spatulas, gently toss the shrimp in the dredge in batches, about a dozen at a time. Remove them, shaking the excess loose.

4 Pour the oil into a large skillet to a depth of about ½ inch (about 3 cups for a 10-inch skillet, 4 cups for a 12-inch skillet). Heat the oil over medium-high heat until the temperature on a candy or frying thermometer reads 365°F.

5 Once the oil reaches 365°, transfer the shrimp to the skillet in batches, about a dozen at a time, using a slotted spoon. Fry them until they're evenly golden brown on each side, about 1½ minutes per side. Adjust the heat on the skillet as necessary to maintain the temperature between 350° and 365°F.

6 Transfer the fried shrimp to a heatproof plate lined with a double thickness of paper towels and place the plate in the oven to warm. Repeat until all the shrimp have been fried.

7 Serve fried shrimp with lemon wedges and cocktail sauce.

FRIED OYSTERS   SERVES: 6   TIME: 40 MINUTES

Frying is the most common Charleston treatment for oysters in a restaurant setting; outdoor roasting rules in the backyard environment, where more often than not the oysters are sourced locally, in affordable clusters. Still, we enjoy frying them ourselves at home any time we crave that delectable crisp crust. Paired with Fried Shrimp (page 156) and Conch Fritters (page 150), these make a fried seafood platter that captures the sweetness and salinity of the Lowcountry's best shellfish, and makes a terrific introduction to Charleston for visitors, who—like the oysters and shrimp—may be just off the boat.

Our style of oyster dredge is floury-light, a hint of crisp golden brown, without egg wash (which would make a thicker, puffier shell), so that grease retention is minimized and flavor maximized: the minerally hit of the oyster comes through. The retail epitome of this style is offered up nightly at the restaurant called The Wreck of the Richard and Charlene, on Shem Creek, the home port of a small working fleet of trawlers.

1 cup all-purpose flour

6 tablespoons fine or medium-fine cornmeal

4 teaspoons kosher salt

4 teaspoons freshly ground black pepper

4 teaspoons panko bread crumbs (optional)

72 shucked oysters (about 3 pints), drained

3 to 4 cups peanut or canola oil, or a blend thereof

Lemon wedges

Cocktail sauce

1 Preheat the oven to 225°F.

2 Sift the flour, cornmeal, and salt together into a bowl, and turn out onto a large plate. Sprinkle the black pepper and bread crumbs, if using, evenly over the dredge. Using your hands or two spatulas, gently toss the oysters in the dredge in batches, about a dozen at a time. Remove them by hand, shaking the excess loose.

3 Pour the oil into a large skillet to a depth of about ½ inch (about 3 cups for a 10-inch skillet, 4 cups for a 12-inch skillet). Heat the oil over medium-high heat until the temperature on a candy or frying thermometer reads 365°F.

4 Once the oil reaches 365°, transfer the oysters to the skillet in batches, about a dozen at a time, using a slotted spoon. Fry them, flipping frequently, until they're evenly browned, 30 to 60 seconds. Adjust the heat on the skillet as necessary to maintain the temperature between 350° and 365°F.

5 Transfer the fried oysters to a heatproof plate lined with a double thickness of paper towels and place the plate in the oven to warm. Repeat until all the oysters have been fried.

6 Serve fried oysters with lemon wedges and cocktail sauce.

FLOUNDER IN PARCHMENT WITH SHAVED VEGETABLES

According to Middleton Foundation president Charles Duell, Edna Lewis's flounder in parchment with shaved vegetables became a signature dish for the Middleton Place Restaurant during her time there (see page 168). The preparation is classic Lewis: an almost monastic focus on the purity and freshness of a small number of ingredients. In fact, Duell claims that no matter how busy the dining room might have been on a given evening, Lewis wouldn't begin shaving the vegetables until an order arrived in the kitchen. This made for some intense moments as certain diners grew impatient.

If you've never attempted cooking in parchment, you should do so now. We promise our instructions are easy to follow, it doesn't have to take long, and the technique, which melds flavors in a steamy capsule, will impress your family and friends. The pocket allows the fish to cook at an even temperature, in its own juice. When vegetables are all at the peak of freshness, and the butter and lemon of great quality, this dish soars.

In the first preparation here, perfect for springtime, a small saladlike garnish of shaved radishes and tender, fragile chainey briar (see page 96), gets scattered over the fish after the parchment is cut open. In the second, more wintry recipe, the fish is steamed on a layer of thinly sliced sweet potatoes that have been gently pickled.

SPRING FLOUNDER IN PARCHMENT WITH SHAVED RADISH AND CHAINEY BRIAR

SERVES: 4   TIME: 35 MINUTES

1 tablespoon extra-virgin olive oil

1 tablespoon dry white wine, such as sauvignon blanc or pinot grigio

2 teaspoons white wine vinegar

Kosher salt

2 ounces chainey briar (or about 3 stalks asparagus, shaved lengthwise with a vegetable peeler)

2 ounces radishes (about 3 radishes), shaved with a vegetable peeler

4 sheets parchment paper, about 13 by 16 inches

4 (4- to 6-ounce) fillets skinless flounder or other tender white-fleshed fish, such as sole or snapper

3 tablespoons unsalted butter, cut into 8 pats

1 lemon, cut into 8 slices

Freshly ground black pepper

1 large egg white

1 Preheat the oven to 400°F.

2 In a shallow bowl, whisk the olive oil with the white wine, white wine vinegar, and ¼ teaspoon salt. Add the chainey briar and the radishes, toss to coat with the dressing, and reserve.

3 For each of the fillets, fold the parchment paper in half lengthwise so it opens like a book, with the seam at the left. Place a fillet with its leftmost, longest edge in the crease of the seam and centered vertically. Season each fillet with 2 pinches of salt. Put 2 pats of butter and 2 slices of lemon on top of each fillet. Grind some black pepper over the fish.

(recipe continues)

4 Make an egg wash by whisking the egg white with 1 tablespoon of water. Brush the three open edges of the bottom layer of parchment with the wash, and lay the top side of the parchment over the fish top. Press on the edges of the parchment to seal. Lift the bottom left corner of the parchment up, and fold it over crisply to create a small triangular fold. Then place your index finger in the center of the long edge of that fold, and make another triangular fold. Continue folding the edge of the paper from the middle of the previous fold until you've sealed up the fish in a half-moon-shaped package.

5 When all the parchment packages are sealed, put them on a rimmed baking sheet and bake for 12 minutes. Remove from the oven and let rest for 3 minutes. Toss the chainey briar and radishes again in the dressing, then cut each packet open. Working quickly, remove the lemon slices (if desired) and strew a portion of the chainey briar and radishes over the fish, and serve immediately, placing each packet of fish directly on a dinner plate.

WINTER FLOUNDER IN PARCHMENT WITH SHAVED SWEET POTATO
SERVES: 4   TIME: 45 MINUTES

¼ cup cider vinegar

1 teaspoon sorghum syrup or honey

Kosher salt

1 sweet potato, shaved lengthwise on a mandoline into 8 planks about ⅛ inch thick

4 sheets parchment paper, about 13 by 16 inches

4 (4- to 6-ounce) fillets skinless flounder or other tender white-fleshed fish, such as sole or snapper

3 tablespoons unsalted butter, cut into 8 pats

1 lemon, cut into 8 slices

8 sprigs thyme

Freshly ground black pepper

1 large egg white

1 Preheat the oven to 400°F.

2 Heat ½ cup of water, the cider vinegar, sorghum, and ½ teaspoon salt in a small saucepan over high heat. Add the sweet potato, reduce the heat, and simmer until it is almost soft, about 8 minutes. Remove the potato from the pickling liquid and set aside. Discard the pickling liquid.

3 For each of the fillets, fold the parchment paper in half lengthwise so it opens like a book, with the seam at the left. Place a slice or two of the sweet potato with its leftmost, longest edges in the crease of the seam and centered vertically. Lay the fish on top of the sweet potato. Season each fillet with 2 pinches of salt. Place 2 pats of butter, 2 slices of lemon, and 2 sprigs of the thyme on top of each fillet. Grind some black pepper over the fish.

4 Seal the packets as in step 4 and cook as in step 5 of preceding recipe. To serve, simply place each packet directly on a plate and bring to the table for each diner to cut open.

SHRIMPING

"SHRIMPING IS DEAD," said Thomas Backman, Jr., who has more than sixty years of perspective on the family business. "All the honey gone—it's down to the vinegar now. My kids tried it, but they had to get jobs, one in landscaping in Columbia and one on the waterfront in Charleston."

Backman sat atop an enormous pile of olive-green shrimp nets, sharpening his thin fillet knife on a brick and using it to chisel away at some yellow rope knots in the sea of green. He was cutting out the aluminum gates that were stitched into the netting to allow sea turtles to escape alive. Each Turtle Excluder Device (TED) is worth about $10 used; the shredded netting he'll sell to restaurants seeking a nautical vibe.

Getting rid of legally mandated TEDs is every shrimper's dream—they're convinced that shrimp and flounder exit through the TED along with the turtles—but today's is not a happy activity. Backman's one remaining trawler, the *Sue Backman,* named after his mother (see Conch Fritters, page 150), was down in Beaufort and the previous year hit bottom.

"A board went bad, so when the tide comes in, the tide comes in. The engine's still good; it's just going to take so much money to refloat and repair it."

He gestures toward the end of his pier, empty but for a brown pelican on a piling. Two trawlers are visible far in the distance, docked at Crosby's Seafood, on the landward side of Folly Beach, the sandy spit of a sea island where in the late 1920s George Gershwin composed *Porgy and Bess.*

"Fifteen years ago, there were eight boats here, eight boats at Crosby's, and maybe 340 working the South Carolina coast; now, there might be ten total between here and Beaufort. And yet the shrimp are gone, too."

Still, he hasn't abandoned all hope: he harbors a feeling that the shrimp might return. Just before publication, we got word that the *Sue Backman* returned to the end of the pier.

SALT-BAKED SHEEPSHEAD

SERVES: 2 FOR A 2-POUND FISH, 4 FOR A 3-POUND FISH   TIME: 10 MINUTES PREPARATION, 35 TO 40 MINUTES BAKING

The fish species that inhabit South Carolina's precious salt marshes (344,000 acres, the most of any Atlantic state) are some of the feistiest and tastiest imaginable.

Sheepshead (*Archosargus probatocephalus*) and croaker (*Micropogonias undulatus*) are two prime examples, their flavor sweet, complex, and delicious, without being particularly oily. Even so, they rarely make it to restaurant menus, but they are reliably found in the independent fish markets closest to the Atlantic, and on the dinner tables of Charlestonians. They're relatively plentiful and easy to catch using a hook baited with a shrimp or fiddler crab.

Carroll's Seafood, a shop located until the mid-1980s at the traditionally fishy end of the old Charleston Market, closest to the harbor, featured a large painted billboard of a sheepshead, with its rounded sunfish profile and black vertical stripes, on the wall above the entry. As you drove down East Bay Street, you couldn't miss the fish, and it brought a bit of commercial whimsy to the otherwise dead-serious architectural regime of the historic downtown. Today, many of the family-owned markets in the Charleston area (Marvin's Seafood on Dorchester Road in North Charleston has one fine example) feature hand-painted fish murals on their interior or exterior walls.

Sheepshead average about three to five pounds and croakers about twelve ounces to two pounds, and we prefer our sheepshead small and croakers large (both fish approximately two and a half pounds), which makes them ideal for cooking and presenting whole, on the bone—a perfect meal for two. A salt-and-egg-white crust is a basic preparation that keeps these fish extra-moist with no added oils, and allows you to keep the scales on (a blessing if you caught the fish yourself) while infusing the fish very effectively with whatever aromatic flavors—tarragon, thyme, fresh bay, citrus peel, and rosemary come to mind—you're feeling. The chopped herbs that go into the salt crust are more for their pretty visual effect.

1 (2- to 3-pound) whole sheepshead or croaker, gutted, with scales, head, and tail left on

5½ cups kosher salt (about 3 pounds, or 1 box)

10 sprigs thyme; 5 left whole and 5 plucked of their leaves

10 sprigs tarragon; 5 left whole and 5 plucked of their leaves

4 sprigs rosemary; 2 left whole and 2 plucked of their leaves

6 dried bay leaves; 3 left whole and 3 shredded

½ lemon, sliced into thin disks

7 large egg whites

1 teaspoon crushed red pepper flakes or pink peppercorns

Parchment for lining the baking sheet

1 Preheat the oven to 400°F.

2 Season the fish cavity with ½ teaspoon of the salt and stuff with the whole herb sprigs, whole bay leaves, and the lemon slices. Whip the egg whites in a large bowl until frothy and add the remaining salt, whisking to combine. Chop the herb leaves and add them to the paste along with the shredded bay leaves and red pepper flakes, whisk to combine.

3 Lay the stuffed fish lengthwise in a baking dish or baking sheet lined with parchment and pat the herbed salt mixture over the fish in a ¼- to ½-inch layer, until the entire fish is entombed (the tail can stick out, and it can be trimmed with a scissors if it hangs over the edge of the dish).

4 Bake until the salt shell has browned nicely in a few places, 35 to 40 minutes. Crack the salt crust with the back of a large spoon and peel away sections of it along with the skin, and discard. Lift the top layer of meat off the bones with a wide knife or spatula, and pull the tail and spine upward to reveal the lower fillet once you've removed the upper one. Place on a plate and serve immediately.

EDNA LEWIS AT MIDDLETON PLACE

FOR DEVOTEES OF seasonal Southern cooking—and of course, we count ourselves among them—Edna Lewis is our heroine. Her 1976 cookbook, *A Taste of Country Cooking*, brought to life her childhood on a farm in Freetown, Virginia, where her family lived close to the land, preparing meals with a refined simplicity and—a word that had seldom been used until then in the context of cooking in the rural South—sophistication. Lewis was sixty years old when that book was published. She had already been the much-lauded chef of Café Nicholson, hot spot for the New York literati, and a private chef to prominent New York families. She had been the proprietor of a New Jersey pheasant farm, and had also taught for ten years in the African Hall of the Museum of Natural History.

Nearly a decade after *A Taste of Country Cooking* appeared, Lewis spent several years in the Charleston area as chef-in-residence at Middleton Place, a period that coincided with the release of her second volume, *In Pursuit of Flavor*. While we never met "Miss Lewis," as her friends called her, we remember the excitement with which people greeted her arrival in Charleston. Articles appeared in both local papers, and there were national features in the *Chicago Tribune*, *Food & Wine*, *Connoisseur*, and *Diversion*, among others. These stories invariably emphasized the shyness and humility that belied her regal bearing and radiant smile.

At Middleton Place, Lewis lived in a dwelling that had once been the plantation's Rice Mill and, in the twentieth century, a Junior League Tea Room. Her mission at Middleton Place was to develop recipes for the historic plantation's restaurant from the region's first home-cooking bible, *The Carolina Housewife*, by Sarah Rutledge (herself a Middleton descendant). It was an

(WILLIAM ALBERT ALLARD)

intriguing time in Charleston's restaurant history to be looking to the past because the temples of Lowcountry food, like Henry's and the Old Edisto Motel, were in their waning years, as diners flocked to Marianne's and Le Midi, the bistros that had opened in the late seventies and early eighties in the wake of the Spoleto Festival. And this was three years before the new-Southern pioneer Magnolia's opened on East Bay Street (with the motto "Uptown Down South"), serving fanciful, chef-driven Southern fare, like collard-greens-stuffed wontons. Lewis shouted above the din by offering plainspoken Southern food: pan-seared quail with country ham, watercress soup, and caramel cake. According to Charles Duell, president of the Middleton Foundation, Lewis's tenure at the restaurant was a transformative time for the institution, and the impression she made is felt to this day in the kitchen and vegetable gardens of the current young chef, Micah Garrison.

Carol Haddix, longtime food writer and editor for the *Chicago Tribune*, traveled to Middleton Place in 1987 to interview Lewis for a story that appeared in the paper on April 23 of that year. Lewis was quoted as saying, "Even today all Southerners, from Virginia to Mississippi, eat in their homes—that's where you'll find the good food, not so much in restaurants in the South. . . . We in the South don't pick up on all of these food trends, but we like to entertain."

We wonder what Lewis would have made of the new Charleston restaurant landscape today, of chefs like Sean Brock stocking their storerooms with homemade pickles, or Craig Deihl curing country hams at Cypress. Thankfully, home cooking *is* the predominant restaurant trend now!

SHRIMP AND GRITS   SERVES: 4   TIME: 1 HOUR

This dish has become such a popular one in Charleston that it may well be on the verge of displacing She-Crab Soup (page 77) in the pantheon of Lowcountry culinary heroes. No discussion of shrimp and grits would be complete without the mention of chef and cookbook author Bill Neal, who was raised on a farm in Gaffney, South Carolina (upstate, peach-growing country), and opened a fancy French restaurant, La Residence, in Chapel Hill, North Carolina. In 1982, he left "La Res" to open the more casual Crook's Corner, serving the kind of honest, simple, and refined farm cooking he grew up with to UNC students and professors. Though Neal died in 1990, his influence lives on today at Crook's Corner, now helmed by Bill Smith, and also in the kitchens of so many of today's superb Southern chefs, who spent time under his tutelage: Robert Stehling of Charleston's Hominy Grill; John Currence of City Grocery, in Oxford, Mississippi; Karen and Ben Barker of Magnolia Grill (1986–2012) and Amy Tornquist of Watts Grocery, in Durham, North Carolina, to name a few. (Neal's son, Matt, and Matt's wife, Sheila, are proprietors of the excellent Neal's Deli, in Carrboro, North Carolina).

Neal had spent time in Charleston, so she-crab soup and shrimp and grits have always been on the menu at Crook's Corner. When the legendary *New York Times* food writer and editor Craig Claiborne, a Mississippian, wrote a lengthy feature for the paper about a visit he'd made to Neal's kitchen, shrimp and grits achieved national stature—this despite the fact that the basic idea of the dish had been around for a while: a recipe for "Shrimps with Hominy" appears in *200 Years of Charleston Cooking* (1934), and it couldn't be more minimalist—shrimp sautéed in butter with salt and pepper, served with "hominy" (as cooked grits are often called in the Lowcountry). By comparison, the "Breakfast Shrimp" in *Charleston Receipts* is torqued up, with diced onion and green pepper, bacon grease, Worcestershire, catsup, and flour to thicken the deal. In Neal's 1985 recipe, published in the *New York Times,* the shrimp are cooked in bacon fat, then dressed with lemon juice, sautéed mushrooms, and green onion.

These days everyone's got his or her own riff on shrimp and grits, and our own formula seems always to be evolving. This recipe represents our latest take on the dish, influenced by (1) our desire to keep the tomato inflection from the *Charleston Receipts* recipe in the dish, and (2) a technique that a local restaurant of recent vintage, The Glass Onion, introduced to us: the chefs there slice the shrimp in half lengthwise so that when they hit the sauté pan, they twist into corkscrew-like curls. Each shrimp piece is easier to eat in one bite, the twisted shape grabs more sauce and gives the overall impression of a lighter dish. Especially if jumbo shrimp are the only ones available in your area, you'll find this an appealing way to cook shrimp and grits.

1¼ pounds headless large (21 to 25 count) shell-on shrimp	1 teaspoon red wine vinegar, plus more to taste
1 bay leaf	4 ounces slab bacon, cut into large dice
Kosher salt	1 lemon, halved
¾ teaspoon sugar	1 tablespoon all-purpose flour
1 pinch of cayenne	2 garlic cloves, minced
1 pound vine-ripened tomatoes, cored and quartered	Freshly ground black pepper
	Charleston Hominy (recipe follows)

(recipe continues)

1 Peel and devein the shrimp, reserving the shrimp in a bowl and the shells in a small saucepan. Add 2 cups of water, the bay leaf, ½ teaspoon kosher salt, ¼ teaspoon of the sugar, and the cayenne to the saucepan with the shells. With a spoon, tamp the shells down beneath the surface of the water, cover, and bring to a simmer over high heat. Uncover, turn the heat to medium low, and let the shrimp stock simmer until reduced by half, about 10 minutes.

2 Meanwhile, with a sharp knife, slice the shrimp in half lengthwise.

3 Put the tomatoes in a blender or food processor and add the vinegar, ½ teaspoon salt, and the remaining ½ teaspoon sugar. Process to a smooth purée, then strain through a fine sieve, pressing the skin and seeds to extract as much juice as possible. Discard the skin and seeds. You should have 1½ cups of tomato purée.

4 Scatter the bacon in a large sauté pan over medium-high heat and cook, stirring occasionally, until the bacon is alluringly browned and has rendered its fat, about 8 minutes. Using a slotted spoon, transfer the bacon to a small paper-towel-lined plate and cook the shrimp in the bacon fat in batches, taking care not to crowd the pan, and stirring occasionally, just until they've curled into corkscrews and turned pink, about 2 minutes; reserve on a plate. Squeeze half the lemon over the shrimp and sprinkle with 2 pinches of salt.

5 Strain the shrimp stock into the sauté pan, discarding the solids, and stir with a wooden spoon to pick up the tasty browned bits from the bottom of the pan. When the stock simmers, spoon off 2 tablespoons and then whisk them into the flour with a fork in a small bowl to make a paste. Add the tomato purée and the garlic to the pan, stir to combine, and then whisk the flour paste into the sauce. Cook until the mixture thickly coats the back of a spoon.

6 Cut the heat, and fold the shrimp in just to warm through. Season to taste with salt, black pepper, and red wine vinegar. Cut the remaining lemon half into 4 wedges. Serve the shrimp over hot Charleston Hominy, and garnish with the reserved bacon and the lemon wedges.

(recipe continues)

CHARLESTON HOMINY
MAKES: 3 CUPS   TIME: 45 MINUTES

Charlestonians of a certain age tend to call cooked grits "hominy." This causes confusion, because hominy every-place else means nixtamalized—hulled by soaking in a lye solution—corn, which is delicious, but a different food and flavor altogether, more evocative of Chihuahua than Charleston. Whether or not you call cooked grits "hominy," everyone seems to agree that the uncooked raw material is "grits."

After several decades of post-WWII decline, real stone-ground grits (dried corn cracked in a mill and cooked with water to a silky softness) have come back in the South—and well beyond, thanks to the valiant efforts of hard-working millers, along with the crusading flavor-centrism of restaurant chefs in Charleston and beyond, who have encouraged neophytes to experience good grits. What everyone enjoys about corn grits is their mildly earthy grain flavor and their texture, which resembles sticky rice and performs the same task of grounding a plate with a bright, malleable, and still toothsome starch. "Hominy" is employed almost inter-changeably with rice, and is near-essential in Charleston with savory breakfasts of fried fish, eggs, and smokehouse bacon, but also appears at lunch and dinner, especially beneath a buttery slab of fish, or with shrimp.

Charleston breakfast hominy, like Charleston Rice (page 133), is an exercise in simplicity; the dish isn't intended to dazzle, but to be honed to a fine polish by years of intensive use—hominy grits, as some call it, is as familiar as water and salt, but rarely taken for granted.

2 cups whole milk	2 tablespoons unsalted butter
1 cup stone-ground coarse grits	Kosher salt and freshly ground black pepper

1 Pour the milk and 2 cups of water into a 2-quart saucepan, cover, and turn the heat to medium high. When the liquid simmers, add the grits, butter, and ½ teaspoon salt, and reduce the heat to medium. Stir every couple of minutes until the grits have become fragrant, and are the consistency of thick soup, about 8 minutes.

2 Reduce the heat to low and simmer, stirring often and ever more frequently, for about 20 minutes, by which time the bubbles will emerge infrequently as the grits have stiffened and fall lazily from the end of a spoon. Add ½ teaspoon black pepper and cook for about 10 minutes more, stirring constantly to prevent the thickened grits from scorching on the bottom of the pan (appoint someone to the stirring task if you have to step away—a scorched pot of grits is bitter and a total loss). If your grits thicken too quickly, or if they are too gritty for your taste, add water by the half cup, stirring to incorporate, and continue cooking until tender.

3 When the grits are stiff and stick well to the spoon, turn off the heat and stir. Season with salt and black pepper to taste and serve immediately.

ALLIGATOR CREEK AND THE SALT MARSH
BETWEEN JOHNS ISLAND AND KIAWAH ISLAND.

POULTRY *and* OTHER MEATS

JUST BECAUSE WE ORIENT OURSELVES TOWARD THE SEA IN CHARLESTON
doesn't mean our meat chapter runs lean. In fact, one of the more inspiring places in our map of great Lowcountry food destinations is an appointment-only meat market south of town in Hollywood, called Marvin's. It's the kind of place where you take your pigs to be prepped for a whole-hog barbecue and your steer to be dressed for packing into the freezer. And Marvin's sells all manner of delicious bits, like pig ears and oxtails. D.C. Burbage Retail Meats, in Goose Creek, is another great full-spectrum butcher.

This chapter is less about the bits than it is about poultry—which, next to seafood, is the most important of Charleston proteins—and about grand, meaty gestures. Our favorite Thanksgiving turkey recipe is here (page 180)—and, especially if you're indifferent to turkey, it's one you must try. The Roast Fresh Ham (page 185) we serve at Easter is also featured, but you might use it on any occasion when you are cooking for a large crowd (or want to indulge a child; Matt's son Arthur loves this roast). And truly no cookbook of the region would be complete without the weekday classics Fried Chicken (page 186) and Smothered Pork Chops (page 182).

Wild duck (page 198) and venison (page 189) recipes in this chapter reflect the importance of game in Charleston home cooking. We're fortunate to have generous friends who hunt (we don't), but as we've learned, those of us who cook can provide a useful service, helping to keep hunting families' freezers from bursting.

A ROOSTER-LESS FABER'S PILAU

SERVES: 4 TO 5   TIME: 2½ HOURS

Samuel Faber, a butler for the Simons family on Tradd Street, may have been the only African American to have his full name credited to a recipe in the Junior League–published cookbook, *Charleston Receipts* (see page 52). "Faber's Pilau" was often celebrated in the press that surrounded that book's publication, and repeatedly over the next few decades, as the cookbook hit printing milestones. The recipe is interesting, standing as the one classic pilau (puh-LO) in the book, the only chicken dish that uses the pilaf technique—originated in the Middle East—of bringing up the rice with the chickeny broth instead of with plain water; most other recipes in the midcentury used the modern inflection of beginning with water-cooked rice.

The finicky nature of cooking rice with thick liquids is to us a large part of the appeal of this dish: the rice and liquid are calibrated such that a crispy layer develops on the bottom of the pot. This is a desirable hallmark of a Charleston pilau, and it should be scraped off the bottom of the pot and folded into the rest of the rice when it is mounded on a platter. The aroma of the chicken cooking with the toasty rice is incomparable, and the dish will register for many as the flavor of a Sunday afternoon.

We've given this adaptation our own touch by adding a teaspoon of turmeric, to deepen the flavor of the broth and to give the Italianate, tomato-onion-thyme gravy a slight Charleston spin, à la country captain, a curry-seasoned chicken and rice dish. In our research we found that turmeric shows up in more than a few South Carolina recipe books of the nineteenth century, so we know it was present in several kitchens. It's a genial spice, occupying the middle background of the palate and making its presence known more as a color—marigold orange—than as a flavor. We resisted the urge to add a cupful of white wine (to retain the plainspoken goodness of the tomato, chicken, and thyme), though we did modify the recipe for modern realities, since the original calls for a seven-pound rooster enriched with a pound of margarine!

This is true comfort food, and it is even more delicious the day after you prepare it.

1 quart hot water

2 cups finely chopped yellow onion (1 large)

1 tablespoon plus 1 teaspoon kosher salt

6 sprigs thyme

1 (28-ounce) can crushed tomatoes

1 (6-pound) chicken, with livers, giblets, and the neck, if available

1 tablespoon freshly ground black pepper

½ teaspoon crushed red pepper flakes

1 heaping teaspoon turmeric

3 tablespoons extra-virgin olive oil

2 cups Carolina Gold or basmati rice

3 tablespoons all-purpose flour, mixed with enough water or stock to make a smooth paste

1. Set a rack in the bottom half of the oven and preheat the oven to 350°F.

2. Add the water, onion, salt, thyme, and tomatoes to a 5- or 6-quart Dutch oven or covered roasting pan, stir to combine, and then put the chicken—and the livers, giblets, and neck, if using—into the pot; the chicken should be not quite covered with liquid. Cover and bake for 30 minutes, turn the bird over, and bake for another 30 minutes.

3. Add the black pepper, red pepper flakes, and turmeric to the pot, stirring it in around the bird as best you can, and flip the bird once again. Cook for 15 minutes; remove the cover on the pan and cook for 15 minutes more, or until a meat thermometer inserted into the thigh reads 155°F.

(recipe continues)

4 Remove the pan from the oven and transfer the bird to a cutting board; reserve the broth in the pan. Discard the neck and giblets, if they were used, and tent the bird with foil.

5 In a 4-quart saucepan, heat the olive oil over medium heat, and when it shimmers, add the dry rice, stirring it around the pan to coat. Cook, stirring often, for about 3 minutes until a toasty popcorn aroma develops. Add 4½ cups of the cooking liquid from the roasting pan (beware: it will bubble vigorously), cover, and cook over low heat until the liquid is absorbed and a crust has developed on the bottom of the pan, 25 to 30 minutes. The surface of the rice may look damp, but probe down with a spoon and you will find that it is dry. Scrape the bottom layer up and fold into the rest of the rice, cover, remove from the heat, and allow to continue steaming until ready to serve.

6 Season the remaining cooking liquid to taste with salt, then heat the liquid in its pan over medium-high heat on the stovetop. Once it simmers, whisk in the flour paste and cook for 5 to 7 minutes, stirring occasionally, until it is a thick gravy.

7 To serve, loosely mound the rice in a deep serving platter, set carved sections of the bird on top of the rice, and drizzle both the bird and rice with the gravy.

HERB-ROASTED TURKEY WITH MADEIRA GRAVY

SERVES: 8 TO 10   TIME: 24 HOURS BRINING, 1 HOUR RESTING, 4 HOURS 30 MINUTES COOKING

In 1984, when we were twelve and fourteen years old, we attended a potluck Thanksgiving party at the Ansonborough home of our parents' friend David Rawle. We made a baroque French dessert—a mountain of chestnut purée blanketed in sweetened whipped cream, called a montblanc—and the whole family pitched in. The excitement of that Thanksgiving was remarkable: seeing what others had made (we recall, like it was yesterday, the bright colors of one friend's trio of Cuisinart purées: beet, lima bean, and sweet potato); watching the table of dishes come together; tasting everything and accepting compliments from other guests—it was all more fun than we'd ever had with grown-ups. And the even cooler thing was that everyone there treated us like we *were* adults. That Thanksgiving started an almost continuous thirty-year tradition of great conversations and friendships.

In later years of Thanksgivings at David's, we took on more and more responsibility for the food, and one of our favorite parts now is the roasting of the bird. Turkey seems to get such a bad rap—It's a chore! It always ends up dry!—but if you're confident in your recipe, and you have the time to do it, it'll always end up being the centerpiece of a happy occasion. You can give yourself an edge by selecting an heirloom breed like a Bourbon Red, Black, or Narragansett, which will, by virtue of its DNA, be tastier and less likely to dry out.

This is our favorite turkey and gravy recipe. For the turkey, we use an herb-laden salt as a "dry brine"; it's so much easier to manage than all that water in a true brine! And the foundation of our gravy is the fortified wine Madeira, which gives the gently smoky pan drippings a wisp of sweetness. Furthermore, it makes geographical sense for a Charleston turkey because it was the most popular wine in the Holy City during the eighteenth and nineteenth centuries!

TURKEY

2½ tablespoons mixed dried herbs, such as thyme, sage, and marjoram

½ cup kosher salt

1 (14- to 16-pound) turkey

8 tablespoons (1 stick) unsalted butter, softened

¾ teaspoon freshly ground black pepper

8 cups turkey stock or chicken broth

GRAVY

1 cup chopped shallots (3 large or 6 small)

¼ cup all-purpose flour

2 cups Madeira wine (a 5- or 10-year-old blend; not "cooking Madeira")

1 Prepare the turkey: Mix the herbs and salt in a medium bowl until thoroughly combined. Put the turkey in the center of a large roasting pan. Sprinkle all but 1 tablespoon of the herb mixture liberally in the body and neck cavities and all over the skin of the bird. Put the pan with the turkey inside a clean, large kitchen can liner or plastic bag, seal it with a knot, and set in the refrigerator for 24 hours.

2 Remove the pan and turkey from the bag and rinse the turkey thoroughly with cold water. Pat it dry with paper towels. Pour off any liquid from the roasting pan and rinse the pan well. Put a rack in the pan and let the turkey stand in the rack at room temperature for 1 hour.

3 Set the oven rack in the lowest position of the oven and preheat the oven to 375°F.

4 Massage the legs and breast with the butter, and season the turkey with the black pepper and the reserved herb-and-salt mixture. Tuck the neck flap underneath the turkey to close, and loosely tie the turkey legs together with butcher's twine. Pour 3 cups of the turkey stock into the pan.

5 Roast the turkey for 45 minutes, and then baste with the pan juices and rotate the pan in the oven 180 degrees to ensure even coloring. Reduce the oven temperature to 350°F, basting every 45 minutes and adding stock by cupfuls to maintain the level of stock in the pan, until a thermometer inserted into the thickest part of the thigh registers 165°F, 2½ to 3 hours more. Each time you baste, rotate the pan in the oven 180 degrees to ensure even coloring. Transfer the turkey to a platter, tent loosely with foil, and let rest for 30 minutes. Reserve the pan juices for gravy.

6 Make the gravy: Pour the pan juices into an 8-cup measuring cup or large glass pitcher, and allow to settle until most of the fat has risen to the top. Spoon off the fat, discarding all but ½ cup. Pour the reserved ½ cup fat into the turkey pan and set it over two burners set to medium. Scatter the shallots in the pan, and sauté in the fat, stirring occasionally, until the shallots are softened and fragrant but not brown, about 3 minutes. Add the flour, whisking it into the shallots and fat for 2 to 3 minutes, until it's evenly distributed to get rid of any raw-flour flavor. Add the Madeira and bring to a simmer, then pour the degreased pan juices into the pan (if you maintained the level of stock in the pan, you should have about 4 cups; if you have less, simply add enough turkey stock to make 4 cups total). Continue to simmer until the gravy has reduced by a third, 6 to 8 minutes.

7 Carve the turkey, and serve with warm gravy.

SMOTHERED PORK CHOPS   SERVES: 4   TIME: 30 MINUTES

This recipe is an easy weeknight dish we enjoy serving our families. It's also our own tribute to the excellent smothered pork chops we eat at Bertha's Kitchen, a restaurant on the northern tip of the Charleston peninsula, where sisters Sharon Coakley, Julia Grant, and Linda Pinckney carry on the legacy of their mother, Albertha Grant. Mrs. Grant opened the restaurant in 1979, serving made-from-scratch Southern comfort food, like green beans, lima beans, collards, fried chicken, fried fish, and smothered pork chops—which we devour so cleanly you'd think the bones had been bleached. The lines that stretch from the steamtable out the door most days at lunchtime are testament to the sisters' fidelity to their mother's recipes, and also to the fact that most Charlestonians don't mind waiting when we know the food's delicious!

PORK CHOPS

½ cup all-purpose flour

¼ cup coarse, medium, or fine stone-ground cornmeal

2 teaspoons kosher salt, plus more to taste

1½ teaspoons freshly ground black pepper, plus more to taste

½ cup whole milk

1 large egg yolk

1½ cups peanut or canola oil, or lard

4 bone-in center-cut pork loin chops (about 2¼ pounds)

GRAVY

1½ cups diced yellow onion (about 1 large)

4 teaspoons all-purpose flour

1⅓ cups chicken broth

⅔ cup whole milk or half-and-half

1 Cook the pork chops: Whisk together the flour, cornmeal, salt, and black pepper in a broad, shallow bowl until thoroughly combined. Transfer to a large plate, spreading the mixture in a flat, even layer. Wipe the bowl clean with a paper towel, and pour the milk into it. Add the egg yolk and whisk until thoroughly combined.

2 Preheat the oven to 250°F, and place a heatproof platter lined with a double thickness of paper towels inside.

3 Pour the oil into a 10-inch skillet to a depth of about ½ inch, and put over high heat. When the oil reaches 375°F on a frying thermometer, turn the heat down to medium high. Submerge 2 of the pork chops in the bowl of egg wash until they're completely coated, letting any excess drip back into the bowl. Press each chop firmly into the flour mixture on the plate, then flip it to coat the other side. Roll each chop around in the dredge so that the sides get an even coating of flour, too, then slide it gently into the hot oil. When both chops of the batch are in the oil, cover the pan, and fry until the bottom side of the chops is alluringly browned, about 2 minutes. Then flip them and continue to cook for about 2 minutes, uncovered, until the second side is browned. Using sturdy tongs, carefully transfer the chops to the plate in the oven. Repeat with the remaining 2 chops.

4 Make the gravy: Once all the chops are in the oven, pour off all but 1 tablespoon of the oil, and add the onion to the pan. Cook, stirring, until fragrant and translucent, but not browned, about 4 minutes. Scatter the flour in the pan and cook, stirring for about 3 minutes, until the flour is distributed evenly throughout the onion and is toasty. Add the broth and milk, and whisk until smooth. Bring to a simmer and cook, stirring, until the gravy is thickened, about 2 minutes. Season to taste with salt and black pepper.

5 Remove the chops from the oven and arrange them on a long platter. Smother them with the gravy and bring to the table.

ROAST FRESH HAM

SERVES: 12 TO 14   TIME: 4 HOURS 30 MINUTES

Though much ballyhoo is made of pork these days in the South, especially concerning barbecue, the truth is that pork of any kind was relatively scarce on Charleston tables until late in the twentieth century. Sure, a cured country ham might be brought back from the mountains of North Carolina (where pork was more common) on a rare occasion, but according to many Charlestonians we've interviewed over the years, the love for pork chops is a post-Vietnam-era thing, with a few exceptions.

One notable pork event, as recalled by a few locals who otherwise never ate it, was the roasted fresh ham at Easter. This roast, usually around eighteen pounds, happens to be one of our favorites, for the purity of the pork flavor and for its fantastic caramelized fat. And it grants us a perfect excuse to drive to one of the few independent butchers remaining in the area (D.C. Burbage Retail Meats, in Goose Creek, or Marvin's Meats, in Hollywood), the sort of place where a whole fresh ham, trimmed to order, is no problem at all—and inexpensive to boot. (Walk into a supermarket and ask for a whole ham, and you're likely to be treated as if you were speaking a different language.)

A whole fresh ham is now a new tradition for us, and paired with Skillet Asparagus with Grapefruit (page 93) and Sweet Potatoes with Sorghum Marshmallows (page 103), it makes for a magnificent special-occasion dinner for a crowd. Kumquat Chile Paste (page 38) is a perfect complement to the roast pork as well.

1 Set a rack in the lower third of the oven and preheat the oven to 425°F. Trim any remaining skin and excess fat from the ham, leaving a layer of fat up to ¾ inch thick. Score the ham all over in a diamond pattern of ½-inch-deep cuts about 1½ inches apart.

2 In a small bowl, combine the salt, black pepper, thyme, and rosemary, pinching and blending the mixture with your fingers until the thyme is fragrant. Pat the mixture all over the ham and into the crevices.

3 Put the ham, fat side up, on a rack in a large roasting pan and roast for 30 minutes. Decrease the oven temperature to 350°F, and (taking care to avoid pouring the liquid directly into rendered fat) pour 2 cups of the wine and 1 cup of water into the pan; loosely tent with aluminum foil. Continue to roast, basting every hour, and adding water as necessary, to keep a ⅛-inch depth of juices in the bottom of the pan, until a meat thermometer pressed into the thickest part of the ham reads 145°F, about 3½ hours.

4 Let the ham rest for 15 to 20 minutes before carving. Pour the pan juices and remaining 2 tablespoons wine into a small saucepan and simmer for about 2 minutes. Turn off the heat, add the half-and-half, and serve the gravy with the ham.

1 (16- to 18-pound) fresh ham, skin removed but as much fat as possible left on

1½ tablespoons kosher salt

1 tablespoon freshly ground black pepper

2 tablespoons fresh thyme (from about 14 stems)

1 tablespoon minced fresh rosemary (from about 5 stems)

2 cups plus 2 tablespoons dry white wine

¼ cup half-and-half

FRIED CHICKEN

SERVES: 4   TIME: 50 MINUTES

We've swung the pendulum on fried chicken: in childhood and adolescence, we lived for the thick, crunchy cape of batter and skin. Then in our first cookbook, we advocated for a minimalist crust of just flour and cornmeal, like the fried chicken found in Charleston homes. Now, we've come back around to an appreciation of a good homemade batter of the sort we'd find at the Piggly Wiggly in-store buffet, whose only difference from our thin version is a modest amount of egg and buttermilk to puff up the flour and cornmeal. We don't cook fried chicken every day, so when we do, we're not pulling any punches.

1 cup all-purpose flour

6 tablespoons fine or medium-fine cornmeal

2 teaspoons kosher salt

1½ teaspoons freshly ground black pepper

1 large egg

1 cup whole or low-fat buttermilk

6 cups peanut or canola oil, or lard

3 pounds chicken legs and thighs (about 6 of each)

1 Preheat the oven to 250°F.

2 Pour the flour, cornmeal, salt, and black pepper into a large (gallon-size or more) sturdy plastic or paper bag. Shake a few times to combine the dredge ingredients. In a medium bowl, whisk the egg with the buttermilk.

3 Pour the oil into a large skillet (12-inch is ideal) or Dutch oven up to a depth of about ¾ inch, and heat over medium-high until it reaches 325°F on a deep-fry thermometer.

4 Meanwhile, dredge the chicken in the flour mixture in batches by putting a couple pieces at a time in the bag and shaking it a few times until they are evenly coated in the dredge. Shake off any excess, then dip each piece in the egg mixture, and allow the excess to drip off. Finally, dip (but don't shake) the chicken in the bag of dredge, being sure to coat all sides.

5 Fry the chicken 6 pieces at a time, adjusting the heat as needed to keep the oil temperature between 300° and 325°F and turning the pieces every 3 minutes or so, until the chicken is golden brown and cooked through, about 15 minutes.

6 With tongs, transfer the chicken to a paper-towel-lined ovenproof dish and put in the oven to warm. Repeat step 5 with the remaining chicken. Serve immediately.

FRIED CHICKEN WITH FRIED CHICKEN GRAVY

This golden gravy captures the essence of fried chicken flavor and is delicious together with hot sauce on fried chicken. The idea was inspired by Mrs. Harry Salmons's (Rosamond Waring's) recipe in *Charleston Receipts*.

Prepare the Fried Chicken as above, except as follows:

1 Preheat the oven to 350°F.

2 In step 5, fry the chicken pieces just until golden brown on both sides, not a minute further, then remove them wetly—don't allow them time to drain—to an ovenproof skillet. Continue until that second skillet contains all the fried chicken, then transfer the chicken to the oven and bake for 20 minutes, until the chicken is cooked through to the bone.

3 Using tongs, remove the chicken parts from the skillet to a platter and cover. There should be about 2 tablespoons of tasty oil and chicken skin and crust bits remaining in that skillet. Add 2 teaspoons all-purpose flour to the skillet over medium-low heat and stir with a wooden spoon constantly, until the flour begins to turn golden brown, 4 to 6 minutes. Add 1 cup whole milk, a couple pinches of kosher salt, and a few grinds of black pepper and continue stirring until smooth and thickened. Serve with fried chicken and hot sauce.

MULBERRY-GLAZED VENISON LOIN

Buff Ross, a Charleston artist and a great friend of ours, has a day job designing Web sites for clients that range from the local food elite (Husk Restaurant, Roots Ice Cream) to the city's cultural institutions (Halsey Institute for Contemporary Art, Charleston Jazz Initiative). He also might be more of a food nerd than we are, and he's the one who introduced us to what we think is the choicest part of the deer: the short loin, or "backstrap."

This cut of venison is so easy to cook. You just season it with salt and pepper, sear it in a skillet on the stovetop, and then transfer it to the oven to cook through to medium rare. We cook it to an internal temperature of 130°F for rare (it'll come up to 135°F as it rests). We like to brush the loin liberally in the last ten minutes of cooking with a delicious glaze, to create a pan sauce with a thrilling balance of sweet, sour, and savory.

Here, we use syrup that we make from the fruit of mulberry trees in the neighborhood. We got lucky last year: about half an hour after we harvested a couple of quarts from the tree on the sidewalk between Magar Hatworks and Sugar Bakery on Cannon Street, a hailstorm came through and took most of the remaining fruit.

If you can't find a producing mulberry tree, you can still make this dish. Use the bottled mulberry syrups found in specialty-food stores. Mymouné brand is the one we find most often and it's a great value—about three bucks a bottle. Venison tenderloin is an intense, lean, richly flavored cut of meat, so serve it with piquant sides such as Matt's Four-Pepper Collards (page 100) and Butter Beans with Butter, Mint, and Lime (page 110). This recipe also works well with farmed venison and super-lean cuts of beef.

1 (2-pound) venison short loin

3 teaspoons canola or other vegetable oil

¾ teaspoon kosher salt, plus more to taste

¼ teaspoon freshly ground black pepper

½ cup Mulberry Syrup (recipe follows)

2 tablespoons Worcestershire sauce

2 tablespoons red wine vinegar

1 bay leaf

1 Preheat the oven to 350°F.

2 Rub the venison with 2 teaspoons of the oil, and sprinkle all over with the salt and black pepper. Pour the remaining teaspoon oil into a large ovenproof skillet over medium-high heat and brush it around to thinly coat the pan. When the oil in the skillet just begins to smoke, sear the venison until it's nicely browned all over, about 8 minutes total, and then transfer to the oven to roast for 25 minutes.

3 While the venison roasts, mix the syrup with the Worcestershire, vinegar, and bay leaf in a small saucepan, and bring to a simmer over medium heat. Reduce the heat, and let simmer until reduced by a half, 6 to 8 minutes.

4 Baste the roast with the mulberry mixture and continue to roast, basting every 5 minutes with the syrup mixture, until the internal temperature reaches 130°F, about 15 minutes. Only a thin coating of the mixture will adhere to the roast with each basting; the rest will fall to the pan—that is fine. Transfer the roast to a cutting board, tent it with foil, and let rest for 10 minutes.

5 Pour any remaining mulberry baste and any juices collected from the cutting board into the skillet and set over medium heat. If needed, reduce the liquid in the pan until it has a syrupy, glazy texture. Remove the bay leaf and brush the glaze over the tenderloin liberally, reserving some to drizzle over each serving. Slice the roast as thinly as you can and serve with drizzles of the glaze.

(recipe continues)

MULBERRY SYRUP

MAKES: 1 PINT   TIME: 35 MINUTES

In late March and early April, mulberries fall from trees in downtown Charleston, bursting apart and staining the sidewalks, and then get tracked into houses, where they mark up carpets and floors. So help us all out: please harvest them, and make this delicious mulberry syrup. When we asked Alice Waters, for a *New York Times* article, what she perceived to be "the flavor of the future," she said: "Mulberry syrup."

Mulberries are special in their own way, and even more so concentrated and liquefied. We always include a small proportion of underripe berries because they have more natural pectin in them than ripe ones and so will better thicken the syrup. This syrup is fantastic stirred into seltzer to make a refreshing summer cooler.

4 cups (about 1¼ pounds) ripe mulberries

A handful or more underripe mulberries

½ teaspoon kosher salt

2½ cups sugar

1 Put the mulberries and the salt in the bowl of a food processor and process to a loose slurry, scraping down the sides of the bowl as you go. Pass through a fine-mesh strainer, pressing down on the solids to extract as much liquid as possible. (You should have about 1¼ cups juice.)

2 Pour the juice into a large saucepan, add the sugar, and bring to a simmer. Cook gently over low heat until the syrup is thick and, well, syrupy, 20 minutes. (When hot, the syrup will always seem like a thin liquid; you can tell if it's done by dipping a wooden spoon into it, then seeing if the layer of syrup that clings to the spoon thickens as it cools.) Transfer to a clean glass jar with a tight-fitting lid and store in the refrigerator. (Syrup will keep in the refrigerator about 1 month.) When cold, it may become stiff, almost jamlike, but you can loosen it by warming it in a saucepan over low heat or in the microwave with a few drops of water.

BOEUF À LA MODE

SERVES: 8 TO 10   TIME: 3 HOURS

Our friend Sallie Duell alerted us to the genius of Boeuf à la Mode—"fashionable beef," per the French—as we chatted over glasses of iced tea on the third-floor piazza of 21 East Battery, overlooking Charleston Harbor and, by chance, a three-masted ship under sail. Back when we were teens, we spent countless afternoons in the house's backyard, catching air on Sallie's stepchildren's trampoline and quarter-pipe skateboard ramp. And though tourists shuttled in and out the front door—the bottom two floors function as one of the city's great house museums—we were completely oblivious to the history of the place. From the very piazza where we interviewed Sallie, General P. G. T. Beauregard had watched the first shots of Confederate artillery land on Fort Sumter on April 12, 1861.

We were eager to interview Sallie, a Greenville, South Carolina, native, because we'd heard that she learned to cook from *Charleston Receipts* when she moved back to South Carolina from New York City as a young bride, in 1964. Our ears perked up when she mentioned that the Boeuf à la Mode from *Charleston Receipts* had been a favorite; it seemed like one of the more daunting recipes in the book. The one that appears in Sarah Rutledge's *The Carolina Housewife* is even more complicated. And as Sallie assured us, it could not be less fashionable now! (We've never been served the dish in either a home or a restaurant.) She noted that boeuf à la mode was a frequent offering at cocktail parties in the sixties and seventies, as a heavy hors d'oeuvre, "an interesting and different sort of way to serve a large cut of meat at a party—to slow-cook it." Alas, Sallie and Charles recently gave up eating red meat—times and tastes do change—but we're doing our part to bring this superb preparation back in fashion.

Boeuf à la Mode is a fantastic roast. We typically use an inexpensive, lean cut such as eye of round or top round, and we season it with a mixture of onions, allspice, black pepper, and salt, which is stuffed into incisions in the beef. The vinegar-inflected pan gravy spooned over thin, medium-rare slices is absolutely delicious, a refreshing change from heavy, earthy beef gravies. It is, in fact, an elegant dish. While Sallie cooked it for cocktail parties, Boeuf à la Mode makes such a handsome presentation that we serve it for dinners, on occasions when we wish we lived in a museum-quality house.

An interesting note: Elizabeth O'Neill Verner, the preeminent artist of the Charleston Renaissance, contributed the recipe for boeuf à la mode to *Charleston Receipts*, and is also credited with designing the cover illustration for the book. Her early etchings and watercolors of Charleston street life are among the most collectible Charleston artworks of the prewar period and one of her studios during that time was in the garden at 3 Atlantic Street, just around the corner from Sallie.

1 cup finely diced yellow onion (about 1 medium)	1 to 4 slices thick-cut bacon, as needed
1 teaspoon allspice berries, ground fine	¾ cup white wine vinegar, plus more to taste
1 teaspoon freshly ground black pepper, plus more to taste	Low-sodium beef broth (optional)
2 teaspoons kosher salt, plus more to taste	1 cup whole milk
1 (5- to 6-pound) top round or eye-round roast	½ cup all-purpose flour
1 teaspoon canola oil, plus more for brushing	2 tablespoons unsalted butter (optional)

1 Set a rack in the middle of the oven and preheat the oven to 425°F.

2 In a small bowl, mix the onion thoroughly with the allspice, black pepper, and 1 teaspoon of the salt. Set the roast on a large cutting board (both a top round roast and an eye-round will tell you which side is up), and using a paring knife, cut 1½-inch-wide slits 1½ inches deep into the surface of the roast in evenly

(recipe continues)

spaced intervals, leaving only the bottom side of the roast uncut (you should make 12 to 16 cuts). Stuff each of these cuts with the onion mixture, sticking your index finger into them to open them up and facilitate stuffing. (This will be a messy, unscientific process; much of the onion mixture will fall out onto the cutting board and/or stick to the surface of the roast; that is fine. You may also have leftover onion mixture; reserve it to add to the skillet in step 4). Brush any stray pieces of onion from the surface of the roast and let them fall to the cutting board. Brush the roast all over with some canola oil, and season it with the remaining teaspoon salt.

3 Pour the teaspoon of canola oil into a 12-inch cast-iron skillet over high heat and brush it around the pan evenly to coat. When the pan is hot—a small drop of water will hiss and dance vigorously in it—brown the roast on all sides, starting with any surface that may have a layer of fat on it, about 2 minutes per side. Transfer the beef to a 13 by 9-inch roasting pan fitted with a flat rack, draping the bacon over any surfaces of the roast that don't have a layer of fat clinging to them.

4 Add any leftover onion mixture to the fat in the skillet and cook until translucent but not browned, about 2 minutes. Pour the vinegar into the pan to deglaze it, and remove from the heat. With a spoon, scrape any browned bits from the bottom of the skillet, and pour the contents of the skillet into the roasting pan. Add 3 cups of water to the roasting pan.

5 Transfer the roast to the oven and immediately decrease the oven temperature to 250°F. Roast for 30 minutes per pound, until a meat thermometer inserted into the center reads 130°F (for medium-rare), 2½ to 3 hours. Transfer the beef to a cutting board and tent with foil. Let rest for 10 minutes before serving.

6 Meanwhile, strain the cooking liquid through a fine-mesh strainer or cheesecloth into a measuring cup. You should have about 3 cups. Pour the liquid into the skillet you used to brown the roast and taste it. If you prefer to serve it as a simple *jus,* simply season to taste with salt and vinegar (conversely, if the *jus* is too assertively seasoned, add the beef broth and bring to a simmer). To make a thicker gravy, add the milk, and when the liquid simmers, whisk in the flour, stirring until the gravy thickly coats the back of a spoon and no raw flour taste remains, about 3 minutes. If the gravy is still sharp, whisk in the butter, and season to taste with salt and black pepper.

7 Remove the bacon from the roast and chop into small dice to serve as a garnish, if desired. With a carving knife, cut the roast thinly into slices and serve with spoonfuls of jus or gravy and the morsels of bacon.

BAKED CITY HAM WITH PLUM GLAZE   SERVES: 24 TO 26

TIME: 4 HOURS 45 MINUTES

Like most Southerners, we're partial to the intense flavors of a country ham, the kind that's dry-cured in salt and sugar for several weeks, then smoked for another few weeks, then aged for months, losing water weight until it's super-concentrated and salty. But there's another type—a brined ham (sometimes called "city ham")—that is soaked or injected with a brine of water, salt, and sugar before being cooked and then smoked for just a few hours. We see plenty of these glazed brined hams on Charleston tables nowadays, and we're happy when we do: they're delicious, and they make a showstopping preparation for crowds—at Easter, Thanksgiving, and family reunions.

These city hams are almost too easy to prepare. It is fully cooked, so all that's required is a sweet, spicy glaze, brushed on during the last hour of reheating. A glaze is optional—but desired, since it will provide a deliciously spicy, sweet, aromatic counterpoint to the brininess of the pork.

A note on carving: you don't need a special knife to carve a ham, though you'll want to choose the longest, sharpest one you've got. Put the ham on a cutting board, and starting at the narrower shank end, make vertical cuts perpendicular to the bone, about ¼ inch thick. Continue to slice until you have several servings' worth. Then cut horizontally, along the bone, to release all the slices you've made. Once you've sliced through that entire side, you can turn the ham and proceed in similar fashion on the other side.

1 (15- to 17-pound) bone-in, fully cooked, whole brined ham

1 tablespoon whole cloves

1 tablespoon unsalted butter

½ cup chopped shallots (1 large)

1 heaping tablespoon fresh thyme, or 1 teaspoon dried

Kosher salt

2 cups chicken broth

8 ounces pitted dried plums (aka prunes), quartered

2 tablespoons Dijon mustard

2 tablespoons cider vinegar, or red or white wine vinegar

1 Set an oven rack in the lower third of the oven and preheat the oven to 325°F.

2 Put the ham on a cutting board flat side down and score the rounded side all over with diagonal cuts about 1½ inches apart and ¼ inch deep, forming a diamond pattern. In the center of each diamond, insert a single clove.

3 Put the ham in a roasting pan and bake for 3 hours.

4 While the ham bakes, prepare the glaze: Melt the butter in a small saucepan over medium heat until frothy and add the shallots, thyme, and ¼ teaspoon salt. Cook, stirring, until the shallots are soft and fragrant, but not brown, about 3 minutes. Add the chicken broth and the prunes, and bring to a boil. Turn off the heat, cover, and let stand for 10 minutes. Transfer the contents of the saucepan to a food processor, add the mustard and vinegar, and process until smooth. Season to taste with salt.

5 Remove the ham from the oven and remove the cloves; brush the ham all over with the glaze. Return the ham to the oven and continue to bake, glazing the ham once or twice more until a meat thermometer inserted into the thickest part reads 135°F, about 3 to 5 minutes per pound, or 45 minutes to 1 hour 15 minutes longer. Remove the ham from the oven, tent with aluminum foil, and let rest for 10 minutes before carving.

THE GUINEA FOWL OF LAMBOLL STREET

NO ONE KNOWS where they came from, and no one seems particularly concerned where they may end up. In the summer of 2010, a breeding pair of guinea hens appeared in the backyards and alleys around the intersection of Lamboll and Legare Streets, just a few blocks from the Battery, at the end of the Charleston peninsula. The birds, each about the size of a basketball, range freely from backyard to backyard, wallowing in the dirt under the azaleas, pecking in the grass, roosting in the camellias and larger shrubs, and shrieking at high decibel whenever a person or predator gets too close for comfort.

Domesticated "helmeted" guinea fowl (*Numida meleagris*), native to Africa, were actually a common sight in the back alleys and gardens downtown in the eighteenth and nineteenth centuries (as were other domesticated birds, such as chickens, geese, and peacocks), but feathered livestock has been scarce in urban Charleston since the 1960s. Guinea hens prefer not to fly but will do so if required, and can cover long distances; it is possible they migrated here from a farm outside of town. However the guinea hens may have arrived, they landed in perfect terrain—a sheltered, quiet locale with plenty of water and bugs, and little competition. (Having survived over two years in this area, they apparently have nothing to fear from the neighborhood dogs and cats, nor from the many red-tailed hawks and peregrine falcons that call urban Charleston home.)

Some residents enjoy the guinea hens' presence enough to feed them cracked corn, and the birds have become progressively less skittish over the year that we've observed them. The female deposits pretty, buff-colored eggs in the hedgerows, but rarely sits on them, and so a few curious neighbors have incubated and hatched more guineas and are raising them in pens in their backyards. As yet, no one has fessed up to cooking one.

WILD DUCK, OPERA STYLE   SERVES: 4

TIME: 8 TO 12 HOURS MARINATING, 1 HOUR 45 MINUTES COOKING

A three-act preparation of wild waterfowl—parboiling, frying, then braising, with the boiling liquid from Act I reuniting with the birds in the final act—is a drama familiar to many of the most significant Charleston cookbooks, and to other game-centric Lowcountry cookbooks as well. The technique tenderizes and moistens these worldly little birds, and firms up the texture of the delicious skin while making the most of the flavor trapped in the bones (and of what little fat there is on a wild duck). This technique also produces the most luscious, concentrated gravy. For good measure, we preface the entire performance with a tenderizing buttermilk brine overnight.

There are plenty of waterfowl hunters in Charleston who live for that chilly, damp November day in the great outdoors, but we're content to sleep in on Saturday mornings and get cooking in March, when our friends' freezers are packed solid with dressed ducks and with venison—and their spouses are eager to give these treats away, to make room. And for the low entry price, we have the liberty to truly experiment. A recent session led us to embrace this thyme-, chile-, and ginger-inflected version, which we developed to make the most of the basic 1- to 1½-pound ring-necked duck, wood duck, or teal.

The recipe generates a fantastic aroma, not unlike that of an heirloom Thanksgiving turkey midroast, and the duck breast will appear like turkey thigh in its dark richness (though here the goal is three or four perfect bites, not a feast-until-naptime experience). You may be tempted to substitute giant farm-raised ducks in this recipe, but please don't bother; make instead our Duck with Raspberries and Rosé, from *The Lee Bros. Simple Fresh Southern*.

Serve this dish with Dirty Rice and Greens (page 113), with Brussels Sprouts with Benne and Bacon (page 115), or with a simple Hoppin' John (page 91) to absorb the gravy.

3 or 4 dressed ducks, 4 to 4½ pounds total	1 ounce fresh ginger (about 2 inches), peeled and minced
1 quart whole or low-fat buttermilk	1 habañero chile, seeded and minced
2 tablespoons kosher salt	2 cups chicken broth
4 large sprigs thyme	1 cup dry white wine
½ cup (1 stick) unsalted butter	1 teaspoon freshly ground black pepper
¼ cup all-purpose flour	4 slices thick-cut bacon
2 cups chopped yellow onion (about 2 medium)	1 cup peanut or canola oil

1 The day before the meal, rinse the ducks, removing any remaining pin feathers, and put them in one or two large resealable plastic bags. Whisk the buttermilk with 1 tablespoon plus 1 teaspoon salt, and pour into the bag (or bags, dividing proportionally) with 2 sprigs of the thyme. Marinate overnight in the refrigerator. When ready to cook, drain the birds and pat dry, discarding the marinade.

2 In the bottom of a 9- to 12-quart stockpot or Dutch oven, melt the butter over medium-low heat and then add the flour, stirring constantly with a wooden spoon until the flour and butter meld and froth. Continue stirring for 4 to 6 minutes more, until the paste begins to turn golden. As soon as the roux darkens to the color of milky coffee, add the onion, ginger, the remaining 2 sprigs thyme, and the chile, and cook, stirring, until the butter appears to be absorbed and the onion begins to release liquid and become translucent, 6 to 8 minutes.

3 Put the ducks breast side up on top of the onion layer, and pour in the broth, wine, and 2 cups of water (the birds won't be entirely covered). Bring to a simmer over medium-high heat. Simmer for 10 minutes, and then turn the birds so their backs face up. Cook for 10 minutes more and then turn breast side up again. The skin should appear taut and any pink should be gone; if any remains, cook another 5 minutes. Note: we find it's best to turn the ducks end over end rather than barrel-rolling them; the latter often makes a bigger mess and causes more strain on the skin. Remove the birds to a platter and sprinkle them all over with the remaining 2 teaspoons salt and the black pepper.

4 Continue to simmer the broth on low, uncovered, stirring occasionally.

5 Meanwhile, in a separate Dutch oven or pot big enough to hold the ducks, fry the strips of bacon over medium-high heat, turning occasionally, until crispy; remove the bacon and reserve for another use. Add the oil to the bacon fat in the pan, and when it shimmers, brown the ducks on all sides in batches, taking care not to crowd the pan, 2 to 3 minutes per side. When all the ducks are nicely browned, transfer them to a platter and drain all but about 1 tablespoon of the fat from the pan. (If cooking these for a dinner party, this is a natural pause in the preparation; the oil, the birds, and the broth can stay warm for about an hour, until you've prepared your other dishes. The balance of the recipe takes about 30 minutes.)

6 Return the ducks to the Dutch oven. Strain and measure the simmering broth. Add about 4 cups of the simmering broth to the pan, or enough so the liquid comes halfway up the side of the ducks. Cover, bring to a simmer, and then maintain a low simmer for 20 minutes, turning them end over end twice during this time.

7 Remove the ducks to a carving board and tent with foil, allowing them to rest for 5 minutes. To serve, carve each breast and leg in a single piece, and place the two pieces on the plate. Add any meaty shreds you can pick from the rib cage and thighs to each portion. Pour the pan gravy into a gravy boat, skim some of the oil from the top, and pour the gravy generously over each portion.

DESSERTS

TWENTIETH-CENTURY CHARLESTONIANS DIDN'T SEEM TO WEAR their sweet teeth on their sleeves—the most important desserts were the scrumptious but homely Huguenot Torte (page 215) and the subtle sesame goodness of Sweet Benne Wafers (page 221). Today, we seek inspiration in the older cookbooks, those published in the eighteenth and nineteenth centuries, where we find a profusion of fascinating ideas and flavors.

This chapter includes the classics—Caramel Cake (page 223) and Peach Leather (page 210) round out that group—and because we're restless, prone to playing around the kitchen, we couldn't resist teaching familiar ingredients a few new tricks. Sorghum Marshmallows (page 217) is the latest salvo in our quest to vanquish flavorless corn syrup from the pastry kitchen in favor of richly flavored Southern syrups. We are confident that these are the greatest marshmallows you've ever tasted (perfect for topping your Thanksgiving sweet potatoes, page 103). And Pineapple Cornbread Pudding (page 212)? The route to that inspired dish was circuitous: up north of the city a few miles, to Moncks Corner, and down south to Beaufort—read on to find out why.

With publication of this Desserts chapter, we hope to bring back silky, sophisticated Syllabub (page 206). We find it in so many old cookbooks and histories, and yet never on dinner tables. Another revival in the making: Groundnut Cakes (page 211), more delicious than any peanut butter cookie you've ever tasted; they deserve to return to the streets of Charleston—where they were sold by street vendors until the mid-twentieth century. Food truck operators, are you listening?

ESTHER KRAWCHECK'S AND AGNES JENKINS' CHEESECAKE SERVES: 12

TIME: 2 HOURS 30 MINUTES, INCLUDING BAKING, 20 MINUTES COOLING TIME

Esther Bielsky Krawcheck and her husband, Jack, were prominent Charlestonians in the twentieth century, for their generosity to Brith Sholom Beth Israel Synagogue (the oldest Ashkenazi synagogue in continuous existence in the United States), for their vivacious personalities, and for the men's clothing shop that Mr. Krawcheck founded, fitting tens of thousands of men over many generations for Harris Tweeds and seersuckers from 1922 until 1995 (about the time national chains like Brooks Brothers and J. Crew moved to King Street). We remember purchasing our first pairs of khakis at Jack Krawcheck, along with light blue oxford shirts, to wear to seventh grade—this was the unofficial uniform for many Charleston boys and men from that age until the grave.

Mrs. Krawcheck's cheesecake recipe, which was published in *Charleston Receipts,* was a collaboration with Agnes Jenkins, who cooked for the Krawcheck family from the time of Jack and Esther's marriage until after both had died. The recipe caught our attention because of its creamy, flanlike lightness and its perfectly understated sweetness. A cheesecake that is not dense and cloying allows toppings like fruit syrups and preserves (such as the raspberry topping included here and dark caramels like corn syrup and sorghum) to redound positively, to tie the dessert together instead of sending it over the edge. We made a few tweaks to their recipe and fiddled with the technique, but the end result is virtually the same: this is a cheesecake for adults, one you can eat three slices of, gladly (and not feel a tinge of remorse that you did).

Feel free to buck the cold cheesecake pattern and to serve this one warm from the oven; its buttermilk-like sourness and exquisite flavor will be all the more apparent.

2 tablespoons unsalted butter, melted, plus more for the pan

¾ cup graham cracker crumbs (2 to 3 ounces, or 5 full sheets of crackers), ground medium-fine in a food processor

¾ cup plus 3 tablespoons sugar

5 (8-ounce) packages cream cheese, at room temperature

4 large eggs yolks

3 tablespoons all-purpose flour

Kosher salt

¾ cup heavy cream

4 large egg whites

6 ounces fresh raspberries

1 Butter the sides and bottom of a 9-inch springform pan. In a bowl, mix the graham cracker crumbs with 2 tablespoons of the sugar and stir with a fork to combine. Add the melted butter and toss with a fork until the butter has evenly moistened the crumb mixture (take the opportunity to break up any larger crumbs during this process). Scatter the crumbs evenly into the pan and press into it using the bottom of a straight-sided glass to create an even layer on the bottom of the pan.

2 Set a rack in the middle of the oven and preheat the oven to 500°F.

3 With an electric hand-mixer, beat the cream cheese in the bowl with the egg yolks until the cheese is soft and fluffy and the egg evenly blended in, about 2 minutes. Mix the flour with ¾ cup of the sugar and ¼ teaspoon salt, and add to the cheese, blending well with the mixer. Add the cream to the batter and beat until thoroughly blended. Whip the egg whites to soft peaks and fold into the cream cheese mixture with a spatula until it's even and elastic.

(recipe continues)

4 Transfer the batter to the crust-prepared pan, smoothing it down, and bake for 15 minutes. Decrease the oven temperature to 200°F and bake for 1 hour. Turn off the oven, leave the door ajar, and let the cheesecake cool in the oven for 30 minutes (though you can skip this step if you don't have time).

5 Heat the raspberries, the remaining 1 tablespoon sugar, and 2 pinches of salt in a small pan over medium heat, stirring frequently, until the raspberries release some liquid and begin to break down. Remove from the heat, and let cool to room temperature.

6 Cool the cheesecake on a rack for 20 minutes, then serve with the topping, or refrigerate the cake before serving if you prefer the cheesecake cold.

SYLLABUB WITH ROSEMARY-GLAZED FIGS

SERVES: 4   TIME: 1 HOUR 15 MINUTES, INCLUDING CHILLING

Syllabub is a supremely simple and decadent dessert; it's essentially fortified wine (Madeira, sherry, or Marsala) whisked with heavy cream. It came to Charleston with English settlers in the 1700s, and was a fashionable dessert among well-to-do families in the Lowcountry until the early twentieth century. We find references to it, not only in cookbooks—from Sarah Rutledge's *The Carolina Housewife* (1847) to *Charleston Receipts* (1950)—but also in books like Laura Witte Waring's *The Way It Was in Charleston*. Waring's memoir is an unusual portrait of domestic life in Charleston in the years just after the Civil War. Waring was the daughter of a wealthy German immigrant and his wife, whose family escaped the vicissitudes of civil war by moving back to Germany, where they prospered. Upon returning to Charleston, they were among the city's wealthiest residents; the mansion and gardens they built in 1816 are now Ashley Hall, a girls' day school. Waring describes the pride with which her mother—and *only* her mother; no one else was entrusted with the task—made syllabub.

In spite of that, we've never been served this dessert in Charleston—neither in a restaurant nor in a private home—not *once*! And we have no clue why: it's as easy to make as whipped cream, beyond delicious, and a perfectly elegant accompaniment for fruit. Syllabub was typically served in specialized silver-and-glass cups with a spoon and a straw, and a sprig of rosemary for garnish, but we prefer to top it with fresh figs that have been quartered and tossed in a light rosemary simple syrup.

We hope Syllabub comes back in style. It's the kind of uncomplicated and yet slightly surprising dessert we enjoy at the end of a Charleston dinner with all the trimmings.

SYLLABUB

½ cup Sercial Madeira or Amontillado sherry

Peel of ½ lemon

1 tablespoon fresh lemon juice

1½ tablespoons sugar

Pinch of kosher salt

1 cup heavy cream, cold

ROSEMARY-GLAZED FIGS

½ cup sugar

2 (3-inch) long sprigs rosemary

Pinch of kosher salt

4 ounces fresh figs (about 4 large), stemmed and quartered

1 Make the syllabub: Put all syllabub ingredients except for the cream into a large bowl, and whisk until the sugar has dissolved, about a minute. Let stand in the fridge, about 1 hour.

2 Make the rosemary-glazed figs: Heat the sugar and ¼ cup of water water in a small saucepan over medium heat, stirring until the sugar dissolves. Add the rosemary and the salt, stir for about 30 seconds to dissolve the salt and bruise the rosemary, and turn off the heat. Cover and let cool to room temperature, about 20 minutes.

3 Put the figs in a small bowl, drizzle 2 to 3 tablespoons of the rosemary syrup over them, and toss gently to coat. (If the figs are less than ripe, let them stand in the syrup for 30 minutes to sweeten.) Reserve the remaining syrup for another use, such as sweetening lemonade.

4 Remove the lemon peel from the wine mixture. Pour the cream into the wine and whisk by hand until the cream is thick and holds its shape, about 2 minutes. Divide the syllabub among four wine glasses or sundae cups and spoon the rosemary-glazed figs over each serving.

GRAPEFRUIT CHESS PIE   SERVES: 6   TIME: 1 HOUR 10 MINUTES

Crazy-delicious citrus is one of the city's unheralded food assets. We've never heard a Charlestonian go long in praising the scrappy, yard varieties of kumquat, lemon, lime, orange, and grapefruit trees; typically they just pick them in the garden to keep them from mucking up the grass and hand them out to neighbors who appreciate the exotic flavors found in noncommercial citrus.

But some Charlestonians with a taste for citrus will venture onto other people's property to get them. Our friend Will has a thing for citrus trees (pomegranates, bananas, and olives also grow downtown). He recently took us on a citrus-trespassers tour of Charleston, through side yards on Line Street and front yards on Rutledge Avenue, clambering up into boughs and throwing the quarry down to us (as we prayed we wouldn't find ourselves looking down the barrel of a shotgun). Like many real-estate obsessed Charlestonians, Will has a nose for properties that are for sale—and also unoccupied.

Fortunately for us, our friend Anne has a mature grapefruit tree and a prolific kumquat in her yard as well, not far from our test kitchen. Anne and her husband, Mason, are beyond generous with their fruit; we insisted they sample this delicious pie, made from their grapefruit.

And this is probably the best policy: if you see something edible that you want on property that's not yours, offer the owner a bottle of loquat cordial, a batch of mulberry muffins, a fig cake for the privilege. They'd be crazy not to say yes.

2 grapefruits

¾ teaspoon kosher salt

3 large egg whites

2 large egg yolks

½ cup heavy cream, at room temperature

4 tablespoons (½ stick) unsalted butter, melted

1 cup sugar

3 tablespoons all-purpose flour

2 tablespoons fine cornmeal, plus more for sprinkling

1 prebaked (9-inch) pie crust (preferably brushed with 1 egg yolk before baking)

Sweetened whipped cream, for garnish (optional)

1 Set a rack in the top third of the oven and preheat the oven to 300°F.

2 Finely grate the zest of 1 of the grapefruits (you should have 1 teaspoon loosely packed grapefruit zest). Segment the grapefruits (see page 93) over a bowl to preserve the juice. Squeeze the core of pith over the bowl to extract the juice from any remaining pulp. Gently strain the segments, reserving the segments and juice separately. (You should have 1 scant cup grapefruit segments and about ⅓ cup juice; reserve any excess for another use.) Whisk the zest and salt into the grapefruit juice.

3 In a large bowl, whisk the egg whites and yolks together until they're light and creamy in color, then whisk in the cream and melted butter. In a medium bowl, mix the sugar, flour, and cornmeal. Add the dry ingredients to the egg mixture in thirds, whisking after each addition. Stir in the grapefruit juice until thoroughly combined.

4 Pour the filling into the pie crust. Arrange the grapefruit segments artfully in the custard, adding them gently to the top of the pie so they float on the surface. Carefully transfer the pie to the oven rack and bake until the top has nicely browned and the pie surface jiggles stiffly—but does not undulate—when you pull the oven rack, 40 to 45 minutes. Cool completely on a rack, about 10 minutes, before serving with the whipped cream, if using.

PEACH LEATHER   MAKES: ABOUT 30 SERVINGS

TIME: 45 MINUTES, PLUS 2 TO 3 DAYS COOLING AND DRYING

From the early 1800s until recently (the mid-1990s), peach leather was popular in Charleston, a confection sold alongside the benne wafers (page 221) and cheese straws at specialty stores like Harold's Cabin. Very few made peach leather at home, since it was understood to require a large slab of marble and a great deal of elbow grease, to pulverize and liquefy the fruit. Then peach leather vanished altogether.

We've discovered that in the era of electric food processors, this tangy and delicious sun-dried fruit treat is actually quite easy to make, and we've enjoyed finding new applications for its concentrated flavor and addictive texture. Recipes for peach leather were published in *The Carolina Housewife, 200 Years of Charleston Cooking,* and *Charleston Receipts,* and all of those call for a steep proportion of sugar, about 1 quart for every 4 quarts of peaches, which produces a stiff leather but is unnecessarily sweet; 1 part sugar to 8 parts peaches will do very well when lemon juice is in the mix. We've calibrated this recipe for 4 half-sheet pans but if you find yourself a pan or two short, just put into service every ceramic plate, platter, enameled baking pan, and cookie sheet you may have on hand. An electric dehydrator may perform a similar trick on peach puree, but we prefer the slow, gentle effect of fresh air and solar energy on our South Carolina peaches. May the sun shine!

5 pounds medium-ripe peaches (about 16 peaches)

2 cups lightly packed light brown sugar

¼ cup fresh lemon juice (from about 2 lemons)

1 teaspoon kosher salt

3 tablespoons coconut or canola oil, or nonstick spray

2 tablespoons granulated white sugar

1 Remove the pits and stems from the peaches (but leave the skins on). Process on the highest setting in a food processor, in batches if necessary, until they become a smooth, creamy-orange liquid. You should have about 3 quarts.

2 Pour the purée into a 4-quart pot over medium-high heat, add the brown sugar, lemon juice, and salt, and stir well to combine. Stir frequently until the mixture begins to bubble and boil, about 10 minutes, and then constantly for exactly 3 minutes. Turn off the heat, and allow to cool to room temperature on the stove. Chill, covered in the refrigerator, overnight. (The purée will keep for about 3 days.)

3 Lightly but thoroughly grease 4 sheet pans with coconut oil, and then ladle about 2½ cups of purée (for a 13 × 18-inch pan; about 1½ cups for a 9 × 13-inch pan) down the middle of each pan. Tilt the pan forward, backward, left, and right until the purée is an even layer, about the thickness of four credit cards (adding more purée if necessary). Pour any leftover purée into whatever glazed or glass plates or pie pans you may have handy, lightly brushed with oil.

4 Set the pans in direct sunlight on a level surface for as long as possible on day 1, moving them to remain in the sun, if necessary; overnight, set a low fan on the sheets indoors. On day 2, repeat the sun worship (NB: make no attempt to shield the leather from airborne "fallout"; instead excise any insects later, once the leather has set). Test the leather at the edge of one pan by lifting with the tip of a knife and pulling up and away with your fingers. If the leather doesn't pull away cleanly, continue to dry in the sun and indoors.

5 Once the leathers are ready, lightly dust with granulated sugar to keep the leather from sticking to itself, and then cut into 1½-inch-wide strips about 6 inches long. Roll each strip, and cluster the rolls in a shallow rimmed dish or ramekin. Store uncut leathers between sheets of waxed paper in a zippered plastic bag for up to 4 weeks.

GROUNDNUT CAKES   MAKES: ABOUT 36 COOKIES

TIME: 1 HOUR 30 MINUTES IF USING RAW PEANUTS, 1 HOUR IF USING ROASTED PEANUTS

Groundnut" is the term that, up until the twentieth century, was used to refer to peanuts, *Arachis hypogaea,* a member of the legume family, which also includes lentils and peas. Throughout the 1800s and until the middle of this century, small cookies, or "cakes," made from roasted groundnuts were sold by vendors on the streets of downtown. Nowadays, groundnut cakes are rare, if not extinct, in Charleston—Sweet Benne Wafers (page 221) have become most folks' go-to cookie—and their disappearance makes little sense. These cakes are a pleasure to make and extraordinarily addictive, especially if you use raw peanuts and roast them yourself. But note: if you opt for this method, raw peanuts are most often found in the shell, with skins still on, and you'll need to shell them and skin them after roasting, which can be a challenge to do one peanut at a time. This is how we winnow the skins from our home-roasted peanuts: Plug a hair dryer into a kitchen socket. Chop the roasted peanuts coarsely so the skins loosen from the nuts. Transfer the chopped peanuts and skins to a bowl, and pour them in a stream from a height into another to bowl while the hair dryer is trained on the stream of peanuts. (You may have to adjust the velocity of the hair dryer's airstream or its distance, so that it blows out only the skins and not the peanuts!) Don't forget to sweep up the skins from the kitchen floor, if you're crazy enough to winnow indoors.

Of course, you may simply use store-bought roasted peanuts that have already been shelled and skinned, and make your life a lot easier! Either way, serve these cookies with tea, as an after-dinner snack, or as an accompaniment to a frozen dessert.

1 cup raw peanuts or roasted, shelled, and skinned peanuts

3 large egg whites

1 cup tightly packed brown sugar

½ cup all-purpose flour

½ teaspoon kosher salt

1 Preheat the oven to 350°F.

2 If using prepared peanuts, coarsely chop the peanuts, reserve, and skip to step 3. If using raw peanuts, spread them on a large rimmed baking sheet and roast for 20 minutes, until the peanuts are fragrant and gently browned. Transfer to a colander or strainer to cool, and if the peanuts have skins, remove them as indicated in the headnote.

3 Whisk the egg whites to soft peaks, and fold in the brown sugar, flour, salt, and peanuts. With a teaspoon, drop the batter onto parchment-lined cookie sheets and bake until firm and gently browned, 20 minutes. Remove from the oven and with a thin metal spatula, transfer to a rack to cool. (Groundnut cakes will keep about 4 days in a sealed container at room temperature.)

PINEAPPLE CORNBREAD PUDDING SERVES: 6 TIME: 1 HOUR

From nineteenth-century travelers' accounts of the Charleston market, we know that pineapples imported from Cuba were sold there for fifteen cents apiece. And we know from early South Carolina cookbooks that some folks in the Lowcountry preserved them or made sweetmeats—crystallized confections—from pineapples. But aside from the canned pineapple slices that garnish holiday hams, we've rarely encountered a Charleston recipe that celebrates this tropical fruit. So, we were thrilled to learn about a pineapple concoction at a book signing in Moncks Corner just north of Charleston.

Several members of a book club there inquired why we didn't have a recipe for a pineapple casserole in our books. Short answer: we'd never heard of it! Our hostess offered us her own very simple recipe for the dish: sugar, butter, and eggs whisked together with cubed white bread and canned pineapple, spread in a baking dish, and baked until the bread on top browns. It sounded to us like a variant of bread pudding, but we were assured that this casserole was *not* dessert but, rather, a side dish for holiday savories like baked ham or roast turkey.

Our natural inclination is to keep savories and sweets in separate courses, so we got to thinking about a pineapple bread pudding. And then, the following week, we traveled south of Charleston, to Beaufort, where we encountered a fantastic cornbread pudding at Breakwater Restaurant, and the phase shift was complete: this Pineapple Cornbread Pudding is the perfect dessert for bringing a touch of fanfare to the conclusion of a casual supper with friends.

Skillet Cornbread (recipe follows), cut into 1¼-inch cubes (about 5 cups)

2 cups small-dice fresh pineapple chunks

1½ cups heavy cream

⅓ cup whole milk

6 tablespoons plus 1 teaspoon sugar

3 large eggs

1 large egg yolk

1 teaspoon pure vanilla extract

½ teaspoon plus a pinch of kosher salt

1 tablespoon dark rum

1 Set a rack in the top third of the oven and preheat the oven to 350°F.

2 In a 2-quart baking dish, arrange 1½ cups of the cornbread cubes, spacing the pieces evenly apart. Spread 1 cup of the pineapple into the dish, spreading evenly in the spaces between the cubes. Add another 1½ cups of the cornbread cubes spaced evenly apart, followed by a second layer of the pineapple. (Reserve leftover cornbread for another use.)

3 Pour 1 cup of the cream and the milk into a large bowl, add 6 tablespoons of the sugar, and stir to dissolve, about 1 minute. Add the eggs, egg yolk, vanilla, and ½ teaspoon of the salt, and whisk to combine thoroughly. Pour the egg mixture slowly into the pan around its edge, and gently agitate the dish to distribute the custard evenly. Transfer to the oven, and bake on the top rack until the bread cubes on top are gently browned in places and the pudding parts in the center have gelled, about 40 minutes.

4 In a large bowl, whip the remaining ½ cup cream with the rum, the remaining teaspoon sugar, and the remaining pinch of salt, until the cream is stiff and holds its shape. Reserve in the refrigerator.

5 Let the bread pudding cool on a rack for 10 minutes. Serve warm or at room temperature with dollops of the rum whipped cream.

SKILLET CORNBREAD
SERVES: 6 TIME: 30 MINUTES

1 tablespoon lard or unsalted butter

¾ cup cornmeal

¾ cup all-purpose flour

1 teaspoon baking powder

1 teaspoon baking soda

½ teaspoon kosher salt

1 teaspoon sugar

1 large egg

1½ cups buttermilk, preferably whole

2 tablespoons unsalted butter

1 Preheat the oven to 450°F. Grease a 12-inch cast-iron skillet with the lard, leaving any excess in the pan, and place it in the oven.

2 In a large bowl, sift the dry ingredients together. In a medium bowl, whisk the egg until frothy and then whisk in the buttermilk. Add the wet ingredients to the dry ones and mix thoroughly. Melt the butter in a small skillet over low heat, and then whisk the butter into the batter.

3 When the fat in the skillet is smoking, carefully remove the skillet from the oven and swirl the fat around to coat the bottom and sides evenly. Pour the batter into the skillet; it should sizzle alluringly. Bake for 15 minutes, or until the top of the bread is golden brown and the edge has pulled away from the side of the skillet. Remove the skillet from the oven. Invert the cornbread onto a board, to cut and serve immediately with butter, or invert onto a rack to cool completely.

A ST. MICHAEL'S CHURCH GATE.

HUGUENOT TORTE

SERVES: 6 TO 8   **TIME: 55 MINUTES, 10 MINUTES COOLING**

Imagine that a blondie and an apple-pecan pie got into a crusty-gooey, sticky-delicious accident in a baking dish, and you'll approximate the ultra-decadence of this dessert. Until relatively recently, Charlestonians believed that this confection, as the title might suggest, came to Charleston with the French Huguenots, who settled in the city in the eighteenth century, and that it was a rustic cousin of elegant *pâtisseries*. But in the 1990s, the culinary historian and Lowcountry native John Martin Taylor tracked down the woman to whom the recipe is attributed in *Charleston Receipts,* and learned that she'd encountered the dish as "Ozark Pudding" while visiting relatives in Arkansas in the 1940s. She had brought the recipe back to Charleston, and put the dessert on the menu of the Huguenot Tavern, where she was a cook.

The fact that this dessert has become as much an icon of Charleston home cooking as Charleston Okra Soup (page 74) and She-Crab Soup (page 77) seems odd—but it's all part of "Charleston's food pattern," as May A. Pyatt wrote in a 1950 review of *Charleston Receipts* in the *News and Courier.* Another interesting note: not many Charleston restaurants these days offer the torte—or even variants upon it—but it is almost always offered on menus at the tea rooms (see page 79) that open in the spring throughout the area. You should master it yourself; it's easy to make and easy to eat, and nice to have in your repertoire.

When we're serving this dish for guests, we often temper its sweetness by whipping a small amount of buttermilk or sour cream into the whipped cream garnish.

Unsalted butter for greasing the dish

2 large eggs

1⅓ cups sugar

¼ cup all-purpose flour

2½ teaspoons baking powder

¼ teaspoon kosher salt

1 Granny Smith or other tart apple, cored, peeled, and diced (1 cup)

1 cup chopped pecans

1 teaspoon pure vanilla extract

½ cup heavy cream

2 tablespoons whole buttermilk or sour cream

1 Preheat the oven to 325°F. Grease a 2-quart baking dish.

2 In a large bowl, beat the eggs with a whisk until they're creamy and frothy. Add the sugar, flour, baking powder, salt, apple, pecans, and vanilla, whisking to combine after each addition.

3 Pour the batter into the prepared baking dish and bake for 45 minutes, or until the top of the torte is crusty. Remove the torte from the oven and let cool for about 10 minutes.

4 Whip the cream with the buttermilk until stiff peaks form. Cut into individual portions—they will be lumpen and misshapen, with shards of crust and spoonfuls of ooze, but no matter—and serve with dollops of the whipped cream.

PEACH UPSIDE-DOWN SKILLET CAKE

SERVES: 12   TIME: 35 MINUTES COOKING, 35 MINUTES COOLING

This cake is beyond simple, yet impressive and festive—perfect for a casual summer dinner party. We toss wedges of peeled fresh peaches in a small amount of sugar and lemon juice, fan them around the bottom of a skillet, and then pour a vanilla-buttermilk cake batter over them before baking.

When the cake is done, we let it cool in its pan for a half hour. We invert it, and spread the peach surface with lightly sweetened whipped cream. Then we slice the cake. But you could slice it before you top it with whipped cream to give the finished portion on the plate dimension and individuality. Or, alternatively, you could go the à la mode route: let the cake cool in its pan for only 10 minutes, invert while still warm, then top with a scoop of top-notch vanilla or buttermilk ice cream.

4 large, ripe peaches, peeled, pitted, and sliced into wedges

⅓ cup plus 2 tablespoons sugar

1 tablespoon fresh lemon juice

¾ teaspoon kosher salt

2 large eggs

¾ cup whole or low-fat buttermilk

1½ teaspoons pure vanilla extract

4 tablespoons (½ stick) unsalted butter, melted, plus more for greasing the skillet

¾ cup sifted all-purpose flour

1½ teaspoons baking powder

1 Set a rack in the middle of the oven and preheat the oven to 425°F.

2 In a medium bowl, mix the peaches with 1 tablespoon of the sugar, the lemon juice, and ¼ teaspoon of the salt, and toss gently with a spoon until the sugar and salt are mostly dissolved, about 20 seconds.

3 Grease the sides and bottom of a 9-inch ovenproof skillet or deep-dish pie pan with butter, and fan the slices of peach, slightly overlapping, around the bottom of the pan until the pan bottom is covered.

4 Add the eggs to the bowl that contained the peaches (you need not wash the bowl), and beat with a whisk. Pour in the remaining ⅓ cup plus 1 tablespoon sugar, the buttermilk, vanilla, and melted butter, and whisk until completely combined. In a second medium bowl, toss the flour with the baking powder and remaining ½ teaspoon salt until evenly mixed. Add the dry ingredients to the wet ones, and whisk until the batter is smooth, about 30 seconds.

5 Pour the batter slowly and evenly over the fruit, and bake until the top is gently browned and a toothpick or cake tester comes out clean, 20 to 25 minutes. Transfer the skillet or pan to a rack and let cool, about 30 minutes.

6 Run the tip of a knife gently around the edge of the cake to loosen, if necessary. Invert the cake onto a platter and let cool for about 5 minutes before slicing and serving.

SORGHUM MARSHMALLOWS

Whenever we see a dessert recipe that calls for corn syrup, we see an opportunity to electrify the dish with real, flavorful sorghum syrup. This traditional Southern sweetener has a ruddy color and an appetizing, complex flavor (it's squeezed from sorghum, a tall, corn-like plant entirely different from sugar cane). We've performed this trick with pecan pie—you can too!—and here, we do it with simple, homemade marshmallows.

These marshmallows collapse beautifully into the top of a baked sweet potato dish (see Sweet Potatoes with Sorghum Marshmallows, page 103) and, chopped up, make a great addition to an ice-box confection (see Strawberry Delight, page 225). This is a terrific project for expanding your kitchen repertoire while impressing your friends and relatives (especially the kids). Source sorghum online or at a specialty foods store, or use cane syrup, which is more readily available.

3 envelopes (.75 ounce total) unflavored powdered gelatin

1½ cups sugar

1 cup sorghum molasses or cane syrup

¼ teaspoon kosher salt

Unsalted butter, vegetable oil, or nonstick cooking spray for the baking dish and spatula

¼ cup cornstarch

¼ cup confectioners' sugar

1   Pour ½ cup of cold water into the bowl of a standing mixer fitted with the whisk attachment, sprinkle the gelatin powder over the surface of the water, and let stand for about 8 minutes.

2   Meanwhile, in a medium or large saucepan over medium-high heat, combine ½ cup cold water, the sugar, sorghum, and salt. Cover, and cook for 3 to 4 minutes. Uncover, attach a candy thermometer onto the side of the pan, and continue to cook, stirring frequently, until the syrup thickens noticeably and reaches 240°F, 8 to 12 minutes. Once the mixture reaches this temperature, immediately remove from the heat.

3   Turn the mixer on low and slowly pour the sugar syrup down the side of the bowl into the gelatin mixture. Once you have added all the syrup, increase the speed to high. Continue to whip until the mixture becomes lukewarm and very thick (but still pourable), 10 to 15 minutes.

4   While the gelatin mixture whips, butter a 9 by 13-inch baking dish. In a bowl, mix the cornstarch and confectioners' sugar thoroughly with a whisk. Dust the baking dish with the sugar mixture by pouring about half of it into the dish and tilting it over the bowl until all the sides are thinly coated. Return any remaining mixture back to the bowl.

5   Pour the marshmallow batter into the prepared dish, using a lightly greased spatula to pat it evenly in the pan. Dust the top with enough of the remaining sugar and cornstarch mixture to lightly cover and reserve the remainder. Set the dish in a cool, dry place and let it stand, uncovered, until the mass is dry enough to release from the pan, stiffly pliable, and no longer sticky to the touch (8 to 14 hours, depending on the humidity of your kitchen).

6   Dust a cutting board and a pizza wheel or large chef's knife with the remaining sugar mixture. Turn the marshmallow slab onto the board and cut the marshmallow into 1-inch squares (or into batons if topping a baked sweet potato recipe, page 103). Lightly dust all sides of each marshmallow with some of the remaining sugar mixture. Store in an airtight container at room temperature for up to 2 weeks.

MACAROONS

MAKES: ABOUT 50 COOKIES   TIME: 45 MINUTES, PLUS 1 HOUR CHILLING

Middleton Place Plantation (a former rice plantation, now a foundation and historic site) is one of the great accessible plantations on the Ashley River—the other two being Drayton Hall, owned by the National Parks Service, and Magnolia Gardens. Middleton's gardens are dreamy, combining the formality of an English royal spread with the louche naturalism of a Spanish moss–draped country road. The house was burned in the Civil War, though a side building remains. It was in the archive room upstairs that we searched for anything related to the late Edna Lewis's tenure at the Middleton Place restaurant (see page 168).

We turned up little of Edna Lewis, but were introduced by the clever archivists at Middleton to a handwritten "Receipt Book" in their collection, dating to about 1774 and beautifully scripted by Hester Drayton, a sister of Arthur Middleton, a signer of the Declaration of Independence. She married Charles Drayton, of Drayton Hall, in 1774, and likely lived there, just down the road, when she compiled her recipes.

The twenty-page "book" (marked "H. D." on the cover) is so legible and plainly written that one can cook from it today. It is composed almost entirely of recipes for baked goods—"Long Biscuit," "Nun's Cake," "Shrewsbury Cake," "A Caraway Cake without Yeast," to name a few—that suggest English colonial influences.

The macaroons that Drayton included called to us in particular because of their simplicity—combining lightly toasted almonds, egg white, and sugar—and their hint of exoticism: they use orange flower water instead of the usual vanilla as a flavoring. (Coconut in macaroons is a twentieth-century innovation.) Orange flower water, until recently an esoteric ingredient, is now imported in greater volume owing to the flourishing cocktail culture, and especially the drink Ramos Gin Fizz, of which orange flower water is a component.

Having a great macaroon recipe can be handy in Charleston: they are often a building block for other fantastic local confections, especially in ice-box desserts like Strawberry Delight (page 225).

The chewy-crumbly texture of these macaroons is just what you crave, and their flavor is pure and brilliantly understated, a lightly toasted almond sensation kissed with the gentlest tropical breeze.

4 large egg whites, or more if needed	1¼ cups sugar
	⅛ teaspoon kosher salt
2 cups whole unsalted blanched almonds (about 12 ounces)	1 tablespoon orange flower water

1   In a medium bowl, beat the egg whites to soft peaks and reserve. Process the almonds, sugar, and salt in a food processor until the mixture resembles crumbly, damp sugar, about 45 seconds. Add the egg whites and orange flower water and process until smooth and well whipped, about 30 seconds, pushing the sides down as necessary with a spatula. The mixture will resemble warm breakfast cereal. Set the bowl of the food processor in the refrigerator for about 1 hour, until the mixture is cool and firmed, but still moves slightly when the bowl is tipped (add more whipped egg white if it is too stiff).

2   Preheat the oven to 325°F.

3   Arrange heaping teaspoonfuls of the batter on two parchment-covered baking sheets (about 50 drops total), mounding them as vertically as possible and leaving 1½ inches between mounds (they should have a slight tendency to spread). Bake for 20 to 25 minutes, turning the sheets halfway through, and switching the bottom with the top sheet, to even the browning. When done, the tops of the cookies will turn an oatmeal color with golden highlights. Cool slightly, remove the cookies from the parchment to racks, and allow to cool. (Macaroons will keep in an airtight container in the refrigerator for about 1 week.)

MAGNOLIA GARDENS PANCAKE COOKIES

MAKES: 24 COOKIES   TIME: 45 MINUTES

Winslow Hastie, the director of Preservation and Museums at the Historic Charleston Foundation, spent his graduate-school decade in San Francisco, but grew up playing in the back alleys of downtown and out on his family's Ashley River plantation, Magnolia Gardens, one of the first large properties to open its gates to tourism in 1870. Hastie's grandfather, J. Drayton Hastie (whom Winslow describes as the P. T. Barnum of the family), configured the 500-acre property to emphasize the gardens, developed a tram tour and petting zoo, and erected billboards in the area advertising "The Complete Plantation Experience." Winslow and his family are now moving the site toward an even more whole, if less sensationalist, interpretation of a plantation—one that reveals insights about the lives of all the people who lived there, enslaved and free, that draws upon archaeological digs, oral histories, archival material, and historical data.

We sat down with Winslow and the 1950 edition of *Charleston Receipts,* and asked him to identify family recipes. The recipes he flagged (including "Shrimp Remoulade," "Chicken Mousse," and "Pancake Cookies") were all contributed by his great-grandmother, Sara Simons Hastie, who spent her later years between Magnolia Gardens and Roper House, one of Charleston's most exquisite downtown mansions.

Though the spaces she inhabited were lofty, Mrs. Hastie's "Pancake Cookies" couldn't be more down to earth, and plainly delicious. They're a classic sugar cookie, slightly chewy in texture and loaded with pecans, which grow at Magnolia Gardens and throughout the Charleston area (local trees produce buckets of nuts in some years, almost none at all in others). The cookies have a spreading tendency—hence, the pancake descriptor—on the cookie sheet, and you can expect various sizes to result no matter how precise you think you are in portioning out the dough.

½ cup (1 stick) unsalted butter, at room temperature

½ cup loosely packed dark brown sugar

½ cup granulated sugar

1 large egg yolk

1 cup plus 1 tablespoon sifted all-purpose flour

⅛ teaspoon kosher salt

1 cup unsalted pecans, toasted and roughly chopped

1 large egg white

½ teaspoon pure vanilla extract

1 Set a rack in the upper third of the oven and preheat the oven to 350°F.

2 With a standing mixer or hand-mixer, blend the butter and sugars together until smooth and fluffy, 1 to 2 minutes. Add the egg yolk, beating until it's incorporated, then 1 cup of the flour and the salt. Toss the pecans with the remaining tablespoon of flour, and then fold into the dough with a spatula. The dough will appear very dry.

3 In a separate bowl, whip the egg white with the vanilla until it forms stiff peaks, then fold into the dough mixture until thoroughly combined.

4 Line a cookie sheet with parchment paper and prepare a small bowl of ice water. Begin portioning the cookies by taking a heaping tablespoon of the dough, dipping your fingers in the ice water, and then forming the dough into a glossy round patty about ⅛ inch thick between your hands. Place on the parchment about 1 inch from the edge, and repeat, leaving 1½ inches or more space between the cookies. Bake until crisp and browning around the edge and on top, 15 to 20 minutes. Let cool slightly and peel off of the parchment, then set the cookies on a rack to cool further. (Cookies will keep in a sealed container at room temperature about 4 days.)

SWEET BENNE WAFERS

MAKES: ABOUT 120 COOKIES   TIME: 50 MINUTES

The addictive, sweet-n-salty benne (sesame) wafer is probably one of the most popular souvenirs of Charleston. The Colony House Bakery, on King Street, used to create the defining benne wafer for us: crisp, salty, and blonde. Nowadays, however, we've pushed our favorite wafer recipe into lacier territory, adding even more sesame seeds (but less flour) and generating a darker, more caramelized look overall. They are just as addictive but somehow a little more chewy and delicious.

½ cup sesame seeds

¼ cup plus 1 tablespoon all-purpose flour

¾ cup tightly packed light brown sugar

½ teaspoon salt

¼ teaspoon baking soda

2 tablespoons unsalted butter, cold

1 large egg

½ teaspoon pure vanilla extract

1 Preheat the oven to 375°F. Line a cookie sheet with parchment.

2 In a cast-iron skillet, toast the sesame seeds over medium-high heat, stirring them frequently in the pan with a wooden spoon, until they are the color of unpopped popcorn, about 5 minutes. Keep stirring for a minute more after removing from the heat.

3 Sift the flour with the sugar, salt, and baking soda twice. Cut the butter into the dry ingredients with your fingertips or with a pastry blender until the mixture resembles coarse crumbs.

4 Using an electric mixer, beat the egg on medium until it stiffens, about 2 minutes. Add the dry flour mixture in three parts, beating until the batter is consistently smooth and lustrous, about 2 minutes. Add the toasted sesame seeds and vanilla, and beat on low speed just until the seeds are evenly incorporated. Transfer the batter to a pastry bag fitted with a small round tip or to a plastic bag with a tiny piece of its corner cut out.

5 Working in batches of 30, pipe the batter in very small, ¼ teaspoon–size drops about 2 inches apart onto the cookie sheet. Bake until the cookies turn noticeably chestnut-brown and lacy, 4 to 6 minutes. Transfer the cookie sheet to a rack and cool until the cookies have stiffened, about 10 minutes, then transfer to a plate or open container to dry further. Repeat until all the cookies are baked, and let them cool completely before sealing the container. If the first batch isn't crisp enough after 15 minutes of cooling time (they should be slightly chewy), pipe subsequent batches with slightly more batter and bake slightly longer to stiffen them. (Cookies will keep in a sealed container at room temperature about 4 days.)

CARAMEL CAKE

SERVES: 12   TIME: 2 HOURS

Ask any Southern baker: caramel cake can reduce a fully grown adult to tears—and we don't mean happy tears, either. It's the icing, a challenge that makes fiddly pastries seem like a walk in Washington Park. Caramel icing is made from little more than cooked sugar and milk, but when it comes time to spread it over the cake layers, it has to be just the right temperature—warm enough to be pourable, but cool enough that, when you work it around the cake with an icing spatula, it sets in place. If the icing cools too fast, stiffening as you're spreading, you'll tear your beautiful cake layers, which are nigh impossible to repair. And if the icing doesn't cool fast enough, it will overflow the cake stand and onto the counter.

Stressed yet?

Fear not, because we have all you require here—namely, the right recipe with the right instructions so that you know that you're doing the right thing. And we also have some tips, care of our friend Angie Mosier, the Atlanta-based food stylist, writer, and photographer, and also baker of Ted and E.V.'s wedding cake (she also styled the props for the photos in this cookbook).

According to Angie, even accomplished Southern bakers will lay sheets of waxed paper around the cake stand to catch any too-warm icing that may overflow, so that it can be returned to the bowl to cool further (we prefer to ice the cake on a rack set over a sheet pan lined with waxed paper). Angie recommends having a small amount of hot water and an electric hand-mixer nearby as you ice the cake so that, if the icing seems to be cooling too readily and seizing up, you can quickly soften it by adding a teaspoonful of hot water to the bowl and blending it in to loosen it up. And for those times when icing seizes on the cake before you've had a chance to spread it, keep a hair dryer nearby, too, for spot-heating cooled icing.

If you're up to the challenge, this is truly a fun one, and succeeding is its own special achievement. As for the cake that results, that perfect salty caramel icing, with its burnt-sugar crispiness dissolving almost instantly on your tongue . . . it'll bring the happy tears.

CAKE

1 cup (2 sticks) unsalted butter, softened, plus more for the pans

2½ cups sifted all-purpose flour, plus more for the pans

2 teaspoons baking powder

2 teaspoons salt

¼ teaspoon baking soda

2 cups sugar

3 large eggs

2 large egg yolks

2 teaspoons pure vanilla extract

¾ cup whole milk

ICING

1½ cups whole milk

4 cups sugar

10 tablespoons (1¼ sticks) butter

2 teaspoons kosher salt, plus more to taste

1 tablespoon pure vanilla extract

¼ teaspoon baking soda

Hot water

1 Make the cake: Preheat the oven to 350°F. Grease and flour two round 9 by 2-inch cake pans. Pour about a tablespoon of flour into each of the pans and roll it around, tapping as you go, until the sides and bottom are covered completely with a thin layer of flour. Tip the pans, and tap out excess flour.

2 In a large mixing bowl, mix thoroughly with a whisk the flour, baking powder, salt, and baking soda.

3 In a separate large bowl, beat the butter with an electric mixer until creamy, about 30 seconds. Add the sugar in ½-cup measures, beating about 15 seconds after each addition and scraping down the sides of the bowl if necessary, until the mixture has lightened in color and become fluffy, about 2 minutes. Add the eggs and egg yolks, one at a time, and the vanilla, beating for 15 seconds after each addition.

(recipe continues)

4 Add the flour mixture to the butter mixture in thirds, alternating with additions of the milk. To avoid overmixing the batter, mix gently with a wooden spoon or rubber spatula after each addition, until the ingredient is just incorporated. Beat until all the ingredients have been incorporated, and then just a few strokes beyond. Divide the batter between the cake pans and spread the tops evenly.

5 Bake until a cake tester or toothpick emerges clean, about 30 minutes. Remove from the oven and let the cakes cool in their pans on a rack for 10 minutes, then slide a thin paring knife around the edge of the pans, and invert the cakes. Turn each cake again so its rounded top is facing up, and cool the cakes completely on the rack.

6 Make the icing: Pour the milk and 3 cups of the sugar into a large, deep, heavy-bottomed pot over medium-high heat, mixing with a whisk. Add the butter and the salt, whisking occasionally until the butter melts. When mixture just simmers, cut the heat, but keep over the warm burner.

7 Pour the remaining 1 cup sugar into a saucepan. Cook the sugar over medium-high heat until it becomes a syrup, stirring every so often with a wooden spoon as it begins to brown, until the sugar syrup is evenly amber colored, 5 to 8 minutes. Pour the syrup into the warm milk mixture, being very careful, as the caramel will bubble and sputter when it hits the hot milk. Turn the heat beneath the pot to high and, whisking gently until all the syrup has completely dissolved into the roiling milk mixture, continue to cook to the soft-ball stage, about 238°F; this may take 8 to 12 minutes.

8 Cut the heat beneath the caramel and gently whisk in the vanilla and the baking soda. Dip a spoon into the caramel, and let it cool to taste it. Season the caramel to taste with salt, and pour it into the bowl of a standing mixer (or use an electric hand-mixer and a large bowl). Beat on low speed as it cools, 15 to 20 minutes depending on the temperature of your kitchen, until the icing is creamy and thick (between 100°F and 105°F). Remove the bowl from the mixer stand and let cool 5 to 10 minutes more, until the icing is between 95°F and 98°F—it should fall off your spatula in a ribbon that remains discernible on the surface of the icing for 10 seconds.

9 Set the first cake layer on a rack set over a sheet plan lined with waxed paper. Have an electric hand-mixer and the hot water nearby to blend a teaspoon or two into the icing if it becomes too thick to spread. Pour enough of the icing over the cake to cover the top in a layer about ¼ inch thick (if it drips over the edge in places, that's fine; this is an early test of whether it's going to set in place or not). Top the first cake with the second cake layer and pour the rest of the icing in stages over the top of the cake, letting it run down the sides and using an icing spatula to guide the icing around the cake as it drips, until the entire cake is covered, for a traditional, classic look. (If you prefer the dramatic look of cake layers peeking out from behind a curtain of icing drips, by all means choose that route!) If you need to reuse any icing that overflows into the pan, simply move the cake on its rack temporarily, scrape up the icing from the waxed paper with a spatula and return it to the bowl, replace the rack over the pan, and continue to ice the cake.

10 Once the icing has set, using two spatulas carefully transfer the cake from the rack to a cake stand and let stand at room temperature beneath a cake dome until ready to serve. Only refrigerate if you plan to store the cake for more than 2 days.

Churnless, "ice-box" desserts like this one were common in early-twentieth-century Charleston cookbooks, with appetizing names like "Cherry Bisque Ice Cream," "Macaroon-Apricot Ice Cream," and occasionally flights of fancy like "Ravenel Twins Delectable" or "Strawberry Delight." The key was to begin with a base of whipped cream, add lots of things to the blend that inhibit a solid freeze—cookie crumbles, nuts, marshmallows, and alcohol—and to stir at just the point when the block becomes half-crystallized in the freezer to tenderize the matrix by breaking up the crystals. The end result is a close cousin to churned, custard-based ice cream, and with all those add-ins, it offers many opportunities to personalize the dessert and to punch up the flavor.

Something akin to this strawberry delight was the exciting conclusion to a formal midafternoon dinner cooked and served to us by Delores Rivers, the chef at a private plantation on the upper Cooper River. (This region, about thirty miles from downtown, is a haunting, largely undisturbed rural landscape that manages to combine large expanses of private hunting land with massive industrial plants and refineries.) Mrs. Rivers grew up a Lockwood in the Cainhoy community near the plantation and spent ten years living in upper Manhattan, raising two sons, before returning to the area to work here, in a house built in the 1790s.

The present owners could afford any appliances they wished, but the kitchen was classic Old Charleston—nothing ambitious or showy, and yet just so: an electric coil cooktop was crowded with a collection of aluminum cookware by Revere and Wagnerware that would look at home in an Art Deco villa or a postwar suburban ranch. Dishes and serving pieces were stored in a large cabinet original to the house, a mounted moose head hung over the mantelpiece opposite the stove, and an open rack near the entrance to the kitchen held a handful of sporting guns, their double barrels pointing at the ceiling. The aroma of ducks stewing would have completed the picture, though a delicious venison in gravy,

okra pilau, and corn pudding were on the menu that day, all prepared by Mrs. Rivers.

While extremely generous and forthcoming in the face of our many questions that day, both Mrs. Rivers and the owners guarded carefully the secret to that particular strawberry delight, a prized family recipe, and so when we returned home we were obliged to reverse-engineer it as best we could from our memories. We recall Mrs. Rivers's version as a bit more pink, more scoopable, and more gelatinous than ours (perhaps a Cool Whip base?), but the spirit of the original comes through in our facsimile and serves as a platform for other directions you might be inspired to explore, including adding toasted pecans, a different type of crumbled cookie, a different fruit syrup, or a shot of fortified wine. If the latter, soak the macaroons in the wine before adding to the cream.

1 pound fresh strawberries, trimmed and halved	1 cup buttermilk, preferably whole
2/3 cup sugar	12 macaroons (about 5 ounces), homemade (page 218) or store-bought, crumbled to bean-size bits
1 pint heavy cream	
2 pinches of kosher salt	
1 cup half-and-half	

1 Put the strawberries, 1/3 cup of the sugar, and 2 tablespoons of water in a small saucepan and cook over medium-low heat, stirring occasionally, for 20 minutes, until the syrup is glossy-red but still runny. Allow to cool for 20 minutes. You should have 1½ cups fruit and syrup.

2 In a large bowl, whip the cream with the remaining 1/3 cup sugar and the salt until peaks begin to hold their shape. Whisk in the half-and-half, buttermilk,

(recipe continues)

and crumbled macaroons, in that order, until evenly combined (the macaroon crumbles will mostly sink).

3 Line a 3-quart loaf pan with plastic wrap and pour the cream mixture into it. Then pour in the fruit and syrup from one end to the other, but do not stir. Lightly cover the loaf pan with a sheet of plastic wrap and place in the freezer for about 2½ hours (set a timer), by which time the cap of crystallized cream will be about 1 inch thick.

4 Use a broad serving spoon to break up the cream and fold the ingredients together, taking special care to lift the strawberry pulp and macaroon bits up off the bottom, where they will initially have settled. Return the pan to the freezer for 1½ hours. Fold again, freeze for another hour, and fold a third time. There still may be some liquid areas in the loaf pan. Allow to set for 1 more hour and serve. (It will keep in the freezer, covered in plastic wrap, for a week or two.)

5 To serve, scoop individual portions out into bowls; for a crowd, turn the entire loaf upside down onto an oval platter and surround with greenery and flowers, slicing portions from the loaf with a knife—silver, if possible— warmed in hot water.

½   1 Mile

Spring Street

Cannon Street

Ashley

King Street

Meeting Street

East Bay Street

Cooper River

Calhoun   Street

Rutledge Ave.   Street

Avenue

Anson Street

Wentworth

Colonial Lake

North   Market St.

King

Meeting Street

Church Street

CITY HALL

East Bay St.

Broad Street   St.

Tradd Street

Ashley River

Atlantic St.

East Battery

WHITE POINT GARDENS

Downtown
CHARLESTON
WALKING TOUR

DOWNTOWN CHARLESTON WALKING TOUR

1 98 Broad Street, Gaulart et Maliclet Café
(Tomato and Watermelon Gazpacho with Shrimp, p. 80)

2 64 Meeting Street, Huguenin-Coen residence, site of Clementine Paddleford meal
(Charleston Okra Soup, p. 74)

3 3 Atlantic Street, private home, former Elizabeth O'Neill Verner studio
(Boeuf à la Mode, p. 191)

4 1 East Battery, private home, onetime Gian Carlo Menotti encampment
(Gian Carlo's Pasta, p. 112)

5 9 East Battery, private home, Roper House
(Magnolia Gardens Pancake Cookies, p. 219)

6 21 East Battery, Edmondston-Alston House
(Broiled Shad with Shad Roe Mousse, p. 140; Boeuf à la Mode, p. 191)

7 83 East Bay Street, private home, former Lee residence
(Shrimp Supreme, p. 132)

8 142 Church Street, St. Philips Church Parish Hall
(Huguenot Torte, p. 215)

9 54 N. Market Street, site of the original Henry's Restaurant
(Whole Flounder with Sunchoke and Shrimp Stuffing, p. 122,
and Henry's Cheese Spread, p. 47)

10 75 Anson Street, private home, Lee family Thanksgiving site
(Herb-Roasted Turkey with Madeira Gravy, p. 180)

11 390 King Street, Marion Square Farmer's Market
(Butterbeans with Butter, Mint, and Lime, p. 110)

12 57 Cannon Street, Magar Hatworks Studio, mulberry tree
(Mulberry-Glazed Venison Loin, p. 189)

13 213 Ashley Avenue, private home, former Hasselmeyer residence
(Deviled Crab, p. 153)

14 186 Wentworth Street, private home, Lee Bros. test kitchen
(Wentworth Street Crab Meat, p. 127)

CHARLESTON AND ENVIRONS DRIVING TOUR

1. 1851 Sol Legare Road, Backman Seafood
   (Conch Fritters, p. 150)

2. *4300 Ashley River Road, Middleton Place Plantation Restaurant,
   (Flounder in Parchment with Shaved Vegetables, p. 159)

3. 3380 Ashley River Road, Drayton Hall Plantation,
   (Macaroons, p. 218)

4. *445 Meeting Street, Piggly Wiggly #1 Cafeteria Lunch,
   (Fried Chicken, p. 186)

5. *1068 Morrison Drive, Martha Lou's Kitchen
   (Stewed Cabbage, p. 109)

6. *2332 Meeting Street Road, Bertha's Kitchen
   (Smothered Pork Chops, p. 182)

7. 110 Haddrell Street, Mount Pleasant, SC, C. A. Magwood and Sons,
   (Fried Shrimp, p. 156)

8. *106 Haddrell Street, Mount Pleasant, SC, The Wreck
   (Deviled Crab, p. 153)

(* indicates prepared food available)

BIBLIOGRAPHY

We have attempted to compile the most complete chronological bibliography of Charleston cookbooks (and a few other relevant food books) possible. Some discretion was used in determining the Charleston area; Beaufort in the south and Georgetown to the north were the loose extremes.

All titles compiled from the Lee Bros. collection, catalogues of the Charleston Public Library and the Charleston Library Society, Amazon and Google book listings, Southern Foodways Alliance bibliography and other Southern food text indexes, and several bibliographies housed by the New York Public Library. All books listed in first editions. Reprintings are not noted.

Eliza Lucas Pinckney, *Recipe Book,* South Carolina Society of Colonial Dames, 1756

Richard J. Hooker (ed.), A *Colonial Plantation Cookbook: The Receipt Book of Harriott Pinckney Horry,* University of South Carolina Press, 1984 (original manuscript 1770)

Henrietta Drayton, *H.D. Receipt Book,* Middleton Place Foundation archives, (original manuscript 1774), unpublished

"Lady of Charleston," *The Carolina Receipt Book: Or Housekeeper's Assistant in Cookery, Medicine, and Other Subjects Connected with the Management of a Family,* Burges & James, 1832

Francis S. Holmes, *The Southern Farmer and Market Gardener,* Burges & James, 1842

William Elliott, *Carolina Sports by Land and Water,* University of South Carolina Press, 1846

Francis Peyre Porcher, *Medico-Botanical Catalogue,* Medical College of the State of South Carolina, 1847

Sarah Rutledge, *The Carolina Housewife: Or House and Home,* University of South Carolina Press, 1979 (original manuscript 1847)

Jane W. Fickling (ed.), *Recipes from Old Charleston: Catherine Lee Banks Edwards (1793–1863),* Banner Press, 1989

Francis Peyre Porcher, *Resources of the Southern Fields and Forests,* Walker, Evans & Cogswell, 1863

Henry W. Ravenel, *The Southern Gardener: Short and Simple Directions for the Culture of Vegetables and Fruits of the South,* Walker, Evans & Cogswell, 1871

Mary J. Waring, *The Centennial Receipt Book,* self-published, 1876

Cook Book, The Charleston Exchange for Women's Work, 1895

Mrs. Samuel G. Stoney [ed.], *The Carolina Rice Cook Book,* Carolina Rice Association, 1901

The Southern Cookbook, Women's Department of the South Carolina Interstate and West Indian Exposition, 1902

Milady's Own Book, Children of the Confederacy, Fort Sumter Chapter of the South Carolina Division, 1903

E.L.K., *Charleston Receipts,* privately published, 1910 (unrelated to 1950 *Charleston Receipts*)

Elizabeth Ravenel Harrigan (ed.), *Charleston Recollections and Receipts: Rose P. Ravenel's (1857–1920) Cookbook,* University of South Carolina Press, 1983

Harriette Kershaw Leiding, *Street Cries of an Old Southern City,* Daggett Printing, 1927

Charleston Recipes, The Studio of 61 Tradd St, 1928, (unrelated to 1948 *Charleston Recipes*)

Lettie Gay and Blanche S. Rhett (eds.,) *Two Hundred Years of Charleston Cooking,* Jonathan Cape & Harrison Smith, 1930 (reprinted 1976 by University of South Carolina Press with added foreword by Elizabeth Hamilton)

Mary Scott Saint-Amand, *A Balcony in Charleston,* Garrett and Massie, 1941

Daisy Breaux (Cornelia Donovan O'Donovan Calhoun), *Favorite Recipes of a Famous Hostess,* Polytechnic Publishing Company, 1945

Mt. Pleasant P.T.A., *Mt. Pleasant's Famous Recipes,* 1945

Don Richardson (ed.), *Carolina Low Country Cook Book,* Woman's Auxiliary of Prince George, Winyah, Protestant Episcopal Church, 1947

Margaret B. Walker and Martha Lynch Humphreys (eds.), *Charleston Recipes,* the Junior League of Charleston, 1948

Charleston Receipts, Junior League of Charleston, 1950

South Carolina Council of Farm Women, *South Carolina Cook Book,* University of South Carolina Press, 1954

Officers' Wives Club, Charleston Naval Base, *Plum Duff,* Nelsons' Southern Printing & Publishing, 1955

Popular Greek Recipes, Greek Orthodox Ladies Philoptochos Society, 1957

Charlotte Walker (ed.), *The Post-Courier Cookbook,* Evening Post Publishing Company, 1966

Linda G. Cohen and Joanne Spector (eds.), *From Charleston, With Love,* Synagogue Emanu-El Sisterhood, 1967

Sheralyn Rosenblum and Gloria Taxon (eds.), *Southern Kosher Cookbook,* Sisterhood Emanu-El, 1968

Dorothy Harris, *Cooking For That Man: Plantation Recipes,* Beaufort Gazette, 1970

Mrs. R.L. Kerr and Mrs. I. Grier Linton (eds.), *A Word to the Y's on Cookery,* Christian Family Y of Charleston, 1970

Nancy Chirich, *An Every Day Charleston Cook Book,* Sand Dollar Press, 1972

Catha W. Reid and Joseph T. Bruce, Jr., *The Sandlapper Cookbook,* Sandlapper Press, 1973

The Morsel Board, Medical University Women's Club, 1973

Kathleen S. Lesesne, *The Dinner Bell Is Ringing,* self-published, 1974

Ethel M. Moise, *Cook Book of the Family Favorites,* self-published, 1974

Lowcountry Colonial Receipts, Junior League of Charleston, 1974

Molly Heady Sillers, *Doin' the Charleston: A Gourmet's Guide & Cook Book,* Chrisreed Publishers, 1976

Ethel M. Moise, *Cook Book of the Family Favorites Book II,* self-published, 1977

Bethel Church Records and Recipes, Bethel United Methodist Church Kendrick-Rogers Circle, 1977

Gastronomic Music, Middleton High School Bandbackers, 1977

Grace United Methodist Church Cook Book, United Methodist Women, 1978

Andy Campbell and Barbara Cohn (eds.), *The Wallace Faculty Cookbook,* Wallace Middle School, 1979

Chilton Hammond, Chilton Chevers Pope, and Dede Deane Gray Cheves, *Flavored with Tradition: A Collection of Recipes from Charleston, Atlanta, and Richmond,* Flavored With Tradition, 1979

Laura Witte Waring, Thomas R. Waring Jr (eds.), *The Way It Was in Charleston: Recollections of a Southern Lady (1877–1975),* Evening Post Books, 1980

Recipes, P.E.O. Sisterhood, Chapter E, 1980

Sea Island Seasons: Favorite Recipes, Beaufort County Open Land Trust, Beaufort, SC, 1980

Julie Lumpkin and Nancy Ann Coleman (eds.), *The South Carolina Wildlife Cookbook,* South Carolina Wildlife and Marine Resources Public Affairs Dept Department, Columbia, SC, 1981

Frank P. Jarrell, *Charleston Choices: Restaurants and Recipes,* (1984), Frank P. Jarrell Co., 1984

Zeta Tau Alpha Charleston Alumnae, Cherished Recipes, Fundcraft Publishing, 1984

Anita Bernstein, Florence Kurtz, Bella Wallace, and Pearl Wolfson (eds.), *Historically Cooking,* Kahal Kadosh Beth Elohim Sisterhood, 1985

Not By Bread Alone: a collection of favorite recipes from the people of the Diocese of South Carolina and other friends, Holy Trinity Episcopal Church, 1985

Recipes to Roar About, Charleston County Library, c. 1985

Linda Glick Conway (ed.), *Party Receipts from the Charleston Junior League: Hors D'Oeuvres, Savories, Sweets,* Algonquin Books, 1986

Ernest Matthew Mickler, *White Trash Cooking,* Ten Speed Press, 1986

Charleston Receipts Repeats, Junior League of Charleston, 1986

Robert Dickson, *A Journal of Fine Cooking,* Roberts of Charleston Inc., 1987

Rice-ipes: The Women's Council Special Rice Recipes, Carolina Art Association Women's Council, 1987

Elwood C. Stith, *Rice, A Lowcountry Tradition: The Official Cookbook for the Third Annual South Carolina Rice Cookbook,* South Carolina Electric & Gas, 1989

Jamie Clayton (ed.), *Favorite Recipes from Drayton Hall,* Friends of Drayton Hall, 1990

A Taste of Summer: A Collection of Recipes Using Lowcountry Products, Clemson University Extension Service, 1990

Angela R. Basha and Peggy Joseph (eds.), *Gracious Goodness... Charleston!,* Bishop England High School, 1991

International Association of Personnel in Employment Security. South Carolina Chapter, *Favorite South Carolina Recipes,* Fundcraft Publishing, 1991

Oscar Vick, *Charleston Cookery : Soups, Salads and Sauces: Recipes from the Waters, Woodlands, and Fields Around Charleston, South Carolina,* self-published, 1991

Riverland Terrace Garden Club 50th Anniversary Cookbook, Riverland Terrace Garden Club, 1991

Yachts of Recipes, Charleston Yacht Club Ladies Auxiliary, 1991

Virginia Mixson Geraty, *Bittle en' T'ing': Gullah Cooking with Maum Chrish,* Sandlapper Press, 1992

Michael O'Neill, *Apples, Apples, Apples,* Windsor Hill Elementary School, 1992

John Martin Taylor, *Hoppin' John's Low Country Cooking,* Houghton Mifflin Harcourt, 1992

Charleston Hospitality, Johnson & Wales University at Charleston, 1992

Oscar Vick, *The Coffee Table Cookbook: From Edisto Island, Hellhole Swamp, Jackass Cut, and Pawley's Island, South Carolina, Recipes, Wild Stories, and Tales from the Historic Lowcountry of South Carolina,* self-published, 1994

Blessed Isle: Recipes from Pawley's Island, All Saints Waccamaw Episcopal Church, 1995

Brother Boniface, *Baking with Brother Boniface: Recipes from the Kitchen of Mepkin Abbey,* Wyrick & Company, 1996

Teresa Pregnall, *Treasured Recipes from the Charleston Cake Lady,* William Morrow, 1996

James Island High School Trojans Home Cookin', Fundcraft Publishing, 1996

Music, Menus & Magnolias: Charleston Shares Its Culture and Cuisine, Charleston Symphony Orchestra, 1996

Jane Kronsberg, *Charleston: People, Places and Food,* Wyrick & Company, 1997

John Hammond Moore (ed.), *The Confederate Housewife: Receipts & Remedies, Together with Sundry Suggestions for Garden, Farm, & Plantation,* Summerhouse, 1997

John Martin Taylor, *Hoppin' John's Charleston, Beaufort & Savannah: Dining at Home in the Lowcountry,* Clarkson Potter, 1997

Tested by Time: A Collection of Charleston Recipes, Porter Gaud Parents Guild, 1997

Karen Hess, *Carolina Rice Kitchen—The African Connection,* University of South Carolina Press, 1998

Zoe D. Sanders, *Entertaining at the College of Charleston,* College of Charleston Foundation, 1998

Emily Whaley with William Baldwin, *Mrs. Whaley Entertains: Advice, Opinions, and 100 Recipes from a Charleston Kitchen,* Algonquin Books, 1998

Pon Top Edisto: Cookin' 'Tweenst the Rivers, Trinity Episcopal Church, Edisto Island, SC, 1998

Soup to Nuts—A Charleston Collection, Christian Family Y of Charleston, 1998

Louis Osteen, *Louis Osteen's Charleston Cuisine,* Algonquin Books, 1999

Sara H. Shawal (ed.), *A Garden of Eatin' Cookbook,* Beth Shalom Beth Israel, 1999

Teresa Pregnall, *Special Recipes from the Charleston Cake Lady,* HarperCollins, 2000

Thomas A. Stumph, *Charleston Cuisine: The Culinary Encyclopedia of the Lowcountry,* Feeding Frenzy, 2000

Marvin Woods, *The New Low-Country Cooking: 125 Recipes for Coastal Southern Cooking with Innovative Style,* William Morrow, 2000

Artful Entertaining: The Official Cookbook of the Southeastern Wildlife Exposition, Southeastern Wildlife Exposition, 2000

Episcopal Church Women of St. John and St. Luke Catholic Church, *A Taste of Heaven,* Morris Press, 2001

Stephen G. Kish and Stephen T. Stone, *82 Queen: The Best of Lowcountry Cuisine,* Wentworth, 2001

Jamie Minster, *Silver Spoon Restaurants: A Culinary Tour of Charleston's Finest,* Velocity Publishing, 2001

Faithfully Charleston: St. Michael's Celebrates 250 Years of Meals and Memories, St. Michael's Church, 2001

Millennium Men Cookbook: Fifty-Five of Charleston's Most Prominent Men Find Their Place in the Kitchen and Get Cooking for a Cause, Florence Crittenton Programs of South Carolina, 2001

Jesse Edward Gantt Jr and Veronica Davis Gerald, *The Ultimate Gullah Cookbook,* Sands Publishing, 2002

Maxine and Malyssa Pinson, *Lowcountry Delights: Cookbook & Travel Guide,* Wimmer Cookbooks, 2002

Diana Hollingsworth Gessler, *Very Charleston: A Celebration of History, Culture, and Lowcountry Charm*, Algonquin Books, 2003

Sallie Ann Robinson, *Gullah Home Cooking the Daufuskie Way*, University of North Carolina Press, 2003

Charleston Postcard Company, *Charleston Cuisine*, Feeding Frenzy, 2004

Pat Conroy, *The Pat Conroy Cookbook: Recipes of My Life*, Nan A. Talese, 2004

Frances Ellison Hamby, *Catering to Charleston: Cherished Recipes from a Premier Southern Caterer*, self-published, 2004

Jane and Michael Stern, *Cooking in the Lowcountry From the Old Post Office Restaurant*, Rutledge Hill, 2004

Oscar Vick, *Gullah Cooking: Seafood Cookbook*, self-published, 2004

Oscar Vick, *Gullah Cooking: Creative Recipes from an Historic Past from the Low Country of South Carolina*, Pelican Publishing, 2005

Oscar Vick, *Oscar Vick Cooks Rice: Rice Recipes from the Lowcountry of South Carolina*, Pelican Publishing, 2005

Donald Barickman, *Magnolias: Authentic Southern Cuisine*, Gibbs Smith, 2006

Jason Davidson, *The Boathouse: Tales and Recipes from a Southern Kitchen*, Joggling Board Press, 2006

Nathalie Dupree and Marion Sullivan, *Nathalie Dupree's Shrimp and Grits Cookbook*, Gibbs Smith, 2006

Catherine H. Forrester, *At Home-Charleston: Traditions and Entertaining in a Charleston Home*, Wimmer Cookbooks, 2006

David Gobel, *Old St. Andrew's Parish Church, Through These Doors—Bread of Heaven*, Morris Press, 2006

Craig Deihl, *Cypress*, Gibbs Smith, 2007

Connie Stahl, *Breakfast on the Battery: A Charleston Chef's Collection of Breakfast and Tea Recipes*, Wimmer Cookbooks, 2007

Bob Waggoner, *Charleston Grill at Charleston Place: French Influenced Lowcountry Cuisine*, Gibbs Smith, 2007

Danielle Wecksler, *Taste of the Lowcountry*, Gibbs Smith, 2007

Janice Shay, *Charleston Classic Desserts: Recipes from Favorite Restaurants*, Pelican Publishing, 2008

Robert Stehling, *Hominy Grill Recipes*, self-published, 2008

Holly Herrick, *The Charleston Chef's Table: Extraordinary Recipes from the Heart of the Old South*, Three Forks, 2009

Holly Herrick, *Southern Farmers Market Cookbook*, Gibbs Smith, 2009

Charlotte Jenkins, *Gullah Cuisine: By Land and By Sea*, Evening Post Books, 2010

South Carolina Lowcountry Firehouse Cookbook, South Carolina Project Impact Initiative, 2010

Charleston Culinary Center, *Seafood Favorites: Recipes from the Lowcountry*, Gibbs Smith, 2011

Frank MacMahon, *Cool Inside: Hank's Seafood Restaurant*, Wyrick & Company, 2012

ACKNOWLEDGMENTS

WE'D LIKE TO THANK the many people who shared their time, knowledge, and resources in the production of this book, including Peter Alexandre, Rica Allannic, William Allard, David Anderson, Thomas Backman, Robert Barber, Jr., Grace Barnett, David Belanger, Milena Berman, Warwick Bonsal, Nigel Bowers, Patrick Brantley, Jennifer Bremer, Sean Brock, Deborah and Melvin Brown, Justin Burdett, Mary Calhoun, Hannah Cameron, Meg Cleveland, Jason Crichton, Vereen and Richard Coen, Doris Cooper, Edwin Cooper III, E.V. Day, Craig Deihl, Fred Dockery, Barbara Doyle, Charles and Sallie Duell, Nathalie Dupree, Molly Fair, Alli Foster, Squire and Stephanie Fox, Debra Gadsden, Martha Lou Gadsden, Micah Garrison, John Gaulden, Erica Gelbard, Janet Gregg, Jane and Harry Gregorie, Cynthia Groseclose, Wayne and Katherine Guckenberger, Derrill Hagood, Jimmy Hagood, Deborah Hamby, Frances Hamby, Kat Hastie, Winslow and Katharine Hastie, Kate Hays, Hank Holliday, Sarah and Ozey Horton, Marge Humphreys, Josephine Humphreys and Tom Hutcheson, Stephanie Huntwork, Dana Iselin, Martha Jackson, Marc Jenkins, Hunter and Maggie Kennedy, Jamie Kimm, Natalie Knowlton, Pam Krauss, Lenny and Townie Krawcheck, Lois Lane, Gladys and Al Lane, Arthur Rano Lee, Gia Papini Lee, Jack and Andrea Limehouse, Sidi Limehouse, Daniel Long, Leigh Magar and Johnny Tucker, Wayne Magwood, Allison Malec, Lee Manigault, Mark Marhefka, Adriane McAvoy, Marge McAvoy, William McCord, David McCormick, Terry McCray, Tressy Mellichamp, Peter Milewicz, Beth and Patrick Miller, Will Milner, Lawrence Mitchell, Lauren Mitterer, Benjamin Moise, Sally Montague, Angie Mosier, Vance Muse and Carl Palazzolo, Josef Kirk Myers, Shelby Nelson, Sarah O'Kelley, Robert Paca, Brad Parsons, Alice Patrick, Donna Passannante, Eugenia Payne, John Payne, Scott Peacock, Ashley Phillips, Anne and Mason Pope, Charles and Susu Ravenel, David and Carol Rawle, John Reid, Patsy Richburg, Keith Riddle, Jane Ries, Joseph and Charlotte Riley, Delores Rivers, Buff and Leila Ross, Allen and Dayna Sassard, Gertrude Sassard, Steven Satterfield, Andrew and Cheryl Savage, Fred Scott, Henry Shaffer, David S. Shields, Margaret Smith, Robert Stehling and Nunally Kersh, Chris Stewart, David Stewart, Dru Strickland, Sully Sullivan, John Martin Taylor, Jane Treuhaft, Kate Tyler, Kim Tyner, Sam VanNorte, Caroline Von Asten and Frank Iwanicki, Bette Walker, Latonnya Wallace, Hugh and Blanche Weathers, Brynn White, Capers White, Jaime Wolf, Ada Yonenaka, and the Young family.

INDEX